Personal Computers: A Guide for Seniors

Personal Computers: A Guide for Seniors

Pat Coleman

DORSET PRESS
NEW YORK

This edition published by Dorset Press
by arrangement with Stephen L. Nelson, Inc.

2001 Dorset Press

ISBN 0-7607-2487-3 *paperback*

Printed and bound in the United States of America

01 02 03 04 MP 9 8 7 6 5 4 3 2 1

RRD-C

For grandchildren Daniel, Elizabeth, and Bailey. And in memory of Adam.

Contents at a Glance

Contents

INTRODUCTION

If you've picked up this book, you're probably over 50, you have a computer, and you want to know more about how to use it. You might also want to know something about a person who has the temerity to write a book about computers for seniors. Shortly before I started writing this book, I celebrated my 60th birthday. Yes, I am indeed a member of the club, and I have the gray hair to prove it. I'm a mother and a grandmother, I work out on the treadmill almost every day, and I've been using and writing about personal computers since 1983—which is a long time in computer years.

I also know what it feels like to be frustrated and intimidated by computers. The reason I first started using computers had nothing to do with a passion for technology. I was forced into it because I needed a job, and the one that presented itself was as an editor and writer of computer manuals, those little booklets that come with a computer and that are supposed to tell you everything you need to know about the computer. On my first day at work, I was given a manual about a word-processing program, taken into an office where a computer was located, told to become familiar with the machine, and then was left totally alone. I'd never seen a personal computer before, and frankly I was scared to death. I didn't even know how to turn it on. At lunchtime, I scurried to the nearest bookstore and bought every book I could find about computers, especially the books that looked as if they were written for children.

Regardless of how adept we are in other areas of our lives, those of us who did not grow up in the digital age often feel especially challenged by technology and its rapid development, yet we can also be energized and empowered by it when we take advantage of the opportunities to learn how to use it. And that's the purpose of this book.

How This Book Is Organized

This book is organized in a pyramid fashion, starting with the basics and concluding with the more complex. I explain everything you'll see on your computer screen and show you in step-by-step fashion how to press the key or click the mouse to do something. Really, that's all there is to using a computer. It's like cooking. You collect the ingredients for a dish, and then you follow the steps to create it.

At the back of this book is a glossary of computer and Windows terms. The first time I use what might be called a "technical" term, I'll explain it right then and there, but I've also put the term in the glossary. If in a later chapter, you need to refresh your memory, you can check the glossary.

In this book, I'm using a version of Microsoft Windows called Windows Millennium Edition, or Windows Me, which is the most recent version for home use. If you've acquired Windows Me and want some help installing it, turn to the appendix.

Here is a description of what you'll find in the individual chapters.

Chapter 1: Getting to Know Your Computer

Understanding how your computer works is key if you want to be in charge of it, instead of the other way around. With the information in this chapter under your belt, you'll be on speaking terms with the parts and pieces of your computer and its operations.

Chapter 2: Windows 101

This chapter is a basic course in the Windows operating system, the software that controls computer hardware and is the foundation for the programs you run to get work done, browse the Internet, play games, and so on. I explain the difference between Windows and Windows applications, describe the little pictures (icons) you see when you start your computer, and show you how to use them.

Chapter 3: Using Windows

Windows get its name from the boxes (windows) that open when you start up a program or open a document. This chapter describes all the elements of a window and shows you how to use those elements to tell Windows what you want the computer to do.

Chapter 4: Managing Your Documents

If you want to be able to find what you store on your computer easily and quickly, you need to understand how Windows stores information and how you can work within that system to organize your documents. Using the guidelines in this chapter, you'll seldom, if ever, have to spend any time at all trying to locate something on your computer.

Chapter 5: Printing Your Documents

This chapter not only describes how to print documents but it provides step-by-step instructions for installing a new printer and managing the printing process. I also tell you how a printer works and what to do if you're having a problem with your printer.

Chapter 6: How to Get on the Internet

We seniors are the fastest growing group of Internet users. We're using it to shop, to trace our family trees, to send and receive e-mail, to sign up for Social Security payments, to access information about health and wellness, and to take care of other matters that in the past required a trip to an office or a lengthy postal correspondence. This chapter tells you exactly how to get connected.

Chapter 7: Exploring the World Wide Web

The Internet and the World Wide Web are not the same thing. The Internet is the huge network of computers around the world. The World Wide Web is the collection of resources that is to be found on these computers. This chapter shows you how to use the Microsoft Internet Explorer Web browser to find and access these resources. In addition, a special section is devoted to sites that seniors should definitely visit.

Chapter 8: Sending and Receiving E-Mail

If e-mail is your only reason for having a computer, that's reason enough. Perhaps nothing has changed the way we live and work more than e-mail. In this chapter, I show you how to use Microsoft Outlook Express, the e-mail program that's included with Windows, to send and receive e-mail. I also tell you how to filter out unwanted mail and set up Outlook Express so that each person in your household can have his or her personal, private e-mail space.

Chapter 9: Maintaining Windows and Your Computer

Keeping your computer fit isn't complicated, and it doesn't take much time. Knowing how to use a few simple tools is all that's needed. In this chapter, I discuss these tools, and I also explain computer viruses and how to avoid them.

Chapter 10: Making Your Version of Windows Special

If you have any physical trait that makes using a computer difficult, you might want to read this chapter first. For example, if you're left-handed, you'll want to switch the way the mouse buttons work, and if you have trouble reading the screen, you might want to make the type larger. You'll find instructions for making these changes and many others in this chapter.

Chapter 11: Got a Problem?

When you run into trouble with your computer, don't despair. Take a look at this chapter. I describe some everyday annoyances and what to do about them as well as how to use Windows features and the Internet to become your own "help desk."

Chapter 12: Using the Applications That Come with Windows

Several programs are included with Windows, and you can use them to store contact information, write a letter, create a logo, view your digital photos, and calculate your checkbook balance. These programs are called accessories, and in this chapter I show you how to find and use them.

Chapter 13: Having Fun

I hope that by the time you get to this chapter you'll already be convinced that using a computer is a lot of fun, but if not, maybe knowing how to play some computer games will increase the entertainment value for you. I'll show you how to play games against the computer and with real people over the Internet. In addition, I introduce you to the tools you use to play audio CDs, listen to radio broadcasts over the Internet, and view Internet movies.

Chapter 14: Setting Up a Home Network

If you have more than one computer in your household, you can set up a network so that the user of each computer can access the Internet simultaneously, print from a single printer, and open and use the files on all the computers with the click of a mouse. A home network is not expensive, and it's really easy to set up. In fact, putting together a child's tricycle is more difficult. This short chapter tells you exactly how to do it.

Conventions Used in This Book

Anything that you need to enter from the keyboard is in italics. For example, when I want you to type a word or a series of characters, I'll tell you where to type it by saying something like "In the Open box, type *a:\setup.exe*." You'll then type exactly what is in italic type, including all the symbols, punctuation marks, letters, and numbers.

I'll identify dialog boxes, options, tabs, and the like by capitalizing the first letter of every word, regardless of how the name of the thing appears on the screen. For example, to tell Windows to notify you when you have new e-mail, you click a check box that on the screen is labeled "Play sound when new messages arrive." In this book, I'll use "Play Sound When New Messages Arrive." Although this might look a bit strange at first, it makes it easier to understand some instructions.

Now, a word about Internet addresses. It's become quite common to shorten Internet addresses in printed media, on television, and in conversation. For example, even though an entire Internet address is *http://www.nyt.com*, you'll see and hear this referred to as *nyt.com*. Just so there is no confusion, in this book I'll use the entire address. And though you often see Internet addresses hyphenated in newspapers and magazines, I won't do that in this book because you can never tell whether the hyphen is actually part of the address.

Scattered throughout are Notes, Tips, and Warnings, which point out tidbits of helpful information. You'll also occasionally find sidebars, which deal with topics that are of interest but not necessarily indispensable to the task at hand.

Chapter 1

GETTING TO KNOW YOUR COMPUTER

Featuring:

- Understanding How Computers Work
- What Is Hardware?
- What Is Software?
- Using the Mouse and the Keyboard
- Understanding Bytes, Megs, and Other Measurements

Just as you don't have to understand much of anything about what makes your car run in order to drive it, you don't have to understand how your computer works to use it. But if you have even a limited knowledge of some key parts and pieces of your car, you can take better care of it, drive it more efficiently, and feel more confident about it when you get behind the wheel.

The same goes for your computer—the more you know about it, the less you need to be in awe of it, or fear it, and the more likely you are to take advantage of the features that will make it the useful tool it was intended to be.

In this chapter, I'm not going to get technical, but I am going to introduce you to the components of your computer that you most need to know about. For example, you don't want to mistake your CD-ROM drive for a cup holder, as did the person in one recent urban legend that made the rounds.

Before I get into the details, though, I want to deal with one thing right upfront: unless you do something really goofy, such as pouring a cup of coffee or a can of soda into your computer while it's running, you can't damage your computer. And even then, the only thing you might harm irreparably is the hard drive. When I'm helping new users get acquainted with their computers, I often ask them to sit on their keyboards—really. Now, if they put their whole weight down, they could conceivably dislodge the pull-out slot in which the keyboard is resting, but the point is this: you can press every single key simultaneously without destroying your computer or any program that resides on it. Don't worry about damaging your computer.

And, furthermore, when something doesn't seem to be working quite right, don't start to solve the problem by asking, "What am I doing wrong?" or "What did I do wrong?" The most likely answer to either question is "Nothing." Computers and computer programs are wonderful inventions, but they have a long way to go before they're as reliable as, say, your televisions or your microwave oven. Toward the end of this book, I devote an entire chapter to troubleshooting; you won't find a single troubleshooting tip that has anything to do with the user as culprit.

Understanding How Computers Work

A computer is an electronic device that does its job in three steps:

1. It accepts input.
2. It processes the input according to predefined rules (programs).
3. It produces output.

For example, if you open your word-processing application and type something on the keyboard, you are giving the computer input, which it receives and processes. It then produces output on the screen—what you just typed at the keyboard.

Computers are classified according to their size, speed, cost, and abilities, and their class names give you a clue about how they fit in the classification: supercomputers, mainframes, superminicomputers, minicomputers, workstations, and microcomputers, also known as personal computers, for example.

In this book, I'll be talking about personal computers, which is what you probably have at home on your desk, although you might use one of the other computer types at work. A personal computer is designed to be used by one person at a time, and it doesn't have to use the processing power, disk, or other resources of any other computer, although it certainly can when it's connected to a network. A personal computer contains everything it needs to work all by itself.

The Basic Components of a Computer

A basic personal computer has most or all of the parts and pieces shown in Figure 1-1.

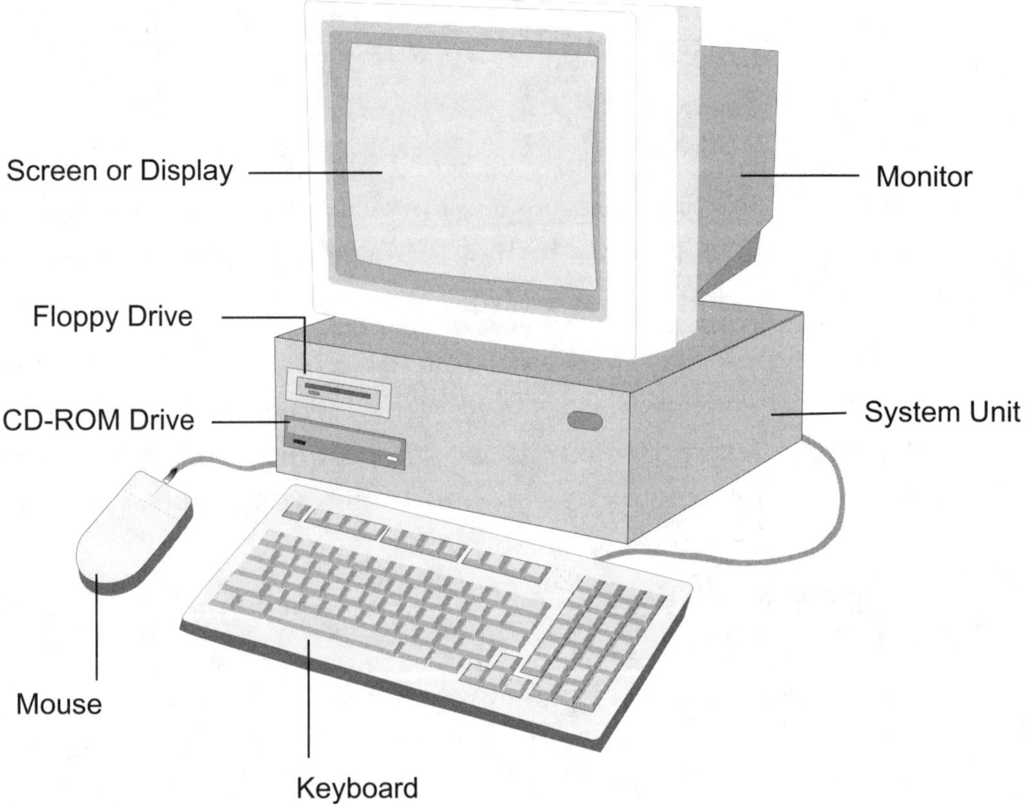

Figure 1-1 The basic components of a personal computer.

Here's a description of what each component does:

- **System unit.** In a personal computer, all the separate components plug into the system unit, which is the large, heavy box part of your computer that stands on the floor or slides into a cabinet.
- **Monitor.** The part of your computer that looks like a TV is the monitor. The monitor has its own On/Off switch usually located beneath the screen. In addition, the monitor usually has brightness and contrast controls, just like a TV.

- **Screen or display.** The part of the monitor that looks like a TV screen is obviously the screen, which is also often referred to as the display. Whatever you type from the keyboard or select with the mouse is displayed on the screen.
- **Mouse.** The mouse is the small hand control with the cord (the "tail") with buttons you can click with your index finger. When you move the mouse on a mouse pad, you can control the position of a cursor (an arrow) on the screen.
- **Keyboard.** The component that looks like a typewriter is, of course, the keyboard. In addition to the keys you'd expect to find on a type-writer, the keyboard includes some special keys.
- **Floppy disk drive.** Most computers have at least one floppy drive on the system unit. A floppy disk is so named because the actual disk that's inside the plastic casing is very thin and floppy. If you were to touch this floppy part, you would ruin it.
- **CD-ROM drive.** CD-ROM stands for Compact Disc—Read-Only Memory. A CD-ROM disc is a storage medium that uses the same technology as music CDs, and the advantage to a CD-ROM is that it can store huge amounts of information, for example, the entire text of *Encyclopaedia Britannica.* Most software manufacturers now deliver their programs on CD-ROMs.

In addition, a computer contains other important parts that you can't see unless you open the case to the system unit:

- **Hard drive.** When you store information in your computer, it is kept on the hard drive. The hard drive is also referred to as the hard disk drive and the hard disk. A hard drive stores data on magnetically coated disks, and the unit is sealed in the factory to prevent contamination.

- **RAM.** An abbreviation for random access memory, RAM is an area in your computer's memory where information is stored while you are working on it. In general, the more RAM you have, the faster your computer works.
- **CPU.** An abbreviation for central processing unit, the CPU is the component that does the real work of computing. The CPU is also referred to as the microprocessor, the processor, or the chip. The speed of the CPU is measured in megahertz (MHz), and the larger the number of megahertz, the faster the processor works. The processor does not store information, as do RAM and your hard drive.

NOTE *If you want to take a look inside the system unit, you can certainly do so. If you haven't done it before, you might want to have the moral support of someone at your side. First, touch a metal portion of the computer while it's on to discharge any static electricity that might have built up in your body and clothing. Next, shut down the computer and unplug it. Now, with a small screwdriver, remove the screws that attach the casing at the back of the system unit, and then slide the casing off. I suggest that you not touch anything unless you know what you're doing, but shine a flashlight on the contents so that you can get a good look. When you're done, slide the casing back on and replace the screws.*

Optional Components

You may well have other additional components attached to your computer, and these days new computers come equipped with various options. Most computer systems that you buy today include speakers, which serve the same function on a computer that they do on a stereo system. Without speakers, you wouldn't be able to hear the sounds that accompany various computer events, be privy to the sound effects on Web sites, or hear the music when you pop in a music CD. (Yes, you can play music CDs on your computer!)

Another option that is available on most computers you buy today is an internal modem. You use a modem to connect to other computers or to the Internet via telephone lines. Many other components are also available, including the following:

- **Printer,** which reproduces on paper the contents of anything you see on the screen.
- **Digital camera,** which lets you take pictures without film and then display, edit, and print them from your computer.
- **Digital video camera,** which lets you record moving images and display them on the computer in real time or create and save them as files to play back later.
- **Scanner,** which lets you convert paper images to digital images and store and display them on your computer.
- **Joystick,** which you need to play certain kinds of computer games.
- **Microphone,** which you can plug into your computer and use to convert speech to text with a speech recognition system or to talk over the phone using your computer.

What Is Hardware?

My favorite definition of hardware is this: if you can stub your toe on it, it must be hardware. (Thanks to my special technical consultant, Peter Dyson, for this definition.) Every component I've described thus far in this chapter is hardware. In other words, all the physical electronic components of a computer system are hardware.

What Is Software?

You can have every single piece of equipment mentioned to this point set up and connected perfectly, but without software, your computer is only useful as a giant doorstop—it won't *do* anything. Software is a collection of computer programs that tell the hardware what to do and how to do it.

By definition, a computer program is a sequence of instructions that a computer can execute, and so you will hear the terms *program* and *software* used interchangeably. Computer programs are written in *programming languages.* Just so you know what a program looks like, here's a little program that displays the text "Hello everybody" on the screen. It's written in the C programming language.

```
main()
{
     printf("Hello  everybody./n");
}
```

If you're like most of us, your eyes start to glaze over at the mere mention of computer programming. But now you have a basic idea of how it works, and this is the last mention of it you'll see in this book.

A computer needs two types of software to function: an operating system and applications. An *operating system* is the software that controls how computer hardware works, and it is the foundation on which applications depend. Here are some examples of operating systems that are in use today:

- Mac OS, which is the operating system in use on Macintosh computers.
- UNIX, which is widely used on network computers and computers that serve as major gateways to the Internet.

- Windows Me (Windows Millennium Edition), which I use in illustrations and examples in this book. Windows is a family of operating systems developed by Microsoft, and I'll describe the various versions in the next chapter. Windows Me is the latest version for use on home computers.

An *application* is the software that performs the tasks that people want to take care of with their computers, and you will also hear the terms *program* and *software* used as synonyms for the term *application*. Here are some of today's most popular applications:

- Corel WordPerfect, a word-processing program.
- Family Tree Maker, a program you can use to enter and arrange genealogical information you've collected, including photographs and anecdotal material. You can also use this program to put your information into a format that you can publish on the Internet and thus share with family and friends.
- Hoyle Card Games, a program you can use to play 16 card games, including Canasta, Cribbage, Bridge, Spades, and Poker.
- MasterCook: The Complete Suite Featuring Betty Crocker, a simple set of programs that you can use to enter and retrieve recipes, calculate nutritional values, plan menus, and search a video library of cooking techniques. MasterCook also includes 6500 recipes.
- Mavis Beacon Teaches Typing, a program that teaches you how to touch type.
- Quicken, a program from Intuit that you can use to manage all your finances. You can bank online, track savings and checking accounts, balance accounts online, plan for retirement, track investments, inventory your home, prepare a will, budget and track your spending, and take care of almost any other financial matter.

- Quicken Turbo Tax, a program that interviews you, places your answers in IRS-approved forms, and performs all tax calculations. You can use this program to print your return or file it electronically.

Using the Mouse and the Keyboard

The mouse and the keyboard are the two primary input devices for a computer.

How the Mouse Works

Most mice have at least two buttons. The one on the left is called the *primary mouse button* or just the *mouse button*. In this book, when I say something such as "click the Start button," I mean for you to place the mouse pointer over the button with the word *Start* on it and then click the left mouse button. You use the left mouse button to point to or select something on the screen.

The button on the right is called the *secondary mouse button* or the *right button*. You click the right button when you want to see options for an object on the screen. In this book, I'll always say "right-click" when you should use the right button instead of the left button.

When you *click* a mouse button, simply press it once and then release it. When you *drag*, click the mouse button, hold it down, move the mouse on its mouse pad, and then release the button. (You can place the mouse directly on your desktop if you want, but you'll get better traction if you use a mouse pad.)

Although the mouse is designed for a right-handed person, you can reconfigure it if you are left-handed. You can also change the graphic that's used for the pointer, adjust the speed of the pointer, and modify how the mouse works in other ways. Chapter 10 gives you detailed instructions about how to make these changes.

How the Keyboard Works

Figure 1-2 shows a Windows keyboard, which contains all the usual special keys plus a couple of others. You don't need a Windows keyboard to work with Windows, but most computers that you purchase these days will come with the Windows keyboard. Table 1-1 describes what happens when you press these special keys.

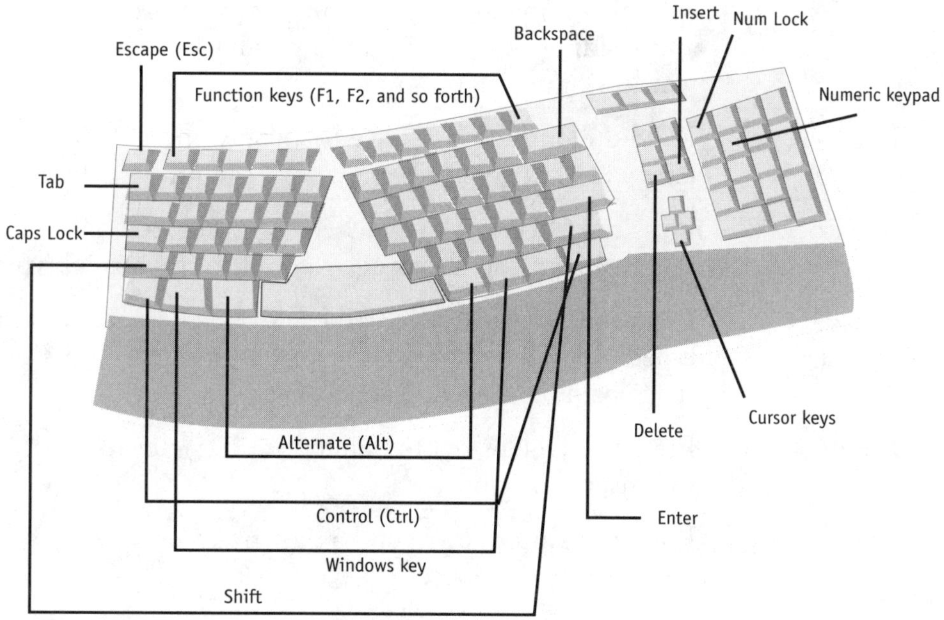

Figure 1-2 A computer keyboard.

KEY	DESCRIPTION
Function	Labeled F1 through F12, function keys perform a special service. For example, in most programs, you can press F1 to open Help. The function of other keys depends on the application.
Esc	Pressing the Escape key typically lets you break out of whatever you are currently doing.
Tab	Pressing Tab in a dialog box moves you back and forth between options. Although you can use tab to indent a paragraph, you don't want to do so. You have many other, better options for formatting a paragraph.

KEY	DESCRIPTION
Ctrl	You press the Control key and then another key to send special commands to the computer. For example, pressing and holding the Ctrl key and simultaneously pressing C copies the current selection to the Clipboard. You can then paste it in another location.
Alt	You press the Alternate key and then another key to send special commands to the computer. For example, pressing and holding the Alt key and pressing F4 closes the current window or exits a program.
Shift	Hold down the Shift key when you want to type a capital letter or a letter on the top row of the numeric keys.
Caps Lock	Press the Caps Lock key when you want to type in all capital letters. Press Caps Lock again to return to normal typing.
Backspace	Press the Backspace key to delete the character you just typed. To delete more characters, continue to press Backspace or hold down the Backspace key.
Delete	Press the Delete key to delete the character to the right of the insertion point.
Enter	Press the Enter key to end a paragraph or to send a command to the computer.
Insert	Pressing the Insert key alternates between Insert and Overwrite modes. In Insert mode, what you type is inserted at the insertion point. In Overwrite mode, what you type replaces existing letters.
Arrow	Also called cursor keys, the arrow keys move the cursor around on the screen when you type or edit.
Numeric Keypad	When you press the Num Lock key, you can use the numbers on the numeric keypad as you would the keys on an old-fashioned adding machine. When Num Lock is off, the numeric keypad functions as cursor keys.
Windows	Pressing the Windows key opens the Start menu.

Table 1-1 The special keys on a computer keyboard.

Typically, you'll use the keyboard to enter text, and you'll use the mouse to select objects on the screen. If you prefer to use only the keyboard or if you have difficulty using the mouse, you can duplicate many mouse functions with key combinations. If you prefer to use the mouse or if you have difficulty using the keyboard, you can display a replica of the keyboard on the screen and use the mouse to "type" by clicking the keys. In Chapter 10, I'll give you detailed instructions about how to do so.

Understanding Bytes, Megs, and Other Measurements

You don't need to be a mathematician to be on speaking terms with the units of measurement that computers use, and from time to time these measurements give you valuable information about your computer. For example, if you're running low on hard disk space, knowing the size of your hard disk and the amount of remaining space will help you decide if you need to delete programs or data from your hard disk or plan to acquire a bigger one.

The basic unit of measure is the *byte,* which is the amount of space it takes to store a single character, such as the letter *d* or the *$* symbol. A space is also considered a character. Computers can store an enormous number of characters, and so we use the terminology in Table 1-2 to describe the various quantities.

TERM	ABBREVIATION	APPROXIMATE NUMBER OF CHARACTERS
Byte	b	1
Kilobyte	KB	1,000
Megabyte	MB	1,000,000
Gigabyte	GB	1,000,000,000
Terabyte	TB	1,000,000,000,000

Table 1-2 Units of measurement used in computers.

In casual conversation, you will hear a kilobyte called a K, a megabyte called a meg, and a gigabyte called a gig.

The Seven Most Important Things to Remember About Your Computer

1. You're the boss, not the computer.
2. In the past, letting a computer run continuously was a safer way to prevent loss of data than turning the computer off and on. That is no longer true, and you can safely turn off your computer at the end of the day or whenever you're finished working with it if you want to do so. But if you want to leave your computer on all the time, that's okay too. Doing so will cause no harm.
3. In general, computers work best in temperatures that are also comfortable for humans, but they can generate a tremendous amount of heat. If you live in a hot climate as I do, you may want to provide some extra cooling in the room or area where you use your computer.
4. Be sure that the cables running to and from your computer are out of any traffic path. The main reason, of course, is that someone could trip over a cable and be injured in a fall, but additionally, unplugging a power source while your computer is running can cause serious data loss.
5. Using a can of compressed air is an excellent way to clean your keyboard and other computer crevices where dust can collect.
6. When your computer is turned off, you can safely clean the screen with window cleaner, and you can wipe down the case with a nonabrasive household-cleaning product.

7. In the past, screens could be imprinted, or burned, with words or images if programs were left running for a long time. Screen savers were invented to prevent this situation. Nowadays, screens no longer are in danger of being burned, and screen savers are just for fun.

Summary

The purpose of this chapter was to help you get on speaking terms with your computer. Becoming familiar with this information takes some of the guesswork out of what to look for when you're buying a computer, and it puts you, not the hardware or software, in the driver's seat when you need to do some work or have fun at your computer. You now have a basic idea of how your computer works, you know the difference between hardware and software, and you know the names and the functions of your computer's parts and pieces.

Chapter 2

WINDOWS 101

Featuring:

- What Is Windows?
- What's the Difference Between Windows and a Windows Application?
- Starting Windows
- Understanding and Using the Desktop
- Using the Taskbar
- Using the Desktop Icons
- Shutting Down Windows

I started using personal computers in the days before Microsoft Windows or the mouse. I typed on the keyboard, and what I typed appeared in white on a black screen. No colors, no little icons, no buttons, no menus. My computer ran an operating system called DOS, and when I wanted to do something such as open or save a document, I had to know a specific command and type it. Thankfully, this is no longer the case for computer users! In Chapter 1, you learned that Windows is an operating system, the software that controls the hardware and that is the foundation on which applications depend. In this chapter, we'll take a closer look at Windows, and then we'll explore the desktop, which is what you see when you first start your computer.

TIP *Learning to use Windows gives you a distinct advantage when you start to learn a new application that runs under Windows. Although specific items might be different, all the basic operations are the same.*

What Is Windows?

Because Windows is an operating system, it's the program that gives you access to all other programs on your computer. It's called Windows because it runs each of those other programs in its own window, or box, on the screen, and you can have as many windows open as you like. In Figure 2-1, I have two windows open. The Paint program is running in the window on the left, and the window on the right is running WordPad, a small word-processing program that comes with Windows.

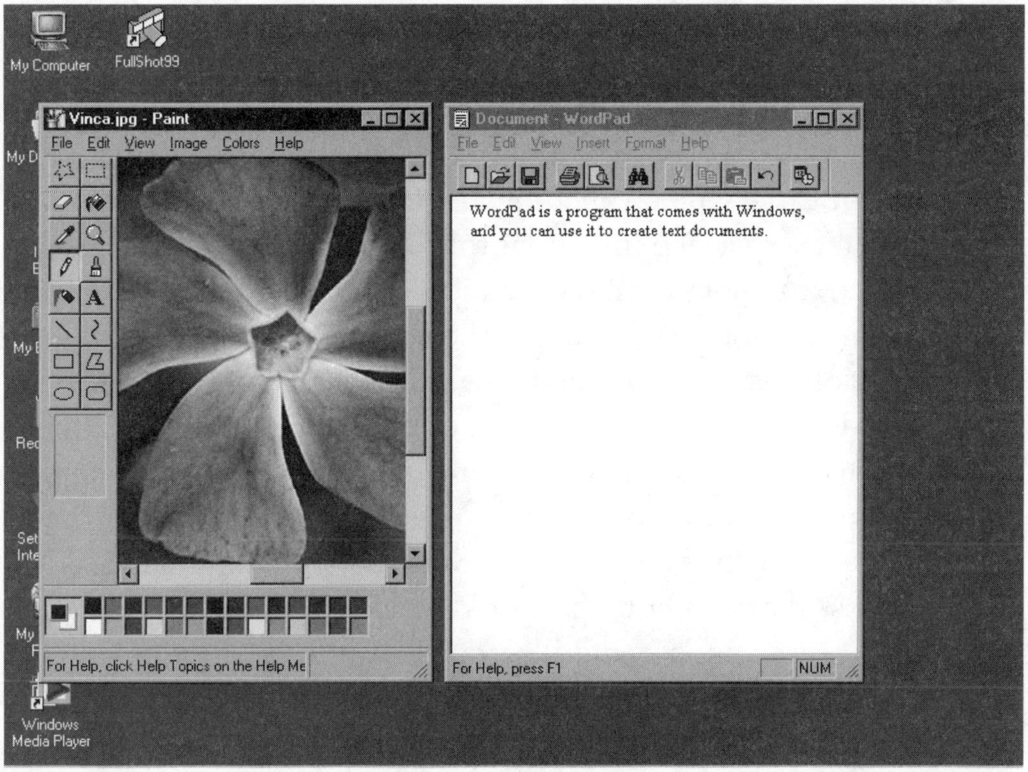

Figure 2-1 Two windows open in Windows.

The word Windows with a capital *W* refers to the program, and windows with a lowercase *w* refers to the boxes on the screen in which other programs run.

What's the Difference Between Windows and a Windows Application?

If you've been following along with the previous chapter and the first part of this chapter, you know the answer to this question. But I want to make a special point about this because I find that many Windows users don't understand the distinction and thus become confused when trying to ask a question or get their computer to do something. I think some of this confusion arises because when you buy a new computer, Windows as well as a number of applications are already installed. Because all these programs come with the computer, people tend to assume that they are all part of Windows, and that's not the case. For example, my newest computer came with a program called Microsoft Works. Works is not a part of Windows; it is an application that you can use to compose and illustrate documents, and, of course, it runs under Windows. Another source of confusion is that as Windows developed, Microsoft began including more and more programs with Windows. Some of the more recent additions are Internet Explorer, Outlook Express, and Windows Media Player.

Windows is the underlying set of programs that make your computer run. An application that runs on top of Windows is a program that you use to perform tasks that are useful to you, such as word-processing, drawing, playing games, accessing the Internet, sending and receiving e-mail, managing your finances, and so on.

NOTE *In this book, I make an effort to explain in context what I think may be terms with which you are not familiar. If you come across a term that isn't explained and that isn't familiar to you, check the glossary. You'll most likely find it there.*

What's All This Version Business About?

In writing this book, I used Windows Millennium Edition, or Windows Me as it is known. Windows Me is the latest version of Windows for the home user. Other versions of Windows are also in use and available in the marketplace. Some are recommended for business use, and others are recommended for home use. Here's a list of those versions now in common use:

- Windows 95, the version of Windows that was released in 1995 and that is still running on many home and business computers. It was a major improvement over its predecessor, Windows 3.1. Usually version numbers are incremental; that is, version 4 follows version 3, version 5 follows version 4, and so on. In this case, Microsoft decided to follow the automobile model and begin naming versions according to the year of their release.
- Windows 98, the version of Windows that was released in 1998 and was an upgrade to Windows 95. Between the release of Windows 98 and Windows Me, Microsoft also released Windows 98 Second Edition, which was a minor upgrade to Windows 98. You may have Windows 98 Second Edition if you bought it in 1999 or in early 2000.
- Windows 2000 Professional, which was the successor to Windows NT Workstation 4.0. Both NT Workstation and 2000 Professional were intended for network use.
- Windows 2000 Server, which is intended for use on a network server computer.
- Windows 2000 Advanced Server, an operating system for enterprises that work with large database applications and online transaction processing. For example, airline reservation systems, banks, and oil companies might use Advanced Server.

- Windows 2000 Datacenter Server, which is for use by large-scale Internet and intranet operations.
- Windows NT 4 Server and Windows NT 4 Workstation, network operating systems that were the predecessors to Windows 2000 Server and Windows 2000 Professional. You will still find many organizations using NT 4 networks because they have not yet upgraded or are in the process of upgrading to Windows 2000.

Why all these versions and why does the software seem to be constantly changing? Because computer technology is constantly evolving. New versions are a good thing because they are an attempt to keep up with the technology.

Do you need to upgrade every time a new version is released? Not necessarily. I do so because I'm in the business, but if you're comfortable with a not-so-recent version of Windows or an application, continue to use it. You will find, however, that eventually you will want to catch up. An excellent example is the recent explosion of the Internet and the way that Windows now makes it easy to connect to and explore the Web. Most likely, you'll want to take advantage of that.

You can get new versions of Windows and applications over the Internet, at computer software stores, at office supply centers, at discount warehouses, and various other places, and they usually are not prohibitively expensive. I recently bought my upgrade to Windows Me for about fifty dollars.

NOTE *If you are using a version of Windows other than Windows Me, the steps you take to perform tasks and what you see on your screen will be similar but not identical to those in this book. You will also not have the features that are new in Windows Me.*

Starting Windows

When you first turn on your computer, you'll hear some whirring sounds and see a short succession of start-up screens while the computer starts. You'll then see the Enter Windows Password dialog box. (A dialog box is a little window-like box that opens on the screen when Windows or a program needs more information from you. In the next chapter, I'll discuss dialog boxes in detail.) If you want to password-protect access to your computer, enter a user name (*you* are the *user*), which can be anything you want, and then enter a password, and click OK. You'll now see the Set Windows Password dialog box, in which you once again enter your password in the Confirm New Password box and then click OK. If you don't want to password-protect access to your computer, simply leave the Enter Windows Password dialog box blank, and click OK.

Under what circumstances might you want to password-protect your computer? If you use your computer at home and you are the only person who uses it, I can't think of any reason to password-protect access to it. Remember, this is a Windows password, not a password that connects you to the Internet or to a network. On the other hand, if other people use your computer at home, at work, or at some other organization and you store information on it that you'd rather others not be privy to, you might want to use a password. Or if you're concerned that others might accidentally erase some important documents that you store on your computer, you might want to password-protect the computer. In any case, it's totally up to you.

If you select a password and then want to change it or you decide you don't want to use a password, you can do so. I'll give you the steps in a later section in this chapter.

Understanding and Using the Desktop

After you deal with the Enter Windows Password dialog box, the next thing you see is the Windows desktop, which is shown in Figure 2-2. You may have more or fewer icons (little pictures) than shown here, depending on what is installed on your system. Except for the FullShot99 icon, the desktop shown in Figure 2-2 is what you'll see the first time you start Windows Me if you or your computer manufacturer hasn't installed additional applications. (FullShot99 is the software program I used to create most of the illustrations in this book.)

Figure 2-2 The Windows Me desktop.

You can get started using Windows by clicking icons on the desktop or by using the Start menu. In this chapter, we'll look first at the Start menu, and later we'll look at how to use the icons.

As we tour the desktop in this chapter, I'll necessarily have to introduce you to some features that I'll explain more fully in later chapters. This chapter isn't meant to take you step-by-step through using the desktop; it is meant to give you an overview of what is on the desktop and how you use the desktop to access the features of Windows. I suggest that as you read this chapter, you open Windows and explore the desktop on your computer. You can use the illustrations as a guide to what to expect.

The Start Menu

The Start button is located on the far left end at the bottom of your screen. Click the Start button, and you'll see a menu similar to the one shown in Figure 2-3. Let's take a look at the items on the Start menu.

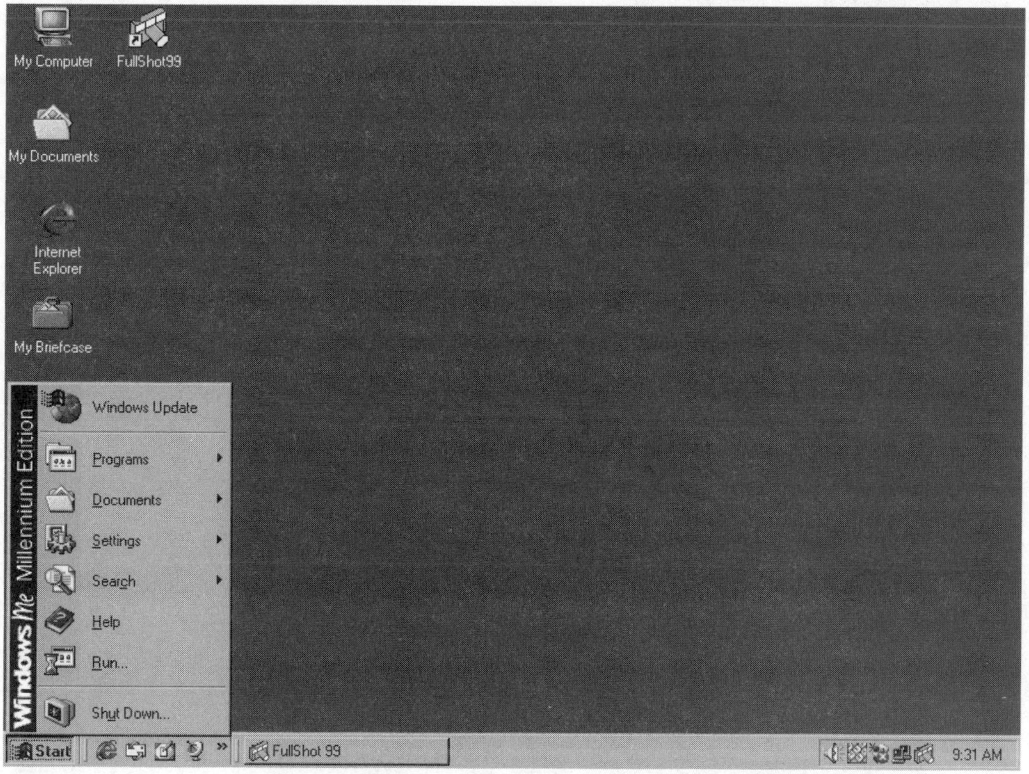

Figure 2-3 The Windows Me desktop and the Start menu.

Connecting to the Windows Update Site

Windows Update is a Microsoft Web site from which you can obtain product updates, technical support, and online help, among other things. If you click Start and then click Windows Update, and you are connected to the Internet, you'll see a Web page similar to that shown in Figure 2-4 open in Internet Explorer. (I'll discuss how to use Internet Explorer and how to connect to the Internet in detail in Chapters 6 and 7. Here I just want to explain what this item on the menu does.) If you want to be notified whenever Microsoft posts a critical new update for Windows Me, click the Product Updates link.

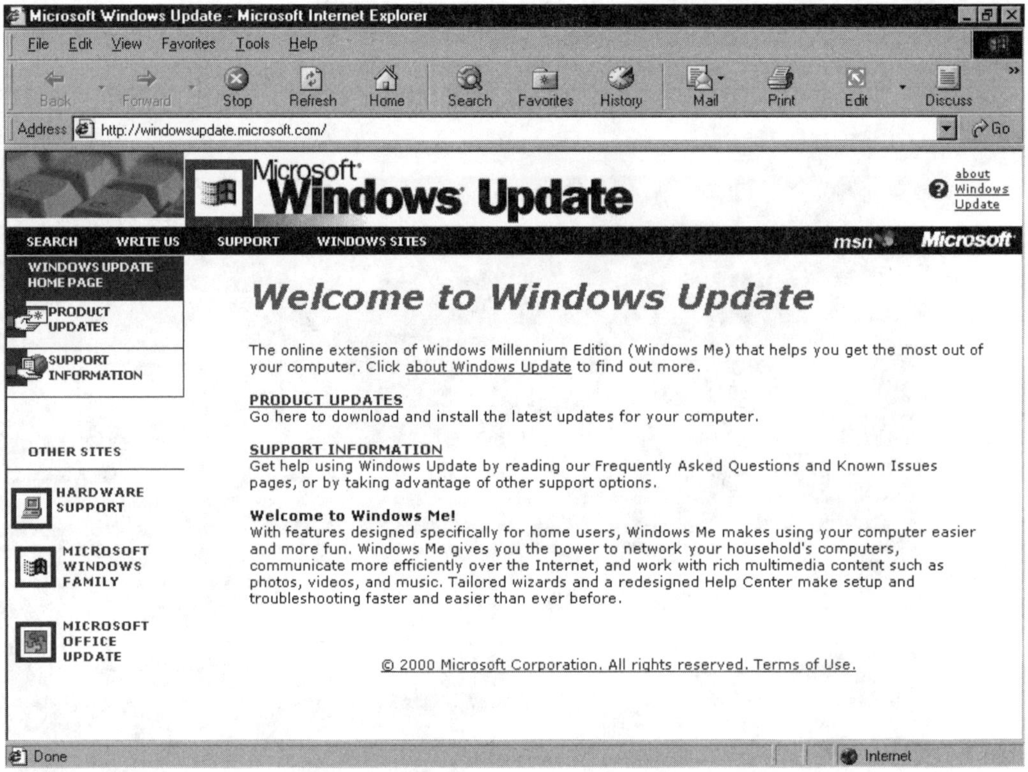

Figure 2-4 The Microsoft Windows Update page.

Finding Programs

As you recall from Chapter 1, the word *program* is often used as a synonym for the word *application* or *software*. Although you can start programs on your system in a number of ways, one of the most straightforward is to use the Start menu. When you click the Programs item on the Start menu, you'll see a submenu that lists all of the programs installed on your computer. Clicking one of the program names either starts that program or displays a submenu that contains a list of programs within that program group. At the very least, you'll see the following items on the Programs menu:

- **Accessories** contains yet another submenu of programs that come with Windows. I'll tell you how to use some of these programs in other chapters in this book, and then in Chapter 12, I'll tell you how to use a group of them that you might use more frequently.
- **Startup** contains the names of programs you want to use every time you start Windows Me.
- **Internet Explorer** is the Web browser included with Windows Me and other recent versions of Windows. In Chapter 7, I'll discuss Internet Explorer in detail.
- **Outlook Express** is the e-mail program that's included with Windows Me and other recent versions of Windows. In Chapter 8, I'll discuss how to send and receive e-mail with Outlook Express.

When you first install Windows Me, a feature called personalized menus is enabled. A personalized menu includes only those items you've used most recently. You can see other items on the menu by clicking the down arrow at the bottom of the menu. Some people find this to be a great way to simplify and streamline the Start menu, while others find it annoying. You can decide for yourself and then disable personalized menus if you don't like using them. To disable personalized menus, follow these steps:

1. **Open the Taskbar And Start Menu Properties dialog box, as shown in Figure 2-5.**

   To do this, click the Start button, click Settings, and then click Taskbar And Start Menu.

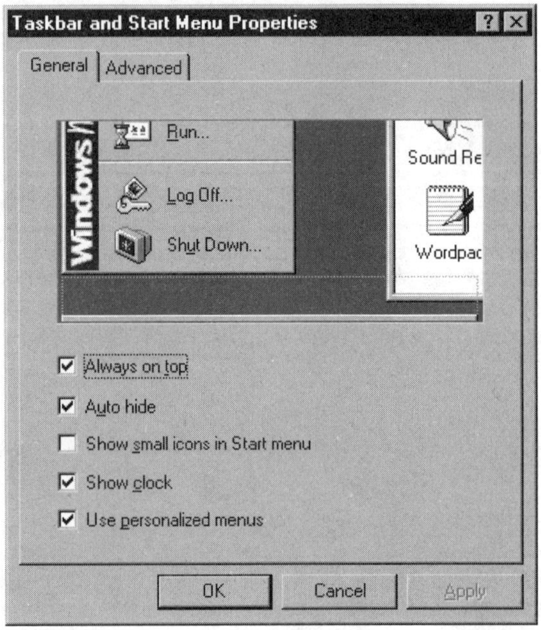

Figure 2-5 The Taskbar And Start Menu Properties dialog box.

2. **Disable personalized menus.**

   On the General tab, click the Use Personalized Menus check box to clear it, and then click OK.

NOTE *If a dialog box involves more information than can be displayed in a single screen, it is divided into tabbed pages, which are referred to simply as tabs. In Chapter 3, I'll give you details about how to use tabs and the other elements in a dialog box. Later in this chapter, we'll look at the taskbar.*

Now that you know how to use the Start menu to find programs, I want to give you the steps to follow if you want to change your password. To do this, we'll use a little program that's found in Control Panel. (I'll tell you all about Control Panel in Chapter 10.) Here are the steps:

1. **Open Control Panel, as shown in Figure 2-6.**

   To do this, click the Start button, click Settings, click Control Panel to open Control Panel, and then click the View All Control Panel Options link (it's in blue and underlined).

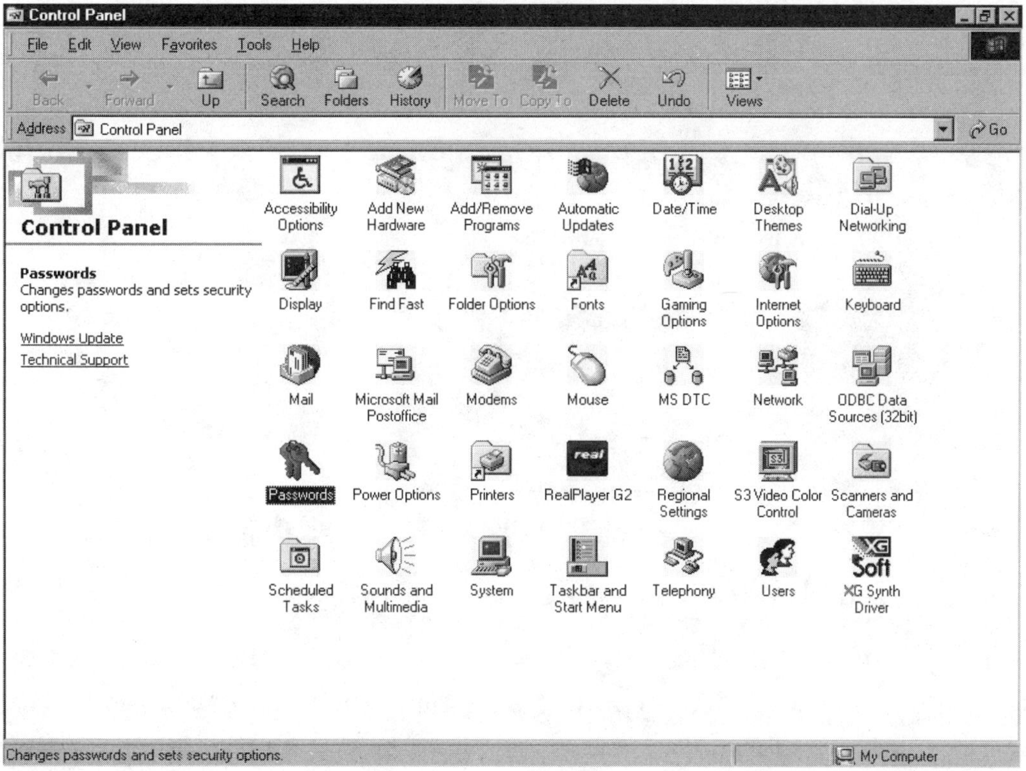

Figure 2-6 The Windows Control Panel.

2. **Open the Passwords Properties dialog box, as shown in Figure 2-7.**

   Double-click the Passwords icon.

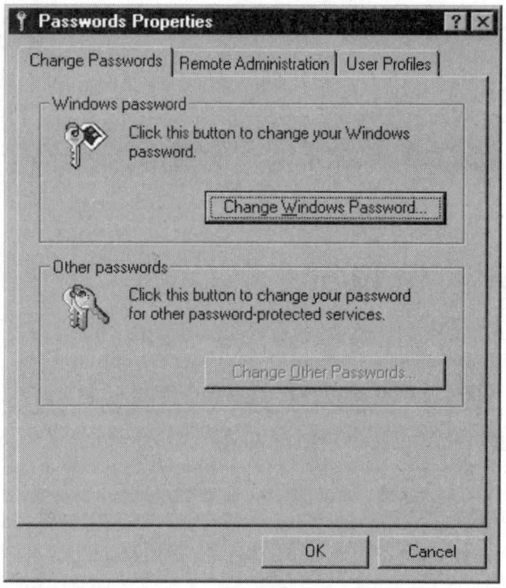

Figure 2-7

The Passwords Properties dialog box.

3. **Open the Change Windows Password dialog box, as shown in Figure 2-8.**

   Click the Change Windows Password button.

Figure 2-8 The Change Windows Password dialog box.

4. **Tell Windows about the new password.**

   In the Old Password box, type your current password. In the New Password box, type the new password, or leave this box blank if you no longer want to use a password. Type the new password again in the Confirm New Password box, or leave this box blank if you don't want to use a password, and then click OK. Click OK again in the Passwords Properties dialog box.

Finding Documents

In Windows, a document is anything you create in an application and then save on your computer system. In the non-computer world, a document is generally considered to contain text, but to the computer, a document is anything that you create. Thus, a document can be a spreadsheet, a drawing, a digital photograph, an e-mail message, and so on.

In Chapter 4, I'll tell you about several ways that you can manage your documents so that you can always easily and quickly find them. In this section, though, we're looking at how to use the items on the Start menu, and the Start menu includes the Documents item, which you can also use to easily and quickly find and open any of the last 15 documents you have used as well as the My Documents folder and the My Pictures folder. (I'll discuss both these folders and explain folders in Chapter 4.)

When you click a document from the list that opens when you click Documents in the Start menu, the document opens immediately in the application with which it was created. One exception, however, is a document that is an image. Clicking an image on the Documents list opens the image in the Image Preview program regardless of the program with which it was created.

To specify the program in which a type of document always opens, follow these steps:

1. Display the Open With dialog box, as shown in Figure 2-9.

Click the Start button, click Documents, right-click the name of a document in the list, and then choose Open With from the shortcut menu.

Figure 2-9

The Open With dialog box.

2. **Associate a program with a document.**

   Select a program, click the Always Use This Program To Open These Files check box, and then click OK.

If you don't see the program you want on the list, click the Other button, select a program, and click Open. Windows Me adds the program to the list. Select the program, click the Always Use This Program To Open These Files check box, and then click OK.

To clear the items from the Documents list and start a fresh list, follow these steps:

1. **Open the Taskbar And Start Menu Properties dialog box (see Figure 2-5).**

   Click the Start button, click Settings, and then click Taskbar And Start Menu.

2. **Tell Windows that you want to start a fresh Documents list.**

   Click the Advanced tab, as shown in Figure 2-10, click the Clear button, and then click OK.

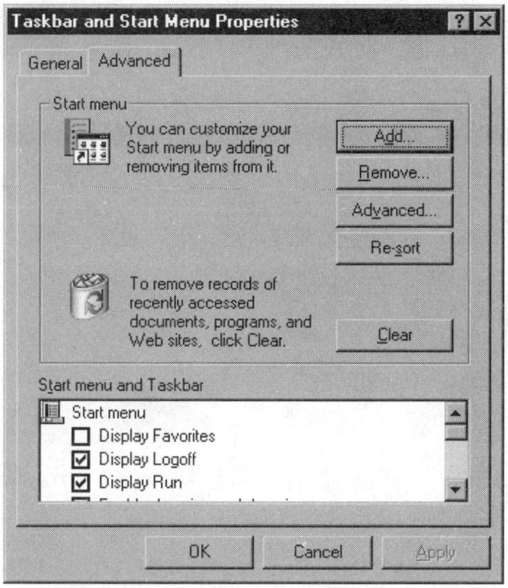

Figure 2-10

The Taskbar And Start Menu Properties dialog box open at the Advanced tab.

Right-Clicking

In Chapter 1, you read how to right-click the mouse, and if you were following along with the steps for opening a document in a specific program, you may have used the right-click method to display a shortcut menu. A *shortcut menu* consists of items that are appropriate to whatever you right-clicked. Sometimes you'll hear this menu referred to as a context menu or a right-click menu.

You can right-click almost anything in Windows and display something useful. In some cases, instead of a shortcut menu you'll see a What's This? box that you can click to get help with the item you right-clicked. Later in this chapter, we'll look at how to get other kinds of help in Windows.

As you become a more-experienced Windows user, you'll quickly see the value of right-clicking. Here's an example of how right-clicking saves you time and effort. Suppose you want to open

Windows Explorer, the tool you use to manage your files and folders. (I'll tell you all about Windows Explorer in Chapter 4.) You can do so in a couple of ways:

- Click the Start button, click Programs, click Accessories to open the Accessories menu, and then click Windows Explorer.
- Right-click the My Computer icon on the desktop, and click Explore.

No question about which technique is quicker, right?

Understanding Settings

In Windows Me, you use the items on the Settings menu to open yet another item with which you can change your computer system in some way. You've already seen how to use the Taskbar And Start Menu item to enable or disable personalized menus. Figure 2-11 shows the items on the Settings menu.

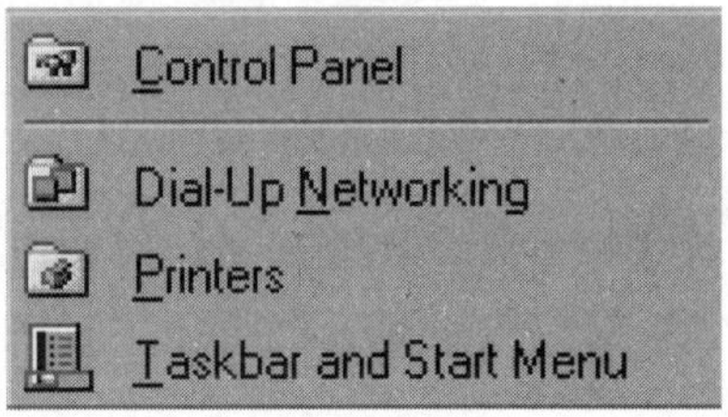

Figure 2-11 The Settings menu.

When you click Control Panel, you'll see the screen shown earlier in this chapter in Figure 2-6. Control Panel consists of *applets,* or small programs, that you use to personalize Windows Me. In Chapter 10, we'll look in detail at how to use the Control Panel applets to customize your system.

When you click Dial-Up Networking, you open the Dial-Up Networking folder, which you can use to create a new Internet connection, check the status of a current connection, or connect to the Internet.

(In Chapters 6 and 7, I'll discuss how to connect to and use the Internet.)

When you click Printers, you open the Printers folder, which you use to install a new printer and get information about the printer or printers installed on your system. In Chapter 5, I'll show you how to use the elements in this folder and how to print.

Searching and Finding

As I mentioned earlier in this chapter, in Chapter 4 I'm going to show you how to organize what you store on your computer so that you can find it easily and quickly. But no matter how well organized you are personally and how diligently you adhere to an organization scheme for storing your computer documents, you will misplace a document or forget where you stored it. Trust me on this.

Just before I started writing this book, my son sent me some photographs of his brand-new baby girl, my second grandchild. I was fortunate that he had acquired a digital camera and was able to transmit these treasures within a matter of hours after her birth. Because he was working quickly, he didn't bother to rename these photos but kept the rather cryptic numeric names that the camera supplied. I downloaded the photos and put them where I thought I'd be able to retrieve them, but I guess in the excitement I forgot the location. I did remember, however, that part of the name of each photo was .jpg. (That part of the filename is called an *extension,* and I'll explain all about filenames and extensions in Chapter 4.) So, I was able to use the Search item on the Start menu to find my pictures and send them off to friends and family. (I'll show you how to do the same thing in Chapter 8.)

Here are the steps I used to locate my pictures:

1. Open the Search Results dialog box, as shown in Figure 2-12.

Click the Start button, click Search, and click For Files Or Folders.

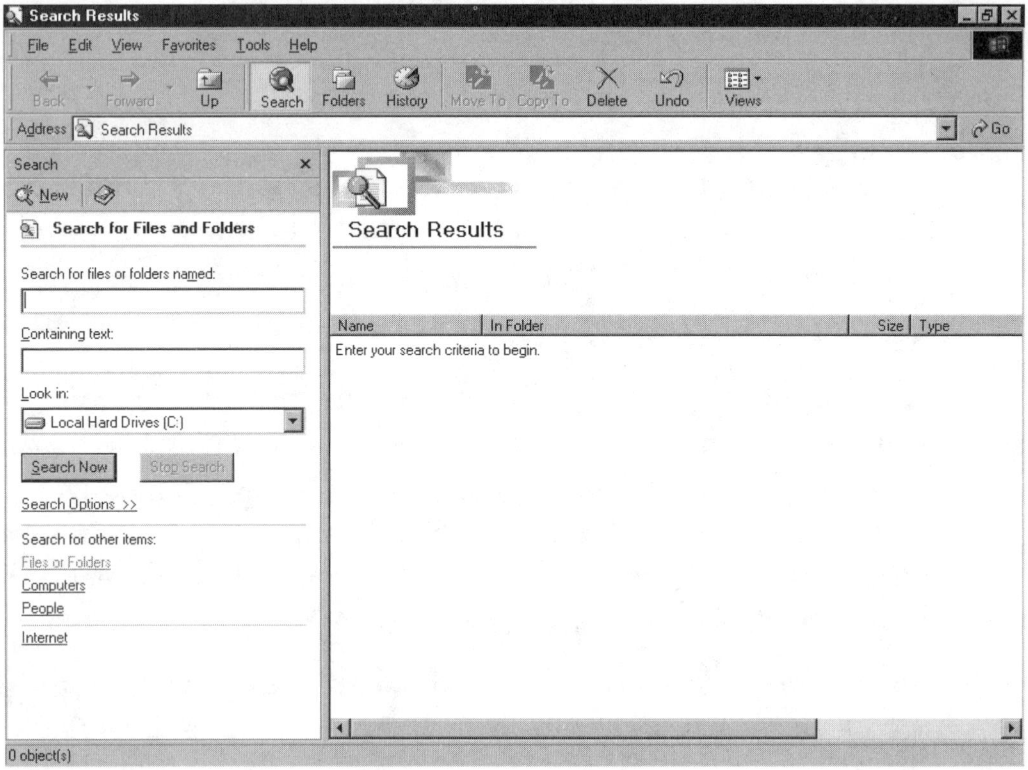

Figure 2-12 The Search Results dialog box.

2. Enter what you want to search for.

In the Search For Files Or Folders Named box, type the part of the filename you know, or, in the Containing Text box, type a term or phrase that you know is contained in the document (if it is a text document). If you have more than one hard drive on your system, select it from the Look In drop-down list box.

NOTE *In my picture search, I typed* *.jpg *in the Search For Files Or Folder Named box. The asterisk (*) substitutes for any character or characters that precede the period.*

3. Begin your search.

Click the Search Now button. You'll see the results of your search in the pane on the right. To open the document, simply double-click it.

You can use the same steps when you need to locate a document, and you can also use Search to locate a person or information on the Internet if you are connected to the Internet. In Chapter 7, I'll tell you how to search the Internet using Internet Explorer.

Getting Help

When you're stumped about how to do something in Windows, where do you go for help? Although you can phone a friend or ask one of your computer-savvy relatives, consider making your first line of defense the Windows Help system. To get to it, click the Start button, and then click Help. Windows displays the Help And Support center, which is shown in Figure 2-13.

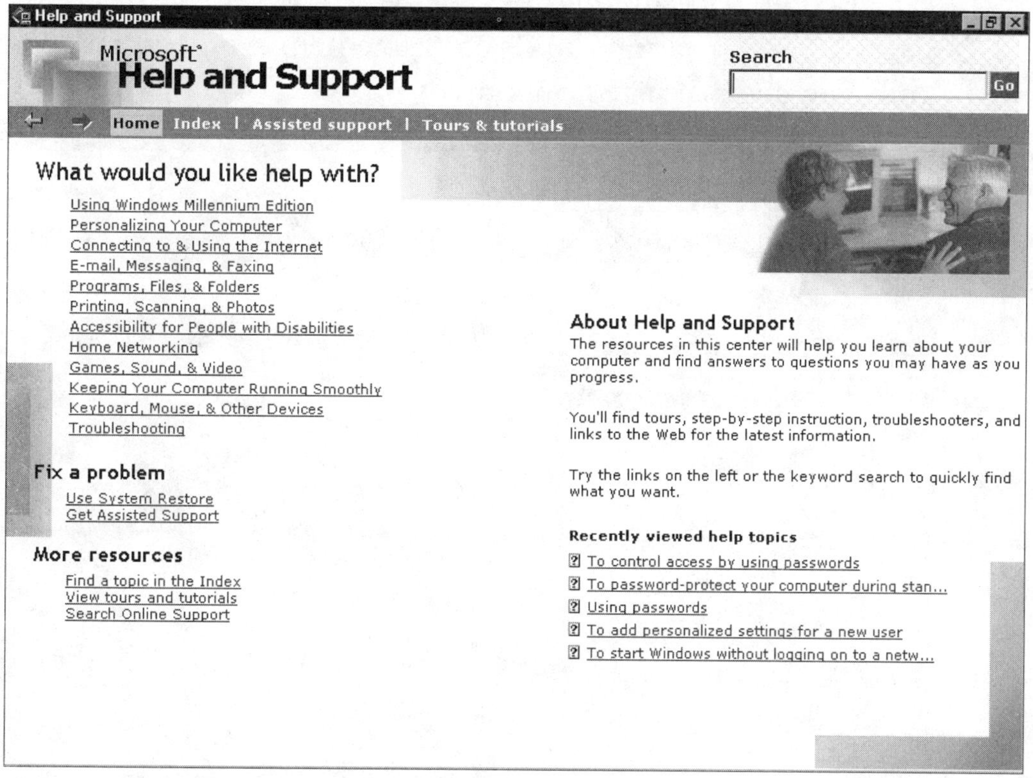

Figure 2-13 The Help And Support center.

This screen looks and acts like a Web page. You can click an underlined phrase to open a page that contains information about that topic. If you're new to using Windows, click Tours & Tutorials in the bar near the top of the page to open a table of contents that lists the available tours and tutorials. Tours and tutorials take the form of little movies or slide shows that you can run yourself.

I usually use the Index page, which is shown in Figure 2-14, when I want to find help on a specific topic. Simply enter a word in the Type In The Keyword To Find box, and then click the Display button to search for information on a specific task or topic. You can then click a link on the left to display its contents in the pane on the right. You can also enter a search term in the Search box at the top right of the page. To access various kinds of online help, connect to the Internet and then click Assisted Support.

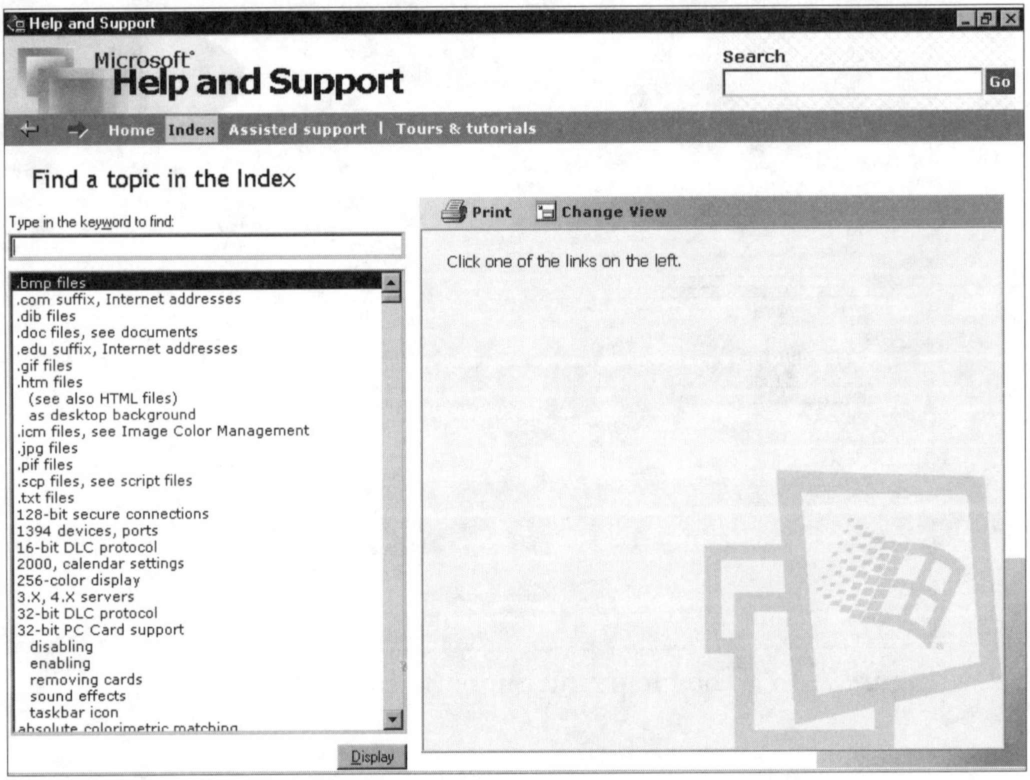

Figure 2-14 The Index in the Help And Support center.

Using the Run Dialog Box

When you're using Windows, you almost always have more than one way to do something—start a program, open a document, or go to an Internet site, for example. Although the Run dialog box might not be your first choice among the many tools at your disposal, you may find that it comes in handy at certain times. And, of course, since the Run item is on the Start menu, you need to know what it's for.

When you click the Start button and then click Run, you'll see the Run dialog box, as shown in Figure 2-15. In the Open box, you simply type the name of a resource—a program, a folder, or an Internet address—and then click OK to open that resource. If you don't know the name, click the Browse button to open the Browse dialog box, which is shown in Figure 2-16, and locate it. When you find the name, select it, and then click Open. Windows displays the name in the Open box in the Run dialog box. Click OK to open the resource.

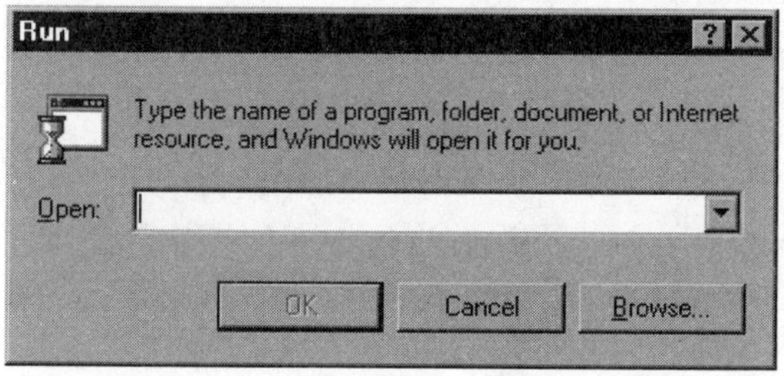

Figure 2-15 The Run dialog box.

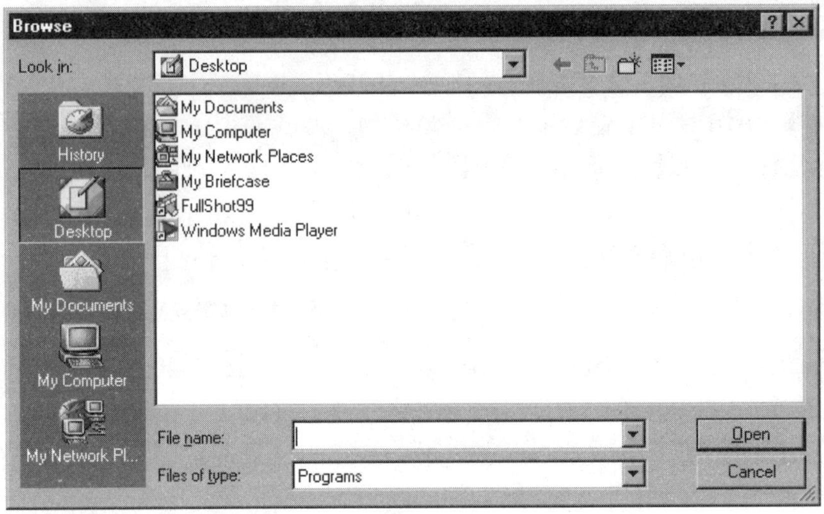

Figure 2-16 The Browse dialog box.

NOTE *You'll find a Browse button in various Windows dialog boxes, and you'll probably use it often to locate precise names of files, folders, and documents. In Chapter 4, you'll find information that will help you understand how this dialog box works.*

This tour of the Start menu is now complete with the exception of the Shut Down item. Shut Down closes your computer when you are finished using it, so I'll discuss this item at the end of this chapter.

Using the Taskbar

The *taskbar* is the bar at the bottom of the desktop, and it's divided into the Quick Launch bar, which is the portion on the left, and the status area, which is at the far right. Figure 2-17 shows the taskbar on my Windows Me system. Clicking an item on the taskbar is the fastest way to access the program.

Figure 2-17 The taskbar in Windows Me.

The Quick Launch Bar

When you start an application, its icon appears on the Quick Launch bar. Icons for Microsoft Internet Explorer and Microsoft Outlook Express always appear on the Quick Launch bar, so you can always quickly start either one. (I'll discuss Internet Explorer in detail in Chapter 7 and Outlook Express in Chapter 8.) To display a ScreenTip that describes each item, simply point to the item. A ScreenTip is a white box outlined in black that contains text telling you what an icon or a button will do when you click the icon or button.

In the next chapter, I'll talk about the elements of a window; how to minimize, maximize, and restore a window; and how to open multiple windows at the same time. If you ever have multiple windows open and need quick access to something on the desktop, click the Show Desktop icon on the Quick Launch bar.

When you click the View Channels icon, you open a Web page in Internet Explorer that contains a link to the WindowsMedia.com site, which is shown in Figure 2-18. WindowsMedia.com is an audio-video guide to sites that let you listen to radio, play and download music, and watch TV, videos, and movies. I'll discuss entertainment features such as these in Chapter 13.

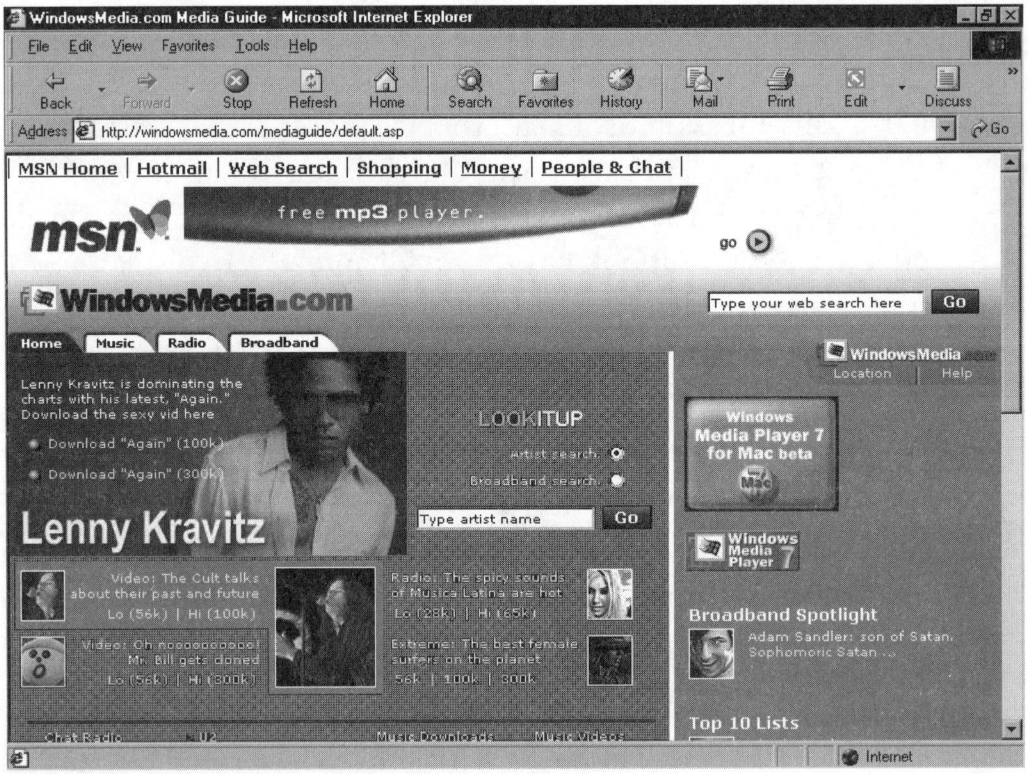

Figure 2-18 The WindowsMedia.com site.

The Status Area

By default, the status area contains the time, the Volume icon, and any other icons that refer to other features that the manufacturer of your computer has installed. If you point to the time, the current day and date are displayed. Windows automatically adjusts the time for daylight saving changes, and for the most part, the Windows clock keeps accurate time. If you live in an area that is subject to power outages, you will need to adjust the time occasionally. You will, of course, need to adjust the time if you move to a different time zone.

NOTE *From time to time in this book, I will use the expression "by default." This is simply a shorthand way to say that a feature or an option is selected when you first start Windows after installing it.*

To adjust the time, you use the Date/Time Properties dialog box. Follow these steps:

1. **Open the Date/Time Properties dialog box, as shown in Figure 2-19.**

   Right-click the time in the status area, and choose Adjust Date/Time from the shortcut menu.

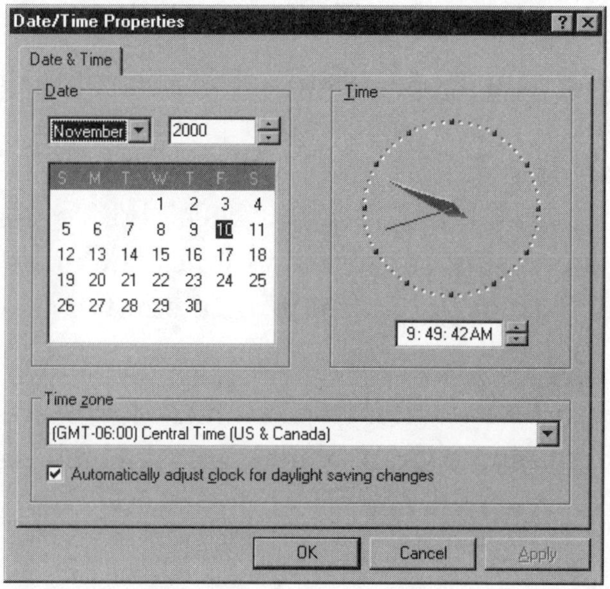

Figure 2-19 The Date/Time Properties dialog box.

2. **Change the date.**

   Click the down arrow for the month, and select a different month. Click the up arrow or down arrow for the year, and select a different year. To change the date, click the date you want in the calendar.

3. **Change the time.**

   Click the up or down arrow next to the current time. To change the time zone, click the down arrow in the Time Zone box, and select another time zone. If you don't want Windows to automatically adjust the time for daylight saving changes, click the Automatically Adjust Clock For Daylight Saving Changes check box to clear it. Click OK.

You can adjust the volume of your speakers in several ways. If your speakers have a volume knob, as mine do, you can simply turn the knob to raise or lower the volume. If you want to mute the sound entirely, you can turn off the power to your speakers by pressing the Power button on the speaker. (Typically, only one speaker has control knobs.) Some keyboards also have buttons for raising and lowering the volume and for muting the sound.

Windows also provides a couple of ways to adjust the volume. Click the Volume icon (the little yellow loudspeaker picture) once to open a slider bar that you can drag to raise and lower the volume. Beneath the slider bar is a Mute check box. Click this check box to mute the sound. If you decide later you want to hear sound, click this check box again. To close this box, click outside it in an empty area on the desktop.

If you want to make even finer sounds adjustments, double-click the Volume icon to open the Volume Control dialog box, which is shown in Figure 2-20. The options that appear in this dialog box depend on your sound system. Use the slider bars in this dialog box to adjust volume and balance; click the Mute check boxes to mute any single aspect of sound, and click the Mute All check box to silence your computer. When you're finished, click the Close button (the X at the top right of the dialog box).

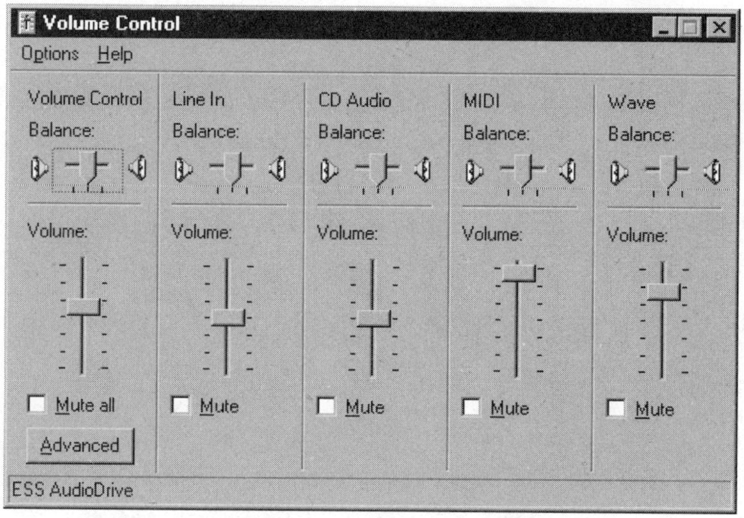

Figure 2-20 The Volume Control dialog box.

Hiding and Displaying the Taskbar

You can completely hide the taskbar, always display it, or choose to hide it unless you point to it. To hide the taskbar completely, click its top edge, and then drag the top edge down to the bottom edge. To display it again, drag the visible edge upward.

To tell Windows how and when to display the taskbar, you select options in the Taskbar And Start Menu Properties dialog box that we have used a couple of times earlier in this chapter (see Figure 2-5). On the General tab (the tab that is displayed when you first open the dialog box), click the Always On Top check box if you want the taskbar visible at all times. (By default, the taskbar is always visible. Clear this check box if you don't want the taskbar visible at all times.) If you want the taskbar hidden unless you point to it, leave the Always On Top check box selected, and also click the Auto Hide check box.

Using the Desktop Icons

The icons displayed on the desktop are *shortcuts;* that is, they are representations of a tool or a program, not the real thing. In this section, I'll describe the basic desktop icons that appear when you install Windows Me. As I've mentioned before, if you acquired your computer with Windows Me already installed, the manufacturer may have also installed other programs whose icons appear on your desktop. To see a description of what each tool or program does, simply point to an icon. To open the tool or program represented by an icon, double-click the icon.

To rearrange the icons on your desktop, simply point to an icon, and then drag it to a new location. Removing an icon does not remove the tool or program, only its representation on the desktop. To remove an icon, simply click it, and then drag it to the Recycle Bin icon (more about the Recycle Bin later in this section). You'll find that you can't remove some icons. When this is the case, a circle with a slash in it will appear as you start to drag the icon.

My Computer

Double-clicking the My Computer icon opens the My Computer folder, which is shown in Figure 2-21. This folder is a window into your computer. From here, you can go to any disk, any program, any folder, or any document. Click an icon to display information about it on the left. For example, if you click an icon for a drive, you'll see a numeric and graphic display of the free and used space.

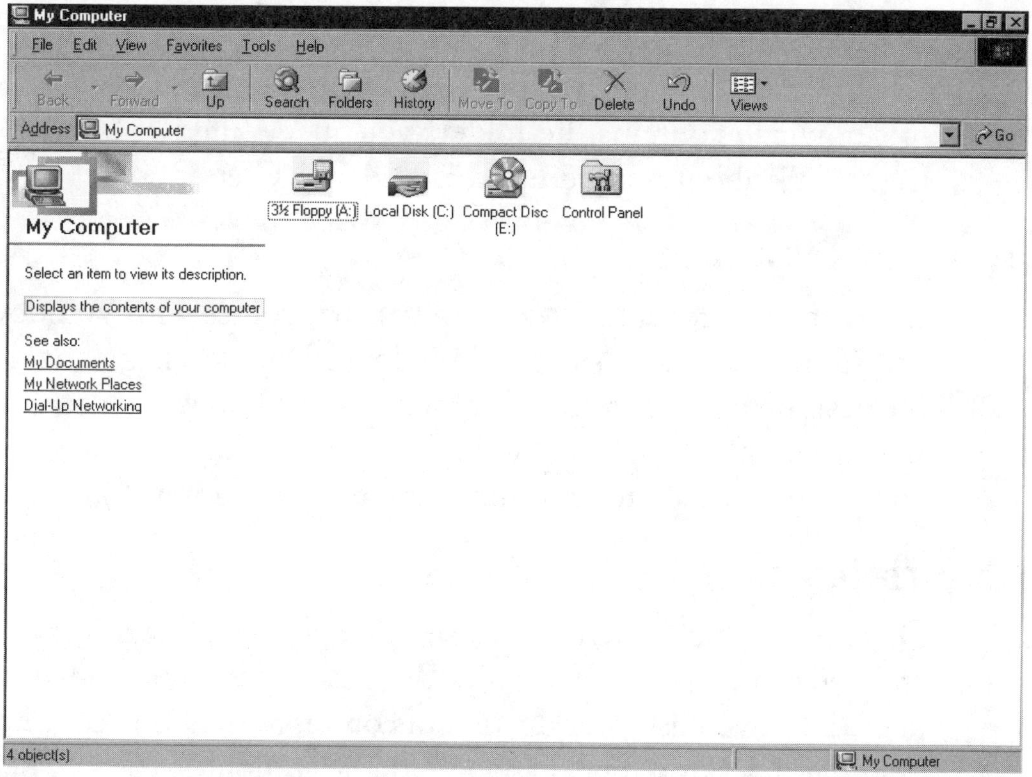

Figure 2-21 The My Computer folder.

If you right-click the My Computer icon once rather than double-clicking, you'll see a shortcut menu. Click Properties to open the System Properties dialog box, which gives you information about your computer system, such as the version of Windows you are running, how much RAM your system has, and so on. You might want to do this if you ever communicate with a technical support person. This is the sort of information that he or she will need to know to help with your problem.

My Documents

Double-clicking the My Documents icon opens the My Documents folder, which contains the folders you and Windows have stored in it. (I'll talk about how to use this folder in Chapter 4.)

Internet Explorer

Internet Explorer is the Web browser that comes with Windows Me and some previous versions of Windows. Double-clicking its icon on the desktop opens Internet Explorer. As you know, you can also open Internet Explorer by clicking its icon on the Quick Launch bar. (I'll give you details about Internet Explorer in Chapter 7.)

My Briefcase

Double-clicking the My Briefcase icon opens the My Briefcase folder and Welcome To The Windows Briefcase window, as shown in Figure 2-22. If you use your documents on more than one computer, for example, a desktop model and a portable computer, you can place the documents in My Briefcase on a floppy disk and transfer them back and forth. I don't think that most home users have occasion to use My Briefcase (I don't), but if this is something you need to do, check out the Help And Support center for more information.

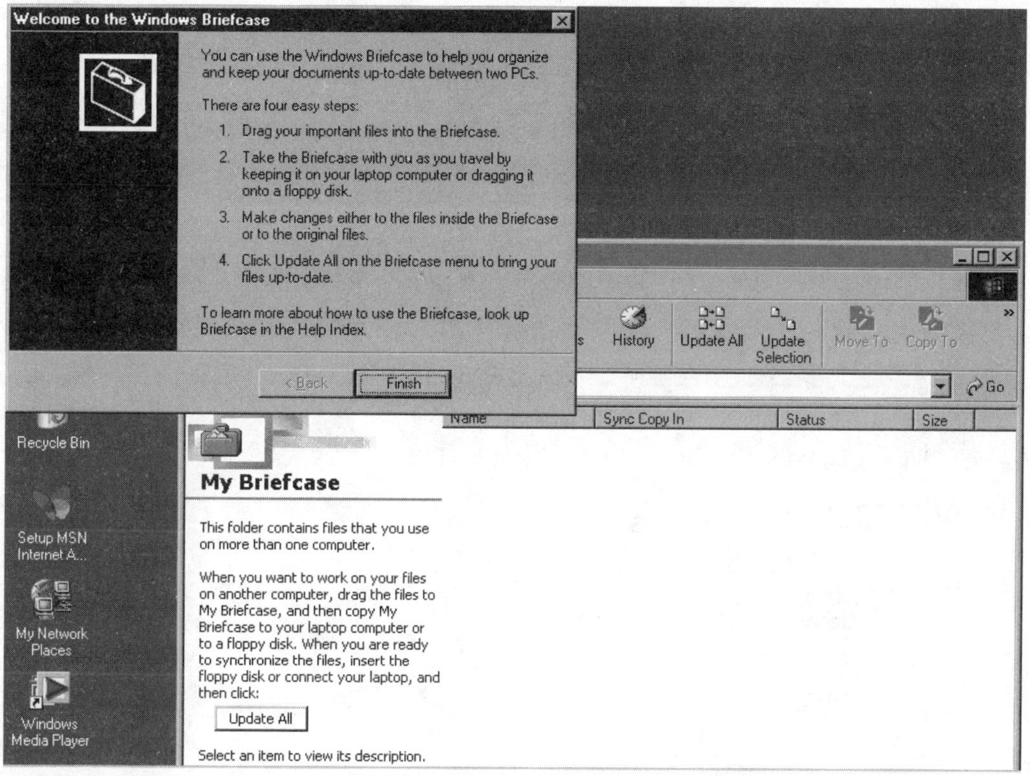

Figure 2-22 The My Briefcase folder and window.

Recycle Bin

In Chapter 4, I'll be explaining how to delete items from your computer. The important point here is that when you delete something, it isn't really gone. Instead, Windows sends it to the Recycle Bin. The Recycle Bin is a safety net because, up to a point, you can retrieve items from it. Only when the Recycle Bin is full are the oldest items in it automatically deleted to make room for other items. Until this stage is reached or until you manually empty the Recycle Bin, you can retrieve an item.

WARNING *Items that you delete from floppy disks are immediately deleted—they do not go to the Recycle Bin first.*

To retrieve an item from the Recycle Bin, follow these steps:

1. Open the Recycle Bin folder.

Double-click the Recycle Bin icon on the desktop. You'll see something similar to what's shown in Figure 2-23.

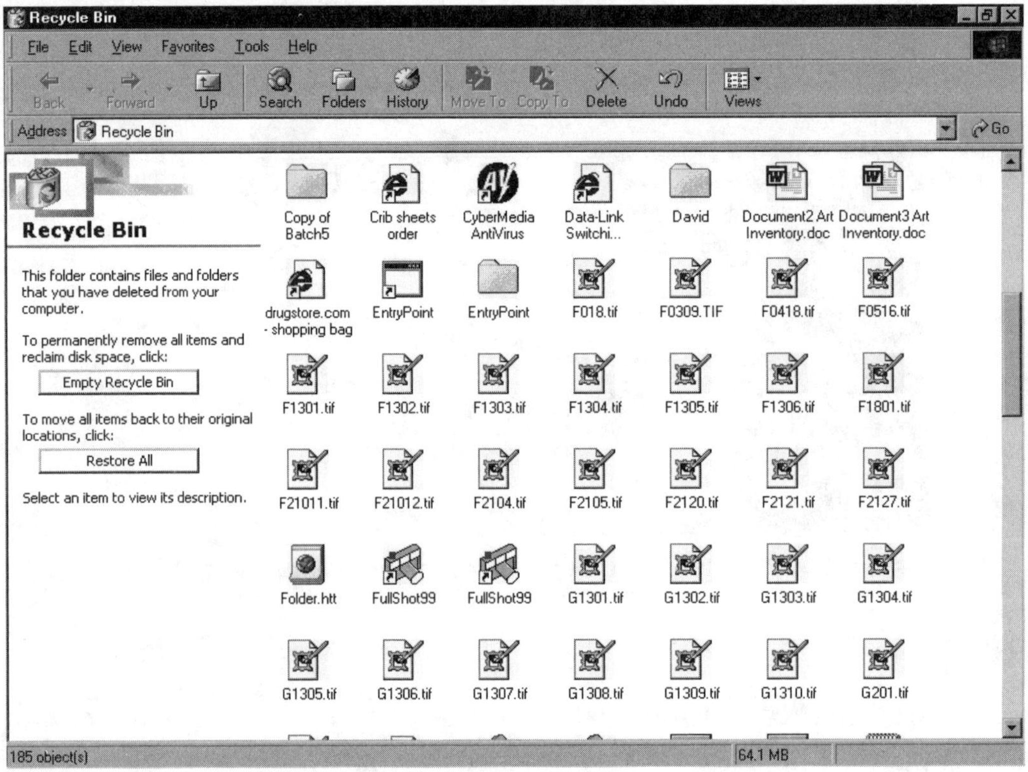

Figure 2-23 The Recycle Bin folder.

2. Retrieve the item.

Click the item you want to retrieve, and then click the Restore button to send the item back to its original location. The Restore button is displayed after you select an item.

To remove all items from the Recycle Bin folder manually, click the Empty Recycle Bin button. To move all items back to their original locations, click the Restore All button.

TIP *Windows provides a safeguard to prevent your deleting an item that you really should keep. When you select an item, its size, date of deletion, and name is displayed on the left.*

If you'd rather not send items to the Recycle Bin but delete them immediately, follow these steps:

1. **Open the Recycle Bin Properties dialog box, as shown in Figure 2-24.**

   Right-click the Recycle Bin icon, and then choose Properties from the shortcut menu.

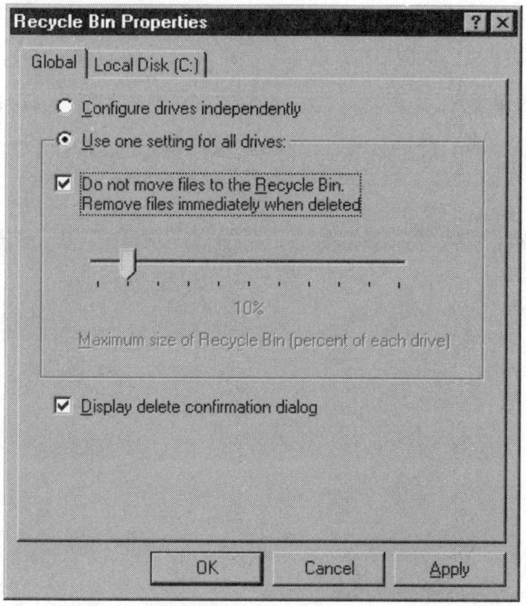

Figure 2-24 The Recycle Bin Properties dialog box.

2. **Tell Windows not to move deleted items to the Recycle Bin folder.**

   Click the Global tab if necessary, and then click the Do Not Move Files To The Recycle Bin check box, and click OK.

To make the Recycle Bin larger or smaller, move the slider in the Global tab of the Recycle Bin Properties dialog box.

Setting Up MSN Internet Access

If you don't have Internet access and would like to use Microsoft's MSN (Microsoft Network) Internet service, click the Set Up MSN Internet Access icon. You'll open a screen that will step you through the process. In Chapter 6, I'll tell you how to connect to the Internet in other ways and explain the differences in the various services that are available.

My Network Places

Double-clicking the My Network Places icon opens the My Network Places folder, which is shown in Figure 2-25. You use the options in this folder to set up and use a local area network or a home network. I'll discuss how to set up a network in Chapter 14 and give you step-by-step instructions.

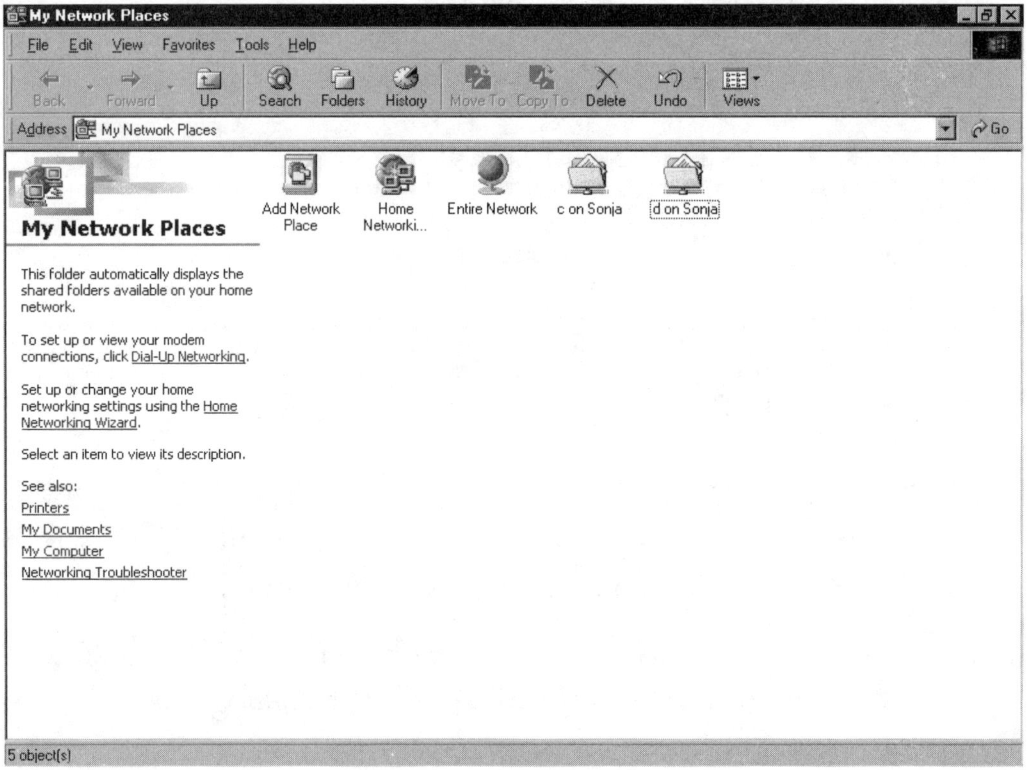

Figure 2-25 The My Network Places folder.

Windows Media Player

Double-clicking Windows Media Player opens the Windows Media Player. I'll discuss this tool and other Windows entertainment features in Chapter 13.

Shutting Down Windows

Windows is a substantial operating system, but it certainly isn't perfect, and users occasionally compile and distribute lists of oddities. How you shut down Windows is always an item on these lists because you click the Start button. In one way, this sounds reasonable because you click the Start button to get to all the tools and programs on your computer. From a plain, old common-sense point of view, you have to chuckle. Nevertheless, when you are finished working with your computer and you are ready to power it down, follow these steps:

1. Open the Shut Down Windows dialog box, as shown in Figure 2-26.

Click the Start button, and then click Shut Down.

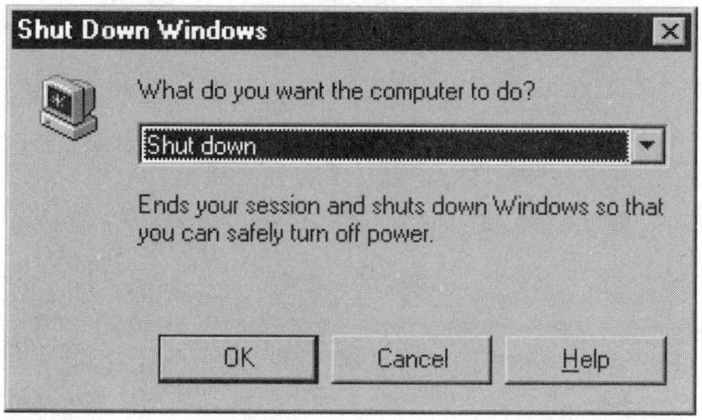

Figure 2-26 The Shut Down Windows dialog box.

2. Shut down your computer.

Click the down arrow, select Shut Down, and then click OK.

You can also use this dialog box to put your computer on standby or to restart your computer:

- Standby turns off your monitor, hard drive, and other devices to conserve power. When you start to use your computer again, it comes to life quickly, and the desktop looks just as it did when you went on standby (unless there is a power failure).
- Restart restarts the system. If you are having difficulty with some program hanging or seem unable to get things working as they should, sometimes the best thing to do is restart. When you select Restart and then click OK, Windows closes and then starts up again. You don't need to shut the power off and turn it back on.

You'll find out soon enough that it's always best to follow the shutdown procedure I've just described. If you don't, the next time you start your computer you'll have to wait while Windows Me checks to make sure that all is well with your hard drives. But even more important, you can lose important information if you don't shut down the computer properly.

Some computers are set up by their manufacturers to power down automatically when the shut down procedure is followed. On other computers, you may see a message telling you that it is now safe to turn off your computer. Only turn off the power after you see this message.

Seven Important Things to Remember About Windows

1. If you don't want to set up password access to your computer, simply click OK in the Enter Windows Password dialog box.
2. Right-clicking an object is a quick way to access options associated with the object, and even if it doesn't, right-clicking can do no harm.
3. You don't need to upgrade every time a new version of Windows is released, but eventually you will want to catch up with the latest version to access features that more recent technology makes possible.
4. Windows with a capital *W* refers to the program; windows with a lowercase *w* refers to the boxes on the screen.
5. In Windows, a document is anything you create in an application and save on your computer.
6. You can open programs quickly from the taskbar.
7. Always shut down Windows properly so that you don't lose important information you've stored on your computer.

Summary

The desktop on your computer screen doesn't seem very big when you compare it with your large-screen TV or a movie screen, but it contains a lot that you need to know about to use your computer effectively. I don't expect you to remember every little nuance of every feature we've looked at in this chapter, but I tried to include everything that you'd normally use and explain some features even though most of us might seldom use them. As you go through the rest of this book and as you use your computer, you can revisit this chapter any time you have a question about your Windows desktop.

Chapter 3

USING WINDOWS

Featuring:

- Understanding the Parts of a Window
- Using Menu Bars
- Using Toolbars
- Using Dialog Boxes

In the process of doing some research for this book, I tried to find some reliable statistics about how so-called seniors were using their computers. Numbers were hard to come by and not up-to-date, but what I did learn was that most seniors use their computers to do the same kinds of things everybody else does: word-process, play games, manage personal finances, desktop-publish, send and receive e-mail, and access the World Wide Web.

Regardless of why you acquired your computer and what you use it for, though, you do yourself a big favor when you take the time to learn how to use windows. (Remember, lowercase *windows* refers to the boxes that open when you start up a program or access a document.) In the previous chapter, we looked at how to use the Microsoft Windows desktop, and along the way, you became familiar with how to use icons and shortcut menus, how to right-click, and how to use other techniques that are also valuable when you work with windows.

In this chapter, we'll look at the elements of a window, and I'll show you some specific techniques that you can use to open windows, close them, resize them, and so on. If you learn to use Windows and windows, you can easily transfer what you know to any application that runs under Windows. Although specific items might be different, all the basic operations remain the same.

Understanding the Parts of a Window

To take a look at the basic parts of a window, let's open WordPad, a small word-processing program that comes with Windows and that is shown in Figure 3-1. Click the Start button, click Programs, click Accessories, and then click WordPad.

Figure 3-1 WordPad is a small word-processing program.

The bar at the very top is the title bar, beneath that is the menu bar, and following the menu bar is the toolbar. The bar at the bottom of the window is the status bar. Here is a description of each of these elements:

- The **title bar** shows the name of the document (if you have saved the document) and the name of the program running inside the window. The title bar also displays the Minimize, Restore, and Close buttons, and we'll look at those next.
- The **menu bar** contains words that are the titles of a list of commands. When you click a menu, you'll see a drop-down list of commands that apply to the menu.
- The **toolbar** contains buttons that are graphic representations of menu items that you frequently use. Rather than clicking the menu and then clicking an item, you can simply click a button.
- The **status bar** contains information from the program that is running in the window.

A window can display in different sizes, and the buttons you see at the far right of the title bar depend on the window's size. If the window fills up the entire screen, it is said to be maximized. In a maximized window, the buttons at the top right of the screen are, in order from left to right, Minimize, Restore, and Close (X). Here is what happens when you click these buttons:

- Clicking the **Minimize** button reduces the window to a button on the taskbar. Clicking the window's taskbar button opens the window again to its full size.
- Clicking the **Restore** button displays the window on the desktop at about one-third its maximized size.
- Clicking the **Close** button closes the window and the program running in it.

In a window that is not maximized, you will see the Minimize, Maximize, and Close buttons. Clicking the Maximize button displays the window in the full size of the screen.

TIP *An even quicker way to maximize and restore a window is to double-click the title bar. When the window is maximized, double-clicking the title bar reduces it to its previous size. When the window is not maximized, double-clicking the title bar displays the window at full-screen size.*

In some windows, you'll see a little sizing pad in the lower right corner. Maximized, the WordPad window does not have a sizing pad, but it does in its restored state, which is shown in Figure 3-2. You can click the sizing pad and then drag it to increase or decrease the size of the window.

Figure 3-2 The sizing pad is in the lower right corner of the screen.

Scroll bars are another important element in a window. You won't see them unless the contents of a window won't all fit on the screen at one time. Figure 3-3 show Windows Explorer open at the My Documents folder. (To open Windows Explorer, right-click the My Computer icon on the desktop, and choose Explore from the shortcut menu.)

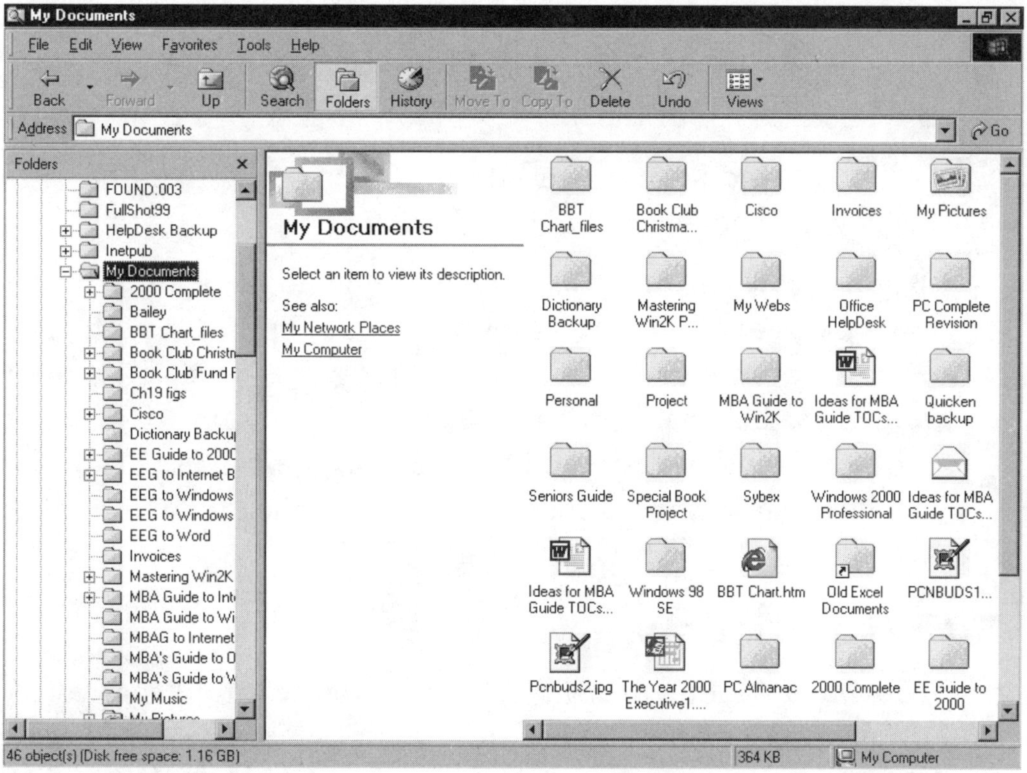

Figure 3-3 Use the scroll bar to view content that is off the screen.

To view the part of the folder that is off the screen at the bottom you use the vertical scroll bar, which is at the far right of the screen:

- To move down one row of folders, click the down arrow at the bottom of the scroll bar once.
- To move up one row of folders, click the up arrow at the top of the scroll bar once.
- To move gradually up or down the screen, drag the scroll bar.

To view the part of the screen that's off to the right, use the horizontal scroll bar at the bottom of the screen in the same way that you use the vertical scroll bar.

Identifying the Active Window

If you have only one window open, it is the active window. If you have more than one window open, you can tell which window is the active window in a couple of ways:

- The title bar of the active window will be in a different color.
- If the windows are stacked one on top of another, the active window is the one on the top.

Knowing which window is the active window is important because only the active window accepts keyboard input. This is a good thing because otherwise you'd end up typing the same thing in all open windows, and that's probably not what you want. If you have more than one window open and the one you want to use is not the active window, you can make it active simply by clicking in it or clicking its button on the taskbar.

Moving a Window

Moving a window is really easy, and you will find that you want to do this more often than you might think. First, be sure that the window you want to move is the active window, and then simply click its title bar, drag the window to a new location, and then release the mouse button.

NOTE *You can't move a maximized window.*

Arranging Windows

If you have several windows open, you can arrange them in several ways, depending on how you are working with them and what you need to do. Here are your options:

- You can *cascade* them. This means stacking them like sheets of paper. To bring any window to the top of the stack you simply click its title bar or click its button on the taskbar.
- You can *tile them horizontally*. This means giving all windows an equal amount of space on the desktop horizontally and arranging them so that their edges don't overlap.
- You can *tile them vertically*. This means giving all windows an equal amount of space on the desktop vertically and arranging them so that their edges don't overlap.

To arrange open windows, right-click an empty area on the taskbar, and then select an arrangement from the shortcut menu, which is shown in Figure 3-4. Open a few windows and experiment by selecting options from this menu.

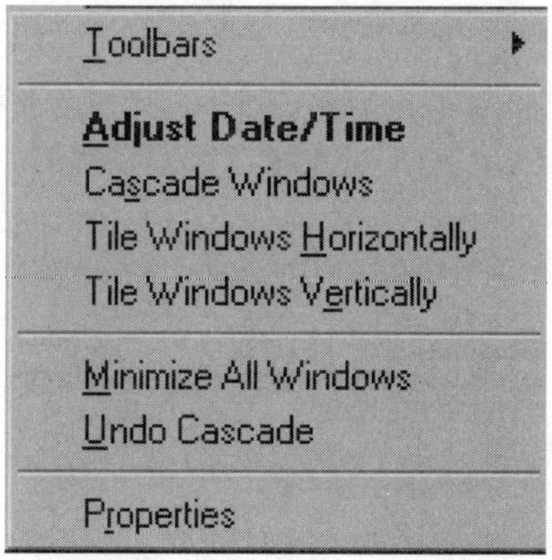

Figure 3-4 Select a window arrangement from this shortcut menu.

WARNING *Sizing or moving a window does not change its contents or close the program. However, when you close a window by clicking the Close button you do close the program. If you have not saved the window's contents (a letter, a memo, a drawing, a worksheet, or whatever), you'll see a message asking if you want to do so before closing the program. If you close the program without saving the contents of the window, you will lose whatever it contains.*

Using Menu Bars

A menu in Windows is analogous to a menu you peruse in a restaurant to select what you want to eat or drink. In Windows and in a restaurant, you open the menu to see the choices. In Windows, the names of the menus available in a program are displayed across the screen in a bar underneath the title bar, as I mentioned earlier in this chapter. To open a menu, you can simply click it.

The items on a menu are often referred to as *commands.* As I mentioned in Chapter 1, in the early days of personal computing you had to type in a command if you wanted to print, open a document, save a document, and so on. Thus, you'll see menu items that are similar to these commands. (A command is simply a word or a phrase that tells the computer to do something.)

As an example, let's look at the File menu in WordPad. Open WordPad (click the Start button, click Programs, click Accessories, and then click WordPad), and then click the word *File* in the menu bar to display a drop-down list that will be similar to that shown in Figure 3-5. The numbered items near the bottom of the list show the names of the last four documents I opened in WordPad. If you've not yet opened any documents, of course, your list won't display any names here.

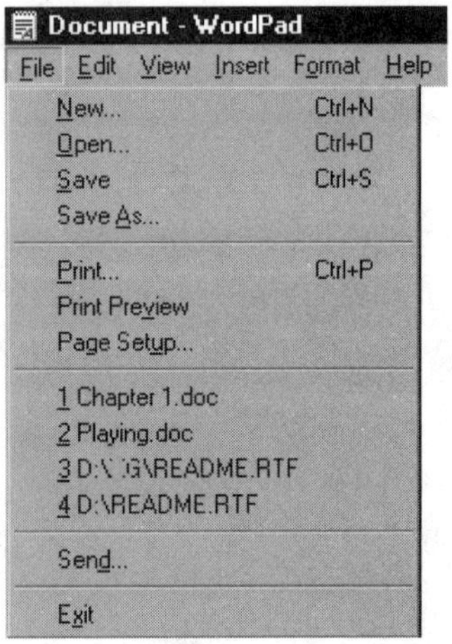

Figure 3-5 The File menu.

As you can see in Figure 3-5, some items on the File menu are followed by an ellipsis, and some are followed by a key sequence, known as a keyboard shortcut. Windows gives you several different ways to accomplish the same thing. For example, instead of clicking the File menu and then clicking New, you could simply hold down the Control key and press the letter *N*. An ellipsis indicates that selecting this menu item will open a dialog box. (In a later section in this chapter, I'll discuss dialog boxes in detail.)

You can also display the File menu by pressing Alt+F. Notice that each menu name has an underlined letter. Holding down the Alt key and pressing the underlined letter opens that menu.

Sometimes a menu item is followed by a right-pointing arrow, which indicates that selecting the item will open a submenu. A submenu is simply another list of choices. At the bottom of some menus you will see a double chevron; pointing to it displays more items in the list, a feature when you are using personalized menus, as I discussed in Chapter 2.

Using Toolbars

As I mentioned earlier in this chapter, a toolbar contains buttons on which are graphic images that represent frequently used menu items. When you point to a button, you'll see a ScreenTip that describes the button. For example, in WordPad, when you point to the first button on the toolbar, you'll see a ScreenTip that says "New." Clicking this button is exactly the same thing as clicking the File menu and then clicking New or typing Ctrl+N. All of these methods allow you to open a new blank document in WordPad.

Many Windows programs contain multiple toolbars, and you can usually select the toolbars you want to display by clicking the View menu, clicking Toolbars, and then selecting a toolbar from a list. You can also add buttons to existing toolbars and create your own toolbars in many applications.

Using Dialog Boxes

As you may recall from Chapter 2, a dialog box is a little window-like box that opens on the screen when Windows or a program needs more information from you. You may also hear dialog boxes incorrectly referred to as *dialogs.* Dialog boxes are so-called because they involve a question-and-answer process. Windows or a Windows program presents some options to you, and you select those that are appropriate for the task at hand.

For example, if you create a document in WordPad and then want to print it, you click the File menu and then click Print, or you can simply click the Print button on the toolbar. If you choose the Print command, you'll see the Print dialog box. You use it to tell Windows what to print, how many copies, and whether to collate the pages and to give Windows any other information it needs before it can print your document. If you click the Print button, you won't see the Print dialog box.

All dialog boxes have certain elements in common, though not all elements are present in all dialog boxes. In the language of Windows, an element in a dialog box is called a *control.* Let's take a look at the kinds of controls you'll encounter.

Tabs

As I also mentioned in Chapter 2, a dialog box is divided into tabbed pages, which are referred to simply as *tabs,* if the dialog box contains more information than can be displayed in a single screen. As you would in a notebook with pages divided by labeled tabs, you flip to the tab to get or enter the necessary information.

Figure 3-6 shows the Display Properties dialog box, which is divided into six tabs. Figure 3-6 shows the first tab, the Background tab, but, for example, to display the options for setting up a screen saver, you would click the Screen Saver tab to display its page of information. (We'll look at this dialog box in detail in Chapter 10.)

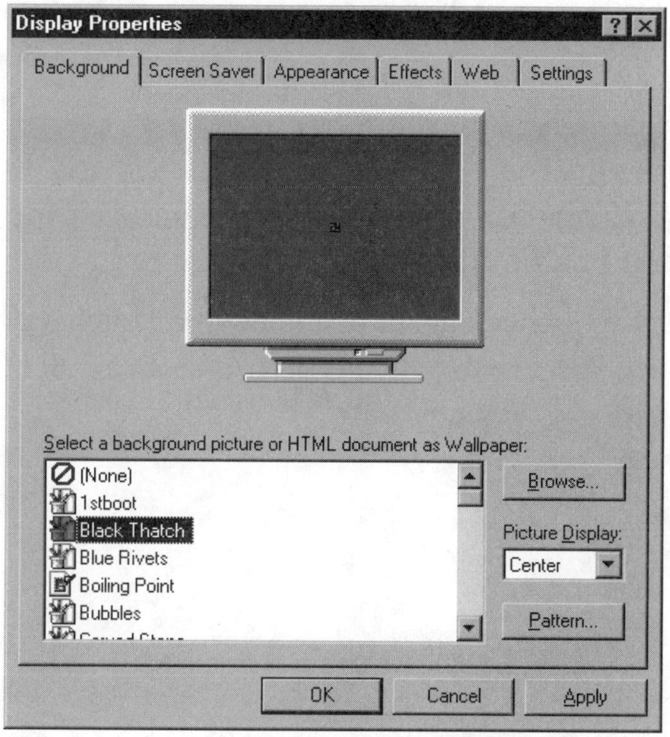

Figure 3-6 The Display Properties dialog box.

Buttons

Some dialog boxes contain several buttons, almost all contain OK and Cancel buttons, and many contain an Apply button as well. If a button's name is followed by an ellipsis, clicking it will open another dialog box. Here is how the OK, Cancel, and Apply buttons work:

- Clicking **OK** applies your selections and closes the dialog box.
- Clicking **Apply** applies your selections but does not close the dialog box. For example, in a tabbed dialog box, you might make selections on one tab, click Apply, and then click another tab so that you can make further selections.
- Clicking **Cancel** closes the dialog box without applying your selections, unless you made some selections earlier and clicked the Apply button.

Check Boxes

A check box looks exactly like the check boxes you've seen on forms all your life, and clicking an empty check box places a checkmark in it. Clicking a checked check box removes the checkmark. In other words, the check box acts like a toggle switch. You click the check box to turn the option on or off.

When you see a group of check boxes in a dialog box, such as the one in Figure 3-7, you can select one of them, some of them, or all of them.

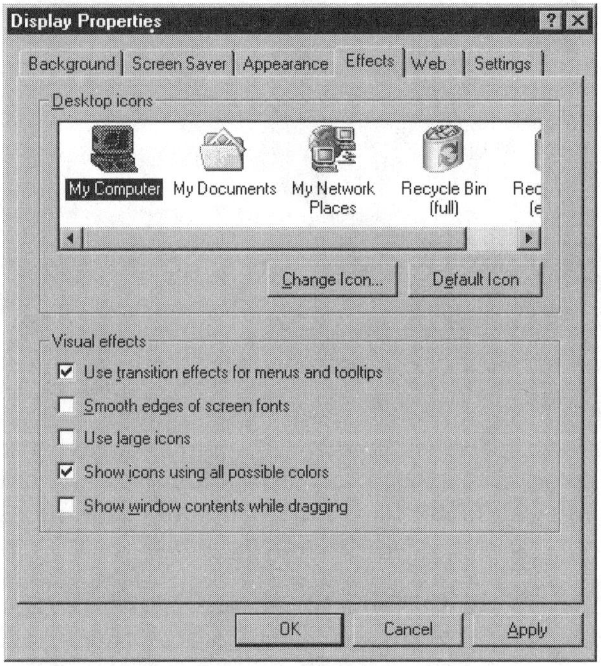

Figure 3-7 You can choose one or several check boxes.

Option Buttons

Option buttons are also called radio buttons because they are mutually exclusive. Like the buttons on your car radio, you can only select one at a time. Figure 3-8, for example, shows the Print dialog box. In the Print Range box, you can select only one of the option buttons. You can print the entire document, specified pages, or a selection.

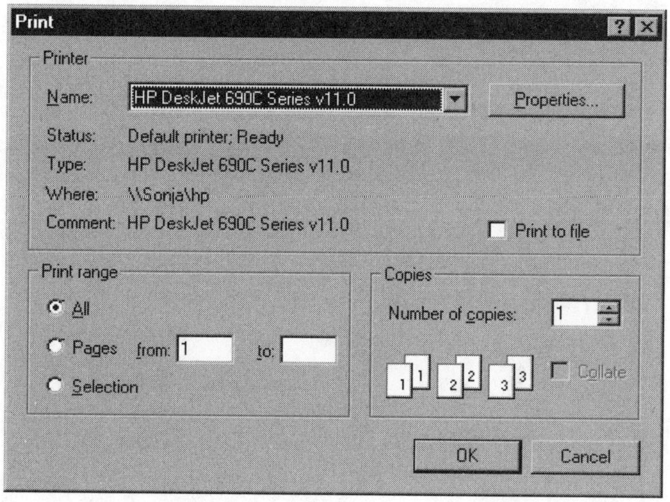

Figure 3-8 Option buttons in the Print dialog box.

Drop-Down Lists

A drop-down list in a dialog box is similar to a drop-list that displays when you click a menu. The list is hidden until you need it. In a dialog box, a drop-down list has a down-pointing arrow that you click to display the list. Figure 3-9 shows a drop-down list before the arrow is clicked on the left and afterward on the right. If you open the list and decide not to make a selection, click outside the list or press the Esc key.

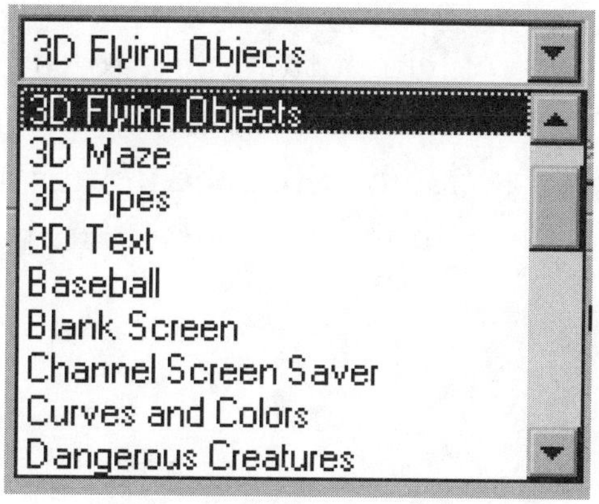

Figure 3-9 The drop-down list before and after you click the arrow.

A list box is similar to a drop-down list but it is already open. To select an item, you click it.

Sliders

You use a slider control to select a setting from a range of settings. In Chapter 2, you used a slider control to adjust the volume on your computer. Look back in that chapter for an example.

Text Boxes

A text box is an area in a dialog box where you type text. In this book, I refer to a text box as simply a "box." To type text, you'll usually need to place the insertion point in the text box, though occasionally you'll find that it's already there. Then simply start typing.

NOTE *Sometimes you'll see that certain controls are "grayed out" in a dialog box. In that case, the control does not apply to the current situation. Nothing is broken, but clicking a grayed-out control is of no avail. It won't become available until the situation or an event calls for it. Not to worry.*

Getting Help in Dialog Boxes

In many dialog boxes, you'll see a question mark button, called the Help button, next to the Close button. You can click the Help button and then click an item in the dialog box to display an explanation of what the item is and how it works. To close the explanation, simply click outside it in an empty area of the dialog box.

Seven Important Things to Remember About Using Windows

1. You can display a window at different sizes by clicking the Minimize, Restore, and Maximize buttons.
2. To move a window, click its title bar and then drag the window to a new location. You can't move a maximized window.
3. A quick way to maximize and restore a window is to double-click its title bar.
4. Use the vertical and horizontal scroll bars to view the hidden content of a window.
5. The active window will have a title bar of a different color than that of other open windows.
6. If an item on a menu or in a dialog box is grayed out, it's simply not available for whatever you are currently doing.
7. You can choose a menu item using the mouse or using the keyboard to type a shortcut key.

Summary

Understanding how to use the components of a window is key to using your Windows computer efficiently and effectively. In this chapter, we looked in detail at windows, menu bars, toolbars, and dialog boxes. Everything I talked about in this chapter also applies to any application you install that runs under Windows. Although certain items will be different, you use the same techniques I've described here. Consequently, once you know how to use and manage windows, you're about 50 percent there when you begin learning how to use a new Windows application.

Chapter 4

MANAGING YOUR DOCUMENTS

Featuring:

- Understanding How Windows Stores Your Documents
- What's the Difference Between a Document, a File, and a Folder?
- Using Windows Explorer
- Creating a Folder
- Creating a File
- Copying and Moving Files and Folders
- Renaming Files and Folders
- Deleting Files and Folders
- Changing the Display in Windows Explorer
- Backing Up Files and Folders
- Using Floppy Disks

I have to confess that I'm not much of a shopper, although I do love a bargain, and I'm in heaven at kitchen stores and office supply stores. Long ago I stopped using index cards for much more than a bookmark or making a grocery list, but I recently couldn't resist a deal on some 1000 of those white 3-by-5 cards with the blue lines. Getting organized around my house or my office usually starts with a trip to the office supply store.

Getting your computer organized doesn't involve shopping, but it does involve understanding how information on your computer is stored and imposing your own sense of order within those boundaries. As I've said before in this book, you don't have to know what's in this chapter to create and store a document on your computer, but without this information, you aren't going to be able to find that document quickly or easily. Just as when organizing paper files at home or in the office, you can set up an elaborate system if you want to do so, or you can create a simple, workable system that anybody could understand and use. The kind of system doesn't matter as long as you have a system.

In this chapter as in the rest of this book, I'm going to be using Microsoft Windows Millennium Edition (Windows Me) and describing how its file system works and how you work within that system. If you are using another version of Windows, you may have a different file system. However, many of the principles about how Windows stores information are the same.

Understanding How Windows Stores Your Documents

Everything that is stored on your computer is stored in a *file*—that includes programs, documents, pictures, drawings, sounds, video clips, and anything else. A *file system* is the overall structure that determines how files are named, stored, and organized. The file system in Windows Me is called FAT32. The *FAT* part of this name stands for File Allocation Table, which is a database of information about the files on your system that is created at the beginning of your hard drive. When you store, or save, a file, Windows places information about that file in the FAT and then uses the FAT later when you want to open the file again. The *32* part of this name refers to the amount of information that your computer can work with at one time. Windows Me is a 32-bit operating system, and so it can work with that amount of information at one time.

NOTE *In Chapter 1, I discussed the units of measurement that a computer uses. You may recall that a byte equals one character. A byte is usually composed of 8 bits, which is the basic unit of information in the binary numbering system.*

In Windows, every file must have a name, and that name consists of three parts: a filename, a period, and an extension. The filename can be a maximum of 255 characters, and the extension consists of the three letters that follow the period. Here are some examples of filenames:

- 2721c05.doc
- Dcp00051.jpg
- F1901.bmp
- My Library.xls
- Map to Terri's House.doc

A filename can contain any characters except back and forward slashes (\ /), the colon (:), the asterisk (*), the question mark (?), quotation marks ("), angle brackets (< >), and the pipe (|). The extension part of the name indicates the file's type or the program with which it is associated. For example, in the list above, .doc is a Microsoft Word file, .xls is a Microsoft Excel file, and .bmp is a bitmap file, which is a type of image.

What's the Difference Between a Document, a File, and a Folder?

As you know, any object on your computer system is a document, and you now know that every document is a file. To keep all these files organized, Windows creates groups of files called *folders,* and you can (and should) create folders as well. In addition, folders may contain *subfolders* and *sub-subfolders,* and so on.

One of the folders that Windows creates and that is present when installing Windows is the My Documents folder. When you create a document in WordPad or any other word-processing program, Windows suggests that you save it in the My Documents folder. I recommend that you follow this suggestion, at least until you really are familiar with the Windows file system structure.

I have hundreds of files on my computer system, and I do use the My Documents folder. When I start a new book project, for example, I create a folder for it in my My Documents folder, and then within that folder, I create subfolders for chapters, artwork, correspondence, and any other groups of documents that I'll collect in the course of the project.

You can do the same sort of thing. For example, if you put together a newsletter for a club or an organization, you might want to create a folder for the group, create a subfolder for the newsletter, create another subfolder for the mailing list, and so on. (I'll show you how to do this in the next section.)

Another folder that exists when you install Windows is the Program Files folder. When you later install applications on your system, Windows always suggests that you place them in the Program Files folder.

NOTE *In earlier versions of Windows, a folder was called a* directory. *Don't be confused if you hear someone refer to a folder as a directory. They are both the same thing, and the person is just using older terminology. Similarly, you may hear a subfolder called a* subdirectory.

When working with files and folders, you'll want to be familiar with the concept of a *path.* The path consists of the exact route Windows must take when opening a file. For example, the file for this chapter is stored in the Chapter 4 folder in the Seniors' Guide to PCs folder in the My Documents folder on the C drive of my computer. Here's how you express that path in the way that the computer understands:

C:\My Documents\Seniors' Guide to PCs\Chapter 4\Chapter 4.doc

It's unlikely that you'll ever have to type this path to get to a file, but now you know what it looks like and what people are speaking of when they refer to a path or a path name. You have many other, easier ways to access your files and folders.

Using Windows Explorer

When I'm helping new computer users get started with Windows, I always place special emphasis on Windows Explorer, the program that you use to "explore" drives and folders on your system. I'm sorry to report that I also encounter many, many people who've been using their Windows computer for years and don't know about or don't know how to use Windows Explorer. Often these same people become extremely frustrated every time they sit down at the computer and claim to be "no good at this computer stuff" or swear under their breath how much they hate computers. I'd be complaining right along with them if I didn't know how to use Windows Explorer.

Windows Explorer is the single most important tool for organizing the information on your computer, and you can open it in the following ways:

- Click the Start button, click Programs, click Accessories, and then click Windows Explorer.
- Right-click My Computer, My Documents, Recycle Bin, My Network Places, or the Start button and choose Explore from the shortcut menu.

Your view of Windows Explorer depends on the way you open it. To display the basic view, right-click My Computer, and then choose Explore from the shortcut menu. You'll see something similar to Figure 4-1. This view shows the highest level folder on each drive, which is called the *root folder* or just *root* for short, and a folder for Control Panel. (You use the settings in Control Panel to personalize your computer, and Chapter 10 will show you how to do that.)

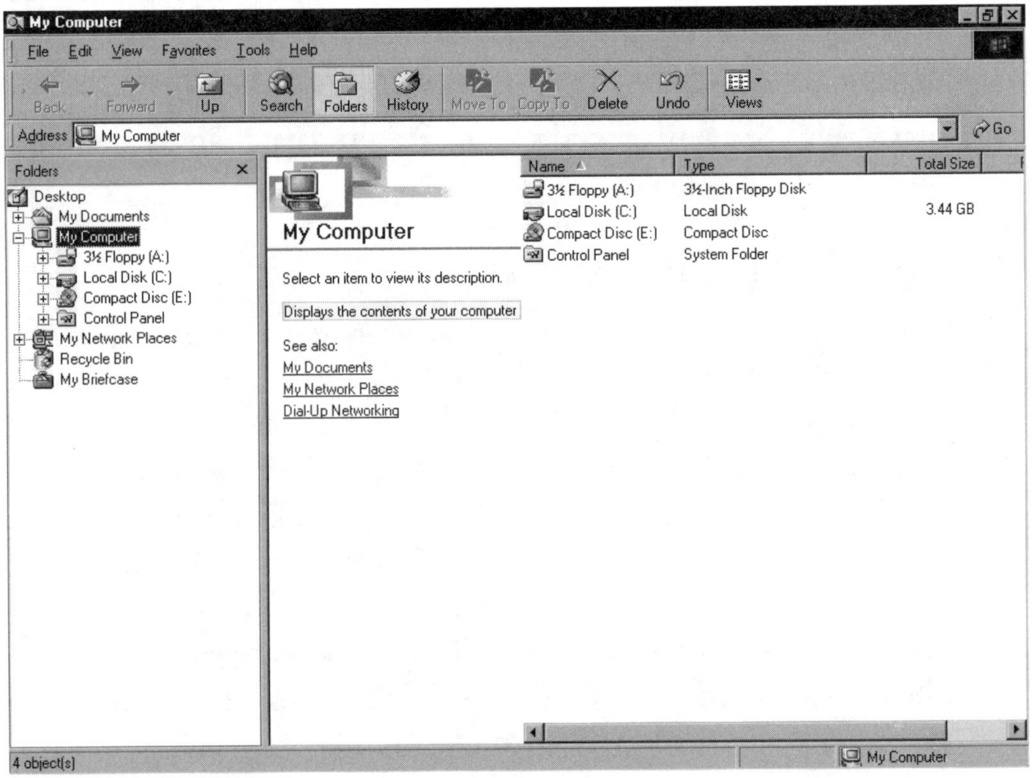

Figure 4-1 A view of Windows Explorer that shows root folders and the Control Panel folder.

To see what's inside a folder whose name is listed in the Folders pane on the left, click the folder. Then in the pane on the right, double-click a folder to display its contents, which could be subfolders or files. If you can't see all the items in the pane on the right, drag the horizontal scroll bar to the right, or drag the vertical scroll bar up or down.

To open a file, simply double-click it. In most cases, it will open in the application in which it was created.

Creating a Folder

You can create a folder from the desktop, from within Windows Explorer, and from within an application.

Creating a Folder on the Desktop

To create a folder on the desktop, follow these steps:

1. **Tell Windows you want to create a folder.**

   Right-click an empty area on the desktop, choose New from the shortcut menu, and then click Folder. You'll see a folder icon on the desktop and a box beneath it containing the words *New Folder.*

2. **Name the folder.**

   Click in the box, type a name for the new folder, and then click outside the box.

   The folder you just created is stored in the Desktop folder, and you can see this by opening Windows Explorer and then clicking the Desktop folder. You can leave the folder there, or you can move it to another folder, as you'll see later in this chapter.

NOTE *The names of files and folders must be unique within a folder. For example, if I create a folder on the desktop named "Pat's Folder," I can't create another desktop folder with that exact same name. I could, however, create a "Pat's Folder" within my My Documents folder.*

If you create a folder on the desktop, you can delete it from the desktop. Simply right-click the folder, choose Delete from the shortcut menu, and then click Yes in the Confirm Folder Delete dialog box.

Creating a Folder from Within Windows Explorer

To create a folder inside another folder in Windows Explorer, open Windows Explorer, and then follow these steps:

1. **Locate the parent folder.**

   Find the folder (known as the parent) inside which you want to create another folder, and click it to select it.

2. **Tell Windows to create the folder.**

   Click the File menu, click New, and then click Folder. You'll see a folder icon in the right pane and a box beneath it that contains the words *New Folder*, as shown in Figure 4-2. This figure shows the My Pictures folder, which is a folder that Windows creates for you. In this case, I'm about to create a new folder in which to store pictures of my new granddaughter, Bailey. As you can see, I already have a folder for Daniel, my first grandchild. (I'll show you how to store digital photos that you receive via e-mail in Chapter 8.) The other pictures in this folder are some that are included with Windows.

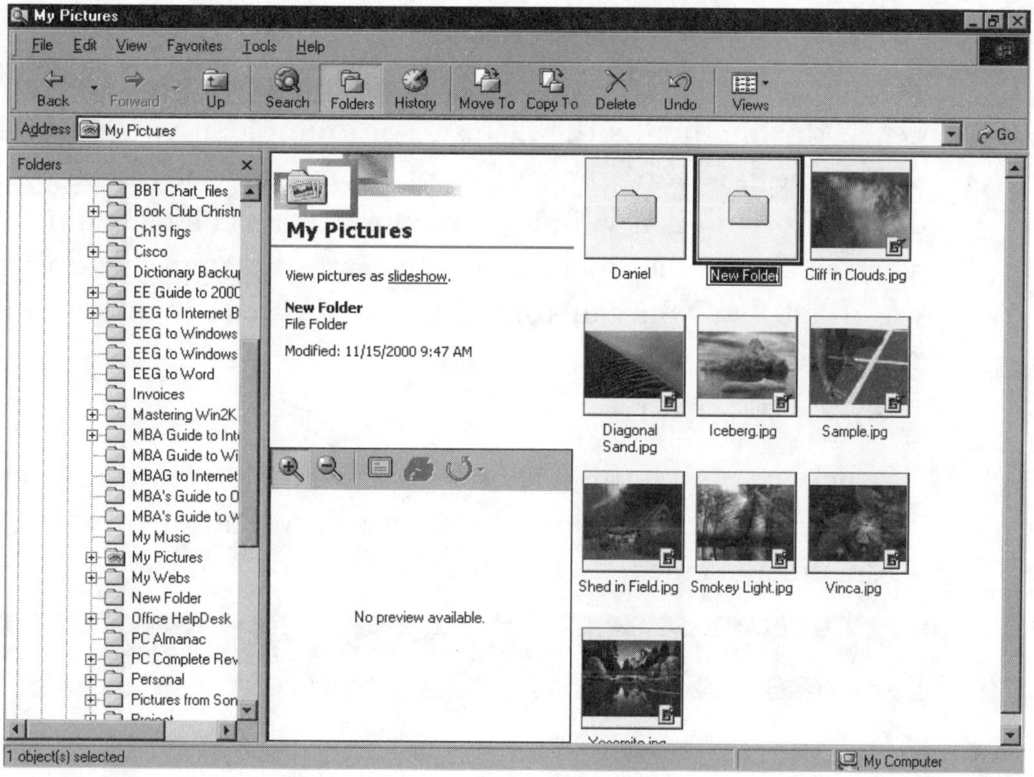

Figure 4-2 Creating a new folder in the My Pictures folder.

3. Give the folder a name.

Click in the box, type a name for the folder, and then click outside the box.

Creating a Folder from Within an Application

Which method you use to create a folder depends on the situation. Often this method is the fastest. For example, if you are creating a document in a word-processing program, you don't need to display the desktop or open Windows Explorer, you can create a new folder when you save the document. Here are the steps for doing so in WordPad, but you can follow the same steps in most Windows applications:

1. **Open WordPad.**

   Click the Start button, click Programs, click Accessories, and then click WordPad. Figure 4-3 shows WordPad open with a blank document screen.

Figure 4-3 A blank document open in WordPad.

2. **Open the Save As dialog box, as shown in Figure 4-4.**

   Click the File menu, and then click Save.

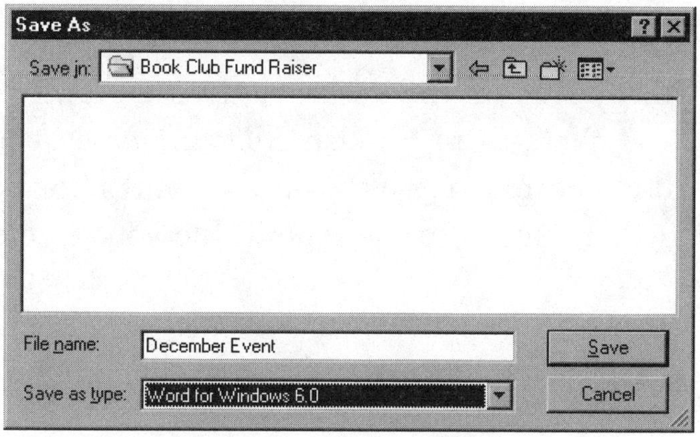

Figure 4-4 The Save As dialog box.

3. **Create the folder.**

   Locate the folder in which you want to create the new folder by clicking the down arrow in the Save In box. When you find it, select it. Click the Create New Folder button. (It's the third button on the toolbar.) You'll see a new folder icon followed by a box that contains the words *New Folder.*

4. **Name the folder.**

   Click in the box, type a name for the folder, and then click outside the box.

Creating a File

As with folders, you can create a file in three ways: from the desktop, from within Windows Explorer, and from within an application.

Creating a File on the Desktop

To create a file on the desktop, follow these steps:

1. **Select a file type.**

   Right-click an empty area on the desktop, choose New from the shortcut menu, and then, from the list, click the type of file you want to create. You'll see an icon on the desktop and a box beneath it containing text that applies to the type of file you selected.

2. **Name the file.**

   Click in the box, type a name for the file, and then click outside the box.

The file you just created is stored in the Desktop folder, which you can see by opening Windows Explorer.

Creating a File in Windows Explorer

To create a file in Windows Explorer, follow these steps:

1. **Open Windows Explorer.**

   Right-click the My Computer icon on the desktop, and then choose Explore from the shortcut menu.

2. **Select a folder.**

   Click the folder that will contain the new file.

3. **Tell Windows to create the file.**

   Click the File menu, click New, and then select a file type from the list. You'll see an icon representing the file type and a box in the right pane.

4. **Name the file.**

   Click in the box, type a name for the new file, and then click outside the box.

Creating a File in an Application

Follow these steps to create a file in WordPad. You use the same steps to create a file in any Windows application.

1. **Open WordPad.**

   Click the Start button, click Programs, click Accessories, and then click WordPad.

2. **Open the Save As dialog box.**

   Click the File menu, and then click Save.

3. **Choose where you want to store the file.**

   Click the down arrow in the Save In box, and select the folder in which you want to save the file.

4. **Name and save the file.**

   In the File Name box, enter a name for the file, and then select the file type in the Save As Type drop-down box. Click the Save button.

Copying and Moving Files and Folders

As I mentioned earlier in this chapter, you can always move a file or a folder to another folder, regardless of where you created it. In addition, you can copy a file or a folder to another folder. When you move a file or a folder, you remove it from its current location and place it in another location. When you copy a file or a folder, the original remains in place, and a copy is placed in another location.

As with many Windows tasks, you can move and copy a file or a folder in several ways:

- Drag and drop with the right mouse button.
- Drag and drop with the left mouse button.

- Copy and paste or cut and paste.
- Use the Send To command.

Which method you use depends on the situation and your personal preference.

Using the Right Mouse Button

To copy or move a file or a folder with the right mouse button, follow these steps:

1. **Open Windows Explorer.**

   Right-click the My Computer icon on the desktop, and choose Explore from the shortcut menu.

2. **Drag the file or folder to its new location.**

   Locate the file or the folder, right-click it, and, while holding down the mouse button, drag the file or the folder to its new folder.

3. **Tell Windows whether to copy or move the file or folder.**

   Release the right mouse button, and choose Copy Here or Move Here from the shortcut menu. If you change your mind about the copy or move, you can choose Cancel from the shortcut menu.

TIP *If you change your mind in the middle of a copy or move operation, press the Escape key to cancel the copy or move.*

Using the Left Mouse Button

As I describe how to copy and move using the left mouse button, it may sound a little complicated, but it's not when you actually do it. Here's how to copy an item:

- If the source and destination file or folder are on the same drive, click the item, hold down the Ctrl key, and drag the item to its new location.

- If the source and destination file or folder are on different drives, click the item, and drag it to its new location.

Here's how to move an item:

- If the source and destination file or folder are on the same drive, click the item and then drag it to its new location.
- If the source and destination file or folder are on different drives, click the item, hold down the Shift key, and drag the item to its new location.

Using the Cut, Copy, and Paste Commands

In Windows Explorer, the Cut, Copy, and Paste commands are on the Edit menu. When you want to copy a file or a folder, you select it, click Edit, and then click Copy. Then, select the destination, click Edit, and click Paste. When you want to move a file or a folder, follow the same procedure, except choose Cut instead of Copy.

An even quicker method is to use the keyboard shortcuts:

- Instead of clicking Edit and then clicking Cut, press Ctrl+X.
- Instead of clicking Edit and then clicking Copy, press Ctrl+C.
- Instead of clicking Edit and clicking Paste, press Ctrl+V.

You can also cut, copy, and paste using shortcut menus, and this is the method I normally use when copying or moving files and folders in Windows Explorer. Right-click the item you want to cut or copy, and then choose Cut or Copy from the shortcut menu. Then, right-click the destination item, and choose Paste from the shortcut menu.

Renaming Files and Folders

Renaming a file or a folder is a simple task. In Windows Explorer, right-click a file or a folder, choose Rename from the shortcut menu, type a new name in the box that appears, and then click outside the box. You can also rename a file or a folder from within an application. Open the Save As dialog box, right-click the file or folder, choose Rename from the shortcut menu, type a new name in the box, and click outside the box.

Deleting Files and Folders

As I mentioned in Chapter 2, whenever you delete a file or a folder, it goes to the Recycle Bin where it stays until the Recycle Bin gets full and empties itself or until you empty the Recycle Bin manually. You can delete a file or a folder in several ways:

- In Windows Explorer, right-click the file or folder name, and then choose Delete from the shortcut menu.
- In the Save As dialog box in an application, right-click the file or folder name, and then choose Delete from the shortcut menu.
- In Windows Explorer, left-click the file or folder name, and then press the Delete key or click the Delete button on the toolbar. (The Delete button has an X on it.)
- If the file or folder is visible on the desktop, click it, and then drag it to the Recycle Bin.

If you delete a file or a folder in Windows Explorer and realize immediately that you've made a mistake in doing so, click the Undo button to restore the file or folder. You must click the Undo button before you do anything else, however, because Undo only undoes the immediately preceding action.

TIP *To bypass the Recycle Bin, hold down the Shift key while choosing the Delete command or pressing the Delete key.*

Changing the Display in Windows Explorer

By default, when you click a folder in the Folders pane, its contents display in the pane on the right in Large Icon view, as shown in Figure 4-5.

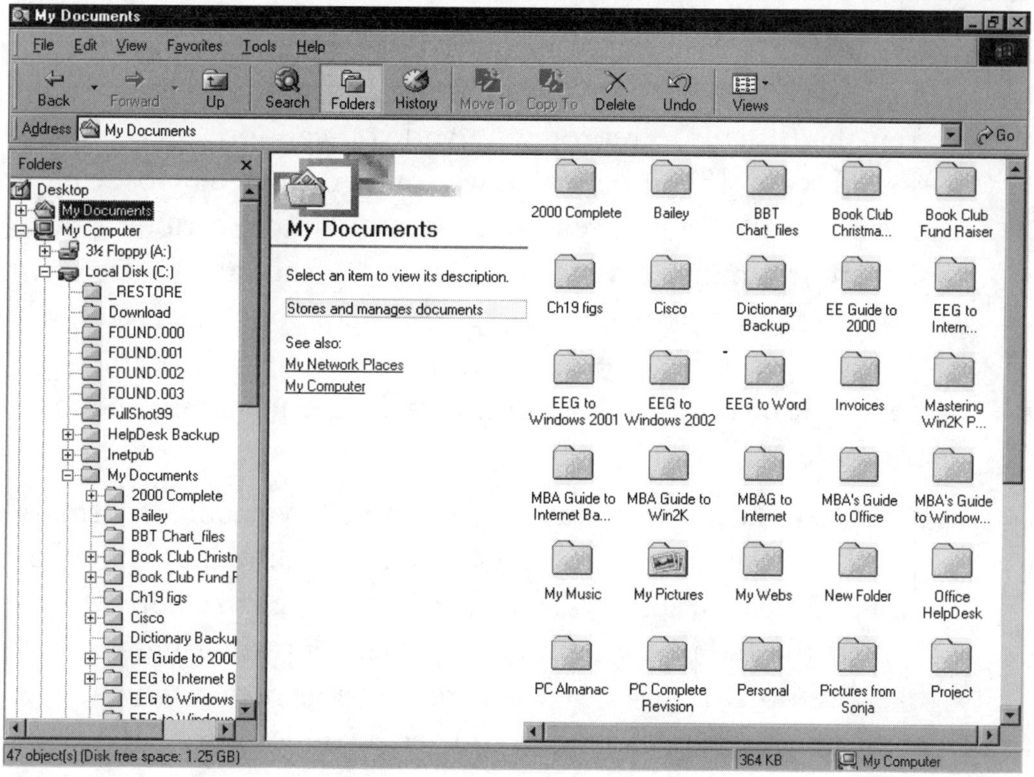

Figure 4-5 Windows Explorer in Large Icon view.

You can also display Windows Explorer in four other views:

- **Small Icons,** which shows a single list of folder names and precedes each name with a small folder icon.
- **List,** which is essentially the same as Small Icons view, but displays the list in more than one column.
- **Details,** which is similar to Small Icons view but also has columns for the file's size and type and the date it was last modified.
- **Thumbnails,** which shows a folder icon in a frame with the file's name beneath the frame.

To see each view, click the View menu in Windows Explorer and then click Large Icons, Small Icons, List, Details, or Thumbnails.

Backing Up Files and Folders

Regardless of how you use your computer, you probably have a lot of information on it that you don't want to lose and that would be extremely difficult to reproduce. And you can lose that information in several ways. If you have a power outage, you may lose any part of a document that you have not yet saved. A more serious loss can occur if there is a major disaster such as an earthquake, a fire, or the like. And then, though we don't like to think about this either, what happens if your hard drive crashes, that is, becomes completely useless? Believe it or not, I've known this to happen to brand-new, expensive computers.

Thus, you need some way to protect your valuable information, and your best insurance policy is a *backup.* A backup is an up-to-date copy of a file. The simplest way to back up a file is to copy it to a floppy disk, if the file isn't gigantic. A single floppy is usually sufficient for backing up a number of word-processing files or spreadsheets, but some graphics are too big to fit even a single file on a floppy. To back up a file to a floppy disk, simply copy it using any of the techniques discussed earlier in this chapter for copying files. Once the file is copied, label the disk with the filename and the date, and put it in a safe place.

Using Floppy Disks

A floppy disk used to be a necessity. Then, with the advent of local area networks and the Internet, a floppy disk tended to become a convenience when some other means of getting a file from one computer to another one wasn't available. Now, a lot of us seldom use floppy disks unless we want to create a backup. So I want to conclude this chapter with some basic information about floppies.

Formatting a Floppy Disk

Formatting a floppy disk means preparing it so that it can store information. Most floppy disks that you purchase these days are already formatted, and you can just pop one in the drive and start using it. If you have a floppy that is not formatted, though, you can format it yourself. Insert the floppy in the floppy drive, and then follow these steps:

1. **Open Windows Explorer.**

   Right-click My Computer, and then choose Explore from the shortcut menu.

2. **Open the Format dialog box, as shown in Figure 4-6.**

   Scroll up the Folders pane until you see the icon for 3 ½ Floppy (A:), and then right-click it. Choose Format from the shortcut menu.

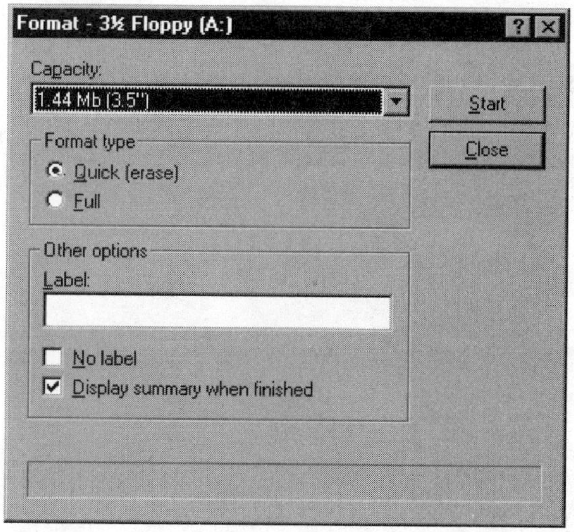

Figure 4-6 The Format dialog box.

3. **Tell Windows how you want to format the disk.**

   In the Format Type section, click the Quick (Erase) option button if you want to reformat a disk that already has information on it. When you format a disk that already contains data, that data is erased. Click the Full option button to format a new disk that is unformatted. If you want to label the disk, type a name in the Label box. Otherwise, click the No Label check box. If you want Windows to display some information about the disk once it's formatted, click the Display Summary When Finished check box.

4. **Format the disk.**

   Click the Start button. When Windows says Format Complete, click OK, and close the Format dialog box.

Copying One Floppy Disk to Another

To copy one floppy disk to another, insert the source disk in the floppy drive, open Windows Explorer, and then follow these steps:

1. **Open the Copy Disk dialog box, as shown in Figure 4-7.**

   In the Folders pane, right-click the floppy disk icon, and select Copy Disk from the shortcut menu. Click the Start button.

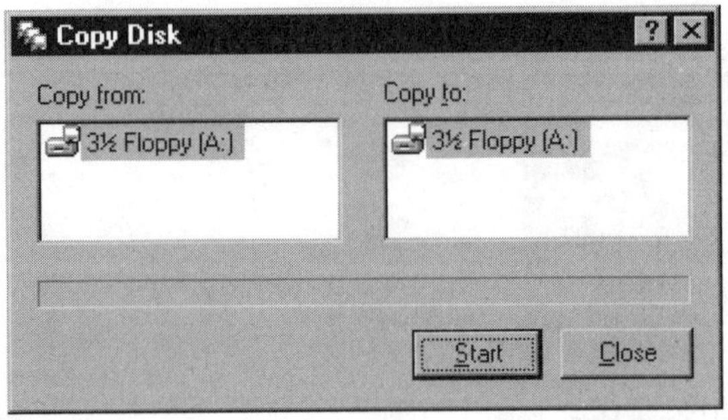

Figure 4-7 The Copy Disk dialog box.

2. **Insert the destination disk.**

   When prompted, remove the source disk, insert the destination disk, and click OK.

When the copy is complete, you'll see the message "Copy Completed Successfully" in the Copy Disk dialog box. Click Close.

Seven Important Things to Remember About Your Files and Folders

1. Everything that is stored on your computer is stored in a file.
2. The Windows file system is called FAT32, and it determines how files are named, stored, and organized.
3. A folder may include subfolders or files, or both.
4. Windows Explorer is the most important tool for organizing information on your computer.
5. You can create files and folders from the desktop, from within Windows Explorer, and from within applications.
6. Right-clicking is often the fastest and easiest way to perform a task relating to files and folders.
7. Make backups of documents that you don't want to lose.

Summary

Knowing how to store and find the documents on your computer will make you a more productive and, thus, more content and secure computer user. In this chapter, we've looked at all the basic skills you need to acquire—using Windows Explorer, creating files and folders, copying and moving files and folders, renaming files and folders, deleting files and folders, and backing up files and folders. We also looked at how to change the display in Windows Explorer, and I gave you a brief explanation of how to format and copy a floppy disk.

Chapter 5

PRINTING YOUR DOCUMENTS

Featuring:

- Understanding How Printers Work
- Installing a New Printer
- Taking Care of Printer-Related Tasks
- Printing Documents
- Managing Your Printer
- Changing Your Printer's Settings
- Installing and Using Fonts

One thing that early computer enthusiasts advocated was that paper documents would become obsolete. You need only take a quick look around your home or office to verify the absurdity of that notion. What has happened, however, is that the quality of printers has increased dramatically while their cost has decreased dramatically. For example, color printing used to be prohibitively expensive and was primarily the domain of commercial printers who worked with large, professional equipment. You can now purchase a color printer for your home office for about $100, and some computer retailers throw in such a printer for free when you buy a computer system.

And what can you print on these modestly priced pieces of equipment? Transparencies, art that you can transfer to a T-shirt, envelopes, labels of all kinds, postcards, newsletters, brochures, photographs, banners, name tags, stickers, greeting cards, invitations, financial statements—the list is really endless.

In this chapter, I'm going to start by briefly describing how printers work, and then I'll walk you through the steps to set up, use, manage, and maintain your printer. As you'll see, not all printers have the same features, nor do they work in the same way. In addition to the information in this chapter, you'll want to consult the instruction manual that came with your printer.

TIP *The instruction manuals that come with computers, printers, and other devices these days have become little more than booklets when compared with the tomes delivered with computers of yore. The reason is that most software developers include extensive online help with the program. Nevertheless, these little pamphlets contain valuable information. It's a good idea to keep them somewhere that you can easily find one when you need it.*

Understanding How Printers Work

Printers for personal computers are of two basic types: impact and nonimpact. An *impact* printer makes an image on paper by hitting a print head or a key against a ribbon. Until the early 1990s, impact printers were the most common type available for use with a personal computer. You may have heard of dot-matrix printers, letter-quality printers, or plotters—they are all impact printers.

Today, the printer market for personal computers is dominated by *nonimpact* printers. Laser printers, inkjet printers, and thermal printers are all nonimpact printers. A laser printer produces an image on paper in the same way a copy machine does. An inkjet printer sprays a fine jet of ink onto the paper, and a thermal printer uses heat to transfer an image onto specially treated paper.

A printer works by putting dots on paper. Printer quality is measured in dots per inch (dpi); the more dots, the higher the quality, and the slower the output. Printer speed is measured in pages per minute (ppm), and color pages print slower than black ink pages. These features are all factors to consider when you buy a printer, and you'll see them listed in advertisements and on the little signs that identify a printer in the store. The type of printer you need, of course, depends on what you'll print with it.

Installing a New Printer

When you acquire a new printer, you first need to connect it to your computer system, and then you need to install it. When connecting it, follow the instructions in the manual that came with your printer. Then, be sure that the printer cable is securely connected to both the printer and your computer and complete any preparatory steps listed in the manual. You are then ready to install the printer. *Installing* simply means identifying your printer to Microsoft Windows and giving Windows some information about the printer.

To install a new printer, follow these steps:

1. **Open the Printers folder, as shown in Figure 5-1.**

   Click the Start button, click Settings, and then click Printers.

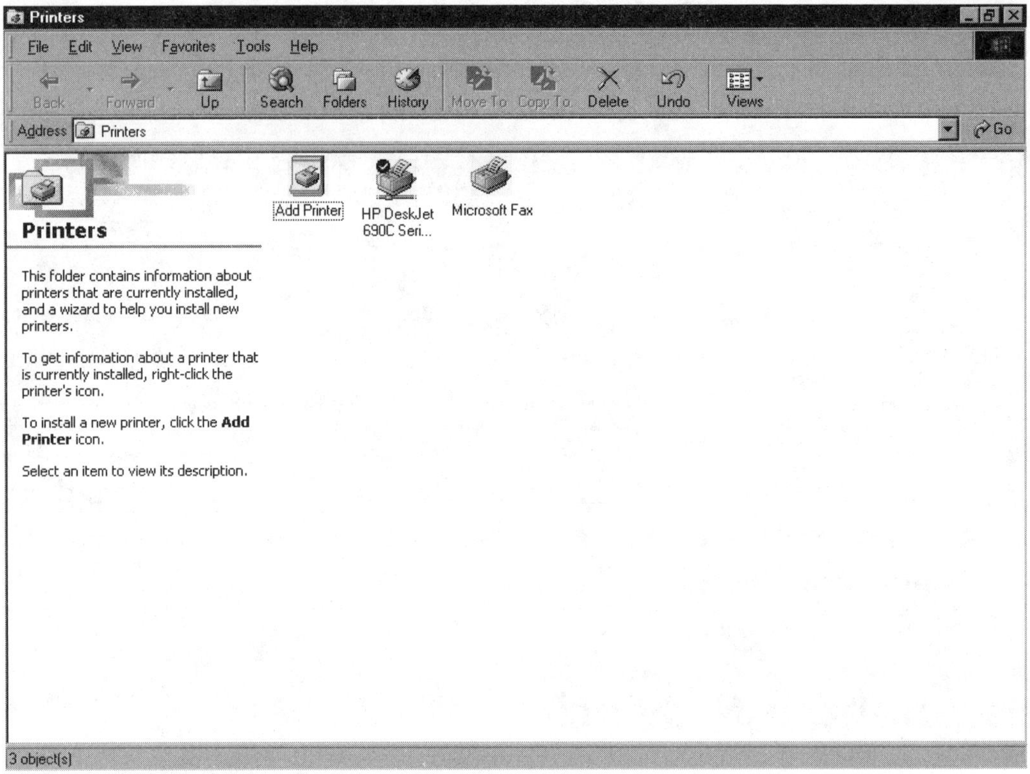

Figure 5-1 The Printers folder.

NOTE *In Figure 5-1, I've already installed a printer and a fax printer on my system. If you have not previously installed a printer, you'll see only the Add Printer icon and the Microsoft Fax icon. When you (or the manufacturer of your computer) installed Windows, the operating system detected your fax modem, installed the fax service, and installed the associated printer.*

2. **Start the Add Printer Wizard.**

   Double-click the Add Printer icon to open the screen shown in Figure 5-2.

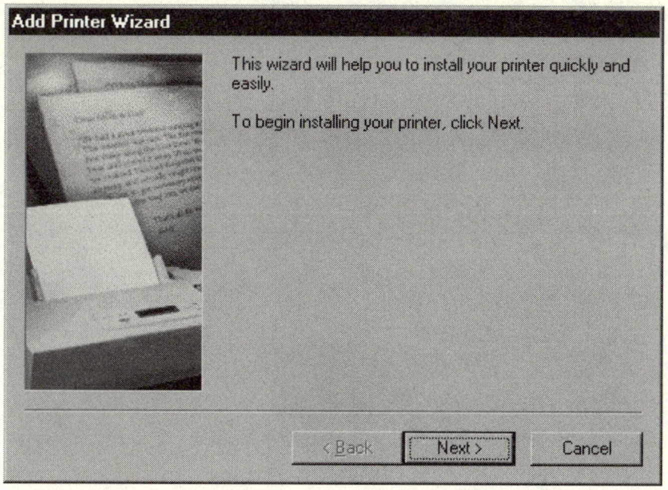

Figure 5-2 Starting the Add Printer Wizard.

NOTE *A wizard is simply a guide that steps you through a process.*

3. **Tell Windows that you want to install a local printer.**

   Click Next, and click the Local Printer option. (A *local printer* is one that is attached directly to your computer. A *network printer* is attached to another computer that is part of a group of computers that are connected.)

4. **Tell Windows the manufacturer and model of your printer.**

   Click Next, and you'll see that Windows is gathering some information about your computer. When it finishes, you'll see the screen in Figure 5-3. Scroll down the Manufacturers list to find and select the manufacturer, and then scroll down the Printers list to find and select the model. If your printer came with an installation disk, click the Have Disk button to open the Install From Disk dialog box. Insert the disk, and click OK to install the printer from the disk. Otherwise, click Next when you have selected the manufacturer and the model.

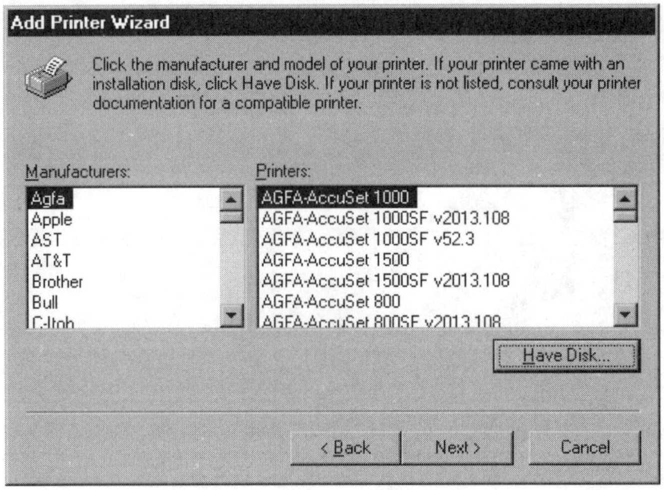

Figure 5-3 Select the manufacturer and model of your printer.

5. **Tell Windows which port to use with this printer.**

   A printer port is the connection through which information between the computer and the printer passes. Normally, printers use LPT1, which is selected by default. Keep this selection, and click Next.

6. **Give your printer a name.**

   In the Printer Name box, keep the name that Windows suggests or type another name. If you want all your Windows programs to print with this printer (and you do if you have only one printer), click the Yes option, and then click Next.

7. **Print a test page.**

   Printing a test page is always a good idea so that you can verify that your printer is up and running. Click the Yes option, and then click Finish. You'll now see an icon for your printer in the Printers folder.

Did Your Test Page Print Correctly?

If your test page didn't print correctly, click No in the dialog box that asks you about this. You'll then see the Printing Troubleshooter open in the Help And Support center, as shown here:

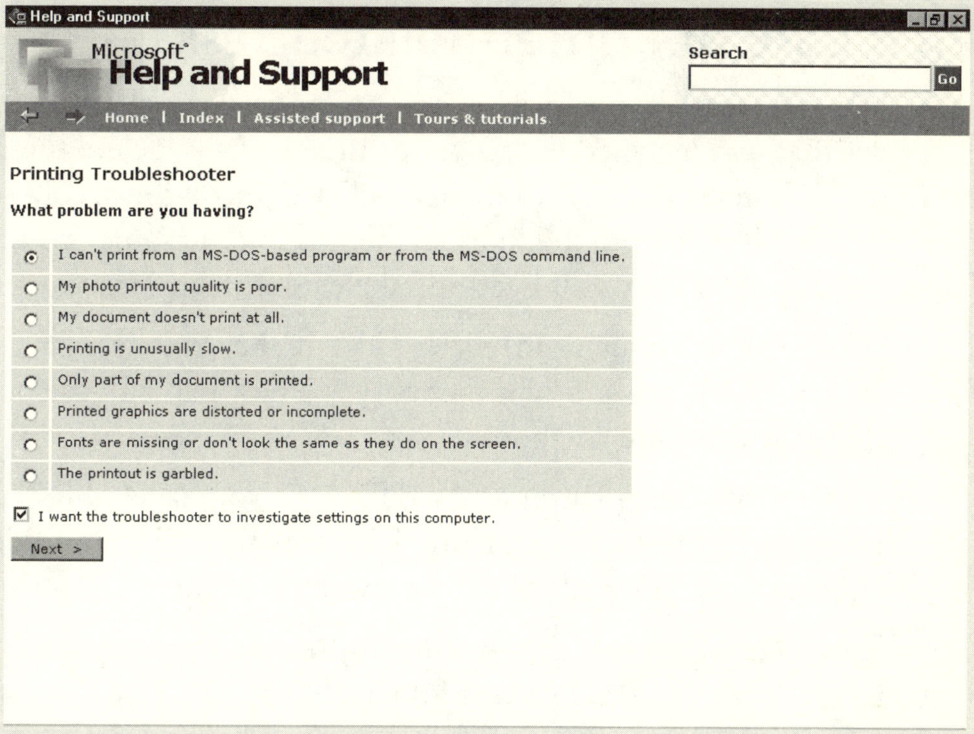

Click an option that applies to your situation, and then click Next. Windows walks you through a series of questions and suggestions to help you solve the problem.

You can also access the Printing Troubleshooter by clicking the Troubleshooting link in the opening screen of the Help And Support center.

If you work through the Printing Troubleshooter and still can't print, contact the manufacturer of your printer. The manufacturer may need to supply you with a different printer driver. A *printer driver* is a little program that lets a computer communicate with and control a printer. Windows includes a number of printer drivers and, in most cases, automatically finds the correct one, but if you have a new printer and are having serious problems, contacting the printer manufacturer is worth a try. You'll probably find contact information in your printer manual.

Taking Care of Printer-Related Tasks

When you install a new printer and no longer have the need for the driver that was installed for an old printer, you can delete the printer from the Printers folder. Simply right-click the icon for the old printer, and choose Delete from the shortcut menu. Here are some other printer housekeeping tasks you'll need to take care of from time to time:

- To **rename a printer**, right-click its icon in the Printers folder, choose Rename from the shortcut menu, type a new name in the box, and then click outside the box.
- To **set a different printer** as the default (if you have more than one printer), right-click the printer's icon in the Printers folder and choose Set As Default from the shortcut menu.
- To **create a shortcut to a printer** on the desktop, right-click the printer's icon in the Printers folder, choose Create Shortcut from the shortcut menu, and click Yes in the Shortcut dialog box. As you'll see in the next section, you'll need a shortcut to your printer on the desktop if you want to use drag-and-drop to print.

Printing Documents

You can print from the desktop or from an application, but in either case, it is Windows that does the printing. A program called the *print spooler* accepts the document and holds it on disk or in memory until the printer is free, and then the printer prints the document.

Printing from the Desktop

You can print from the desktop using drag-and-drop, or you can right-click.

Using Drag-and-Drop to Print

As I mentioned in an earlier section of this chapter, to print from the desktop using drag-and-drop, you need a shortcut to the printer on your desktop, and you need an open folder that contains the file you want to print. In other words, you need to be able to see both the printer icon and the filename or icon. In Figure 5-4, I'm getting ready to drag this chapter from the Chapter 5 folder to the printer icon on my desktop.

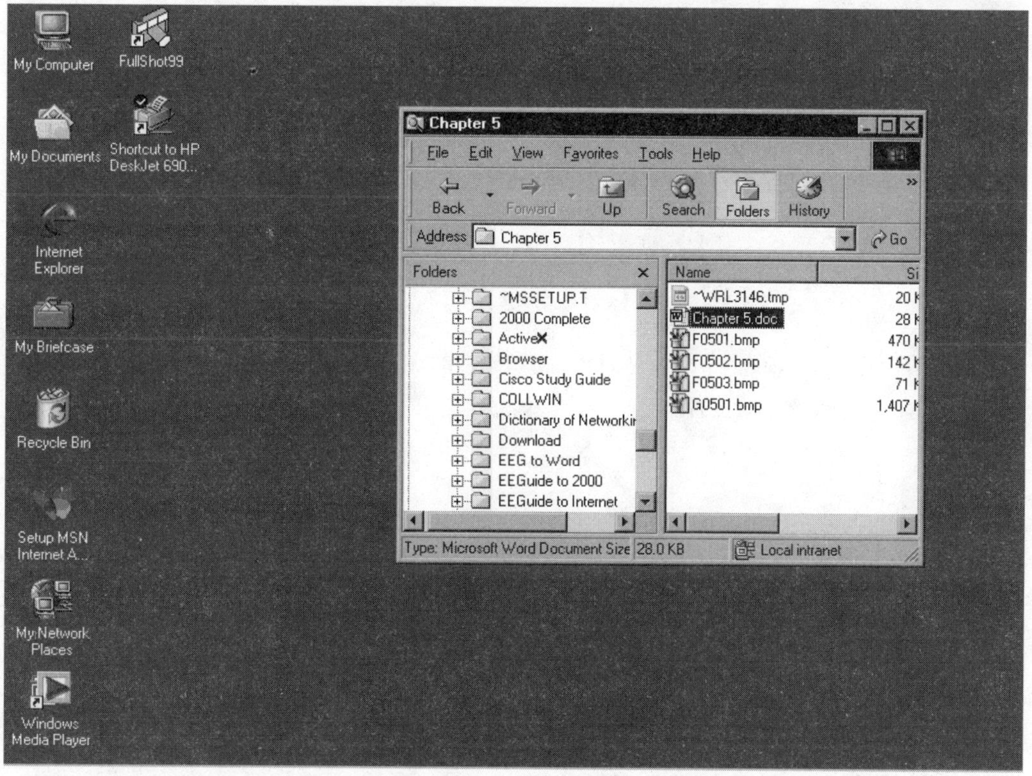

Figure 5-4 Preparing to print using drag-and-drop.

To print using drag-and-drop, create a shortcut to your printer on the desktop (as described earlier in this chapter), and then follow these steps:

1. **Open Windows Explorer.**

   Right-click My Computer, and then choose Explore from the shortcut menu. Find the file you want to print. If Windows Explorer opens in a maximized window, click the Restore button to shrink it somewhat. Click the title bar of Windows Explorer to position it on the desktop so that you can see both the file you want to print and the printer's icon.

2. **Print the file.**

   Click the icon or the filename, drag it to the printer's icon, and release the mouse button.

   The file opens in its associated application and then prints, using the default options in the Print dialog box, which I'll discuss later in this chapter.

Right-Clicking to Print

To print using the right-click method, follow these steps:

1. **Open Windows Explorer.**

   Right-click My Computer, and then choose Explore from the shortcut menu.

2. **Find the file.**

   Open a folder that contains the file you want to print.

3. **Print the file.**

   Right-click the file, and then choose Print from the shortcut menu.

As is the case when you use drag-and-drop to print, the file opens in its associated application and prints using the default options in the Print dialog box.

Printing from a Windows Application

To easily and quickly print from an application, open the application, open the document, and click the Print toolbar button. Clicking the Print button, dragging-and-dropping, and right-clicking all print a document quickly, but, as I mentioned earlier in this chapter, you pick up the default print settings. In other words, the entire file is printed, only one copy is printed, the printed output is in portrait orientation (vertical), and the default paper size and paper tray are used.

To exercise finer control over how a document prints, you need to use the Print dialog box in an application. To print in WordPad, for example, follow these steps:

1. **Open WordPad.**

   Click the Start button, click Programs, click Accessories, and then click WordPad.

2. **Open a document.**

   Click the File menu, click Open to open the Open dialog box, select the file you want to print, and then click Open.

3. **Open the Print dialog box, as shown in Figure 5-5.**

   Click the File menu, and then click Print.

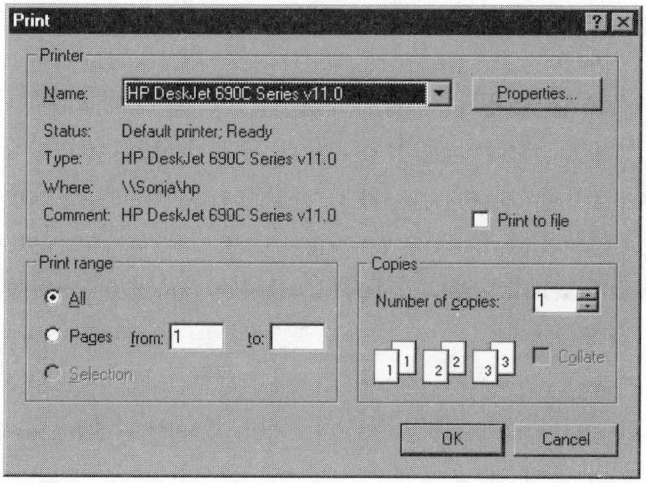

Figure 5-5 The Print dialog box.

4. **Tell Windows what to print.**

   In the Print Range section, click the All option button to print the entire document. To print selected pages, click the Pages option button, and then in the From box enter the number of the first page in the range, and in the To box enter the number of the last page in the range. To print a Selection, such as a paragraph, several paragraphs, or most of a page, make the selection before you open the Print dialog box. Click the Selection option button.

5. **Tell Windows how many copies to print and whether to collate them.**

   In the Number Of Copies box, enter a number or click the arrow to select a number. If you want the pages of multiple copies collated, click the Collate check box.

6. **Tell Windows which page orientation to use, which paper, and any other specifications.**

   Click the Properties button to open the Properties dialog box, which is shown in Figure 5-6. The options you see in this dialog box will depend on your printer. Figure 5-6 shows the options for my DeskJet 697C printer. You may have more or fewer tabs, and options may be arranged differently. In any case, specify the paper size and type and the orientation. Portrait orientation prints vertically, and landscape orientation prints horizontally. When you've made your selections, click OK.

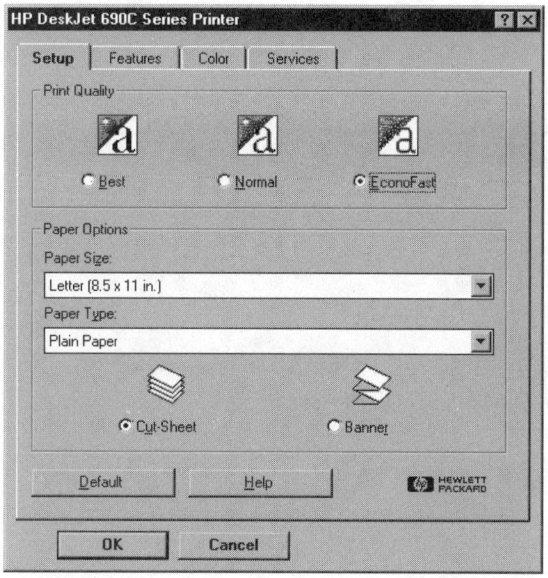

Figure 5-6 The Properties dialog box for a printer.

7. **Print the document.**

   Back in the Print dialog box, click OK to print your document.

Managing Your Printer

After you click OK to print a document, the document wends its way through the printing process. But what if you suddenly realize that you've sent the wrong document to the printer and it's more than 100 pages? You can stop the printer, pause it temporarily, and get information about the printing process by clicking the printer's icon in the Printers folder.

TIP *Got to stop that 100-page document, but you've forgotten how to get to the Printers folder? Don't panic. To get to the Printers folder, click the Start button, click Settings, and then click Printers.*

Figure 5-7 shows the window for my printer, which is in the process of printing a document.

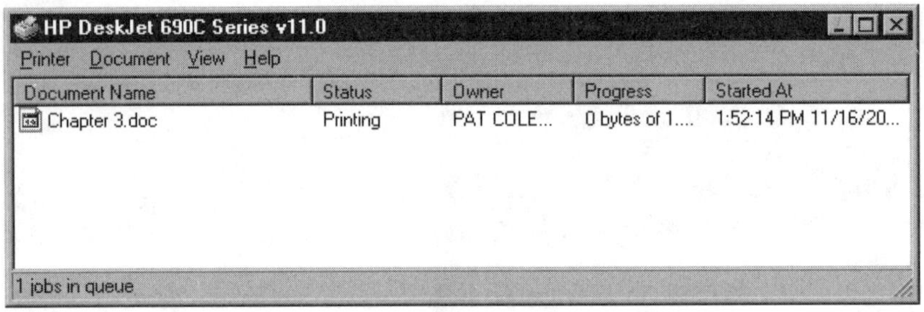

Figure 5-7 The printer window for my printer.

Here's a description of what each column in the printer window displays:

- The **Document Name** column displays the document filename.
- The **Status** column tells you whether the document is being printed, is paused, or has been deleted.
- The **Owner** column displays the name of the person who sent the document to the printer.
- The **Progress** column tells you how many bytes of the total number of bytes have printed.
- The **Started At** column gives you the time and date the document started to print.

Use the following techniques to manage a printer in the printer's window:

- To **cancel the printing** of a document, select it, click the Document menu, and then click Cancel Printing.
- To **temporarily halt the printing** of a document, select it, click the Document menu, and then click Pause Printing.
- To **resume printing** a document, select it, click the Document menu, and then click Resume Printing.

You'll notice that printing doesn't stop immediately when you pause or cancel the printing of a document. Whatever pages have already been spooled to the printer must print before the printing ceases.

Changing Your Printer's Settings

Earlier in this chapter, we looked at the printer's Properties dialog box, which we opened from the Print dialog box. You can also open the Properties dialog box from within the Printers folder and establish settings that become the default for that particular printer. To open a printer's Properties dialog box, open the Printers folder, right-click the printer's icon, and choose Properties from the shortcut menu.

The tabs and options on your printer's Properties dialog box are specific to your printer. If you don't understand some of them, check the manual that came with your printer. You can also click the Help button (the button with the question mark next to the Close button) and then click an item to display an explanation of what it is and does.

Installing and Using Fonts

When you print using any of the methods I've described in this chapter, you use a particular typeface, or *font.* Examples of fonts included with Windows Me are Comic Sans MS (a popular font for use on Web pages), Courier (which looks like a typewriter did the printing), and Times New Roman (the default selection for printing in Windows applications). To see the entire selection of fonts, follow these steps:

1. **Open Control Panel.**

   Click the Start button, click Settings, and then click Control Panel.

2. **Open the Fonts folder, as shown in Figure 5-8.**

   Click the Fonts icon.

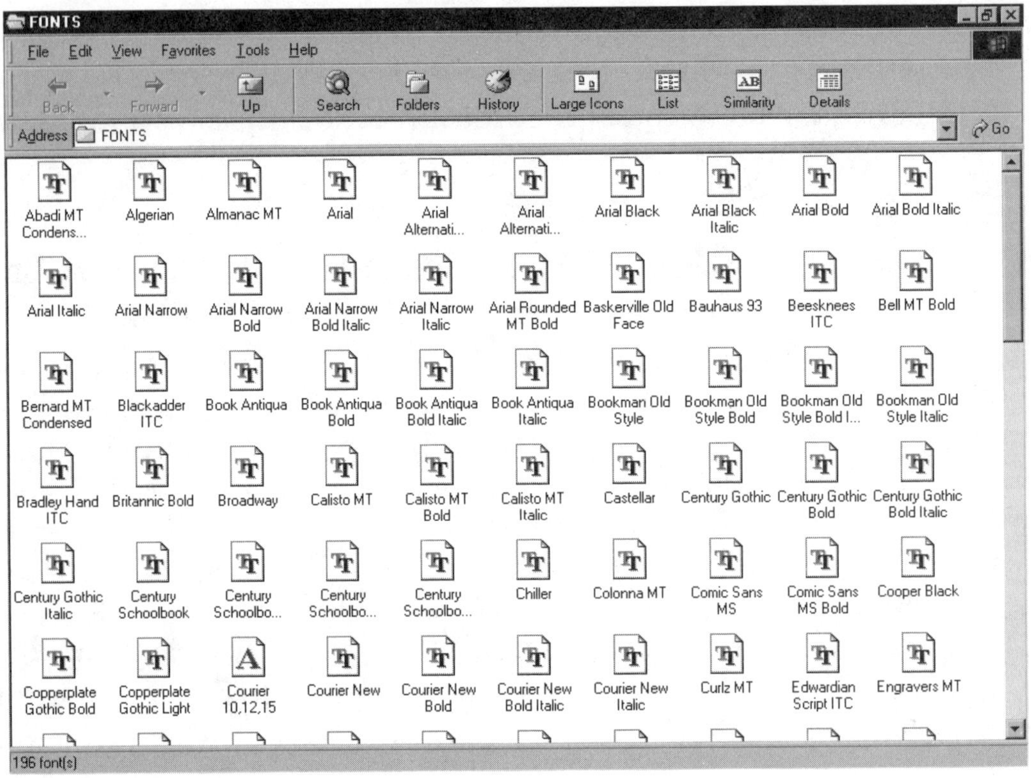

Figure 5-8 The Fonts folder.

Windows Me provides two kinds of fonts. The icon containing the double-letter *T* indicates a TrueType font. The printed output of a TrueType font is identical to what you see on the screen. The icon containing the letter *A* indicates either a vector font or a raster font. Vector fonts are primarily used with plotters; raster fonts are stored as bitmap images and can't be scaled or rotated and won't print if your printer doesn't support them. Courier is an example of a raster font.

A font can have size, which is measured in points (1 point is 1/72 inch) and style (for example, *italics* or **boldface**). To see what a particular font looks like in various sizes, double-click its icon. Figure 5-9 shows how the Comic Sans MS looks in various sizes. To print this screen, click the Print button.

Figure 5-9

Check out the look of a font in various sizes.

Changing the Font in an Application

To print a document in a font that you specify instead of in the default font, you must print from an application. The steps are the same in most Windows applications. To select a font for a printed document in WordPad, open WordPad, and then follow these steps:

1. Open the Font dialog box, as shown in Figure 5-10.

Click the Format menu, and then click Font.

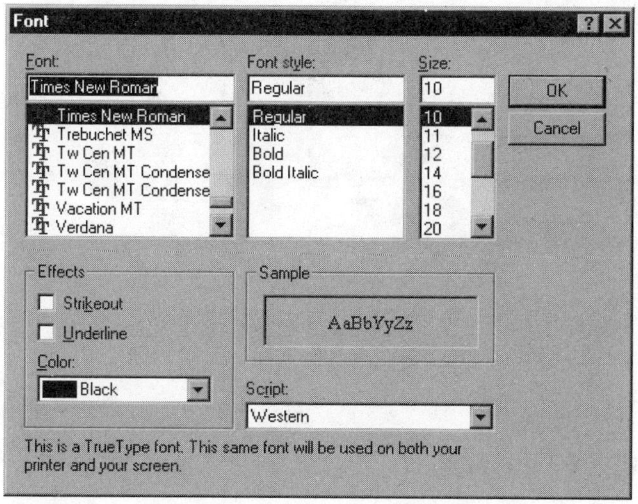

Figure 5-10 The Font dialog box.

2. **Select a font.**

   Select a font, a font style, a size, an effect, and a color, and then click OK.

You can see the result of your selections in the Sample box.

Installing a New Font

Although Windows Me and other versions of Windows includes a great many fonts in all sorts of styles and sizes, you might want to install other fonts for particular purposes such as addressing formal envelopes, creating special invitations, and so on. Additional fonts can be purchased on disk anywhere computer software is sold. To install additional fonts, follow these steps:

1. **Open the Add Fonts dialog box, as shown in Figure 5-11.**

   In the Fonts folder, click the File menu, and then click Install New Font.

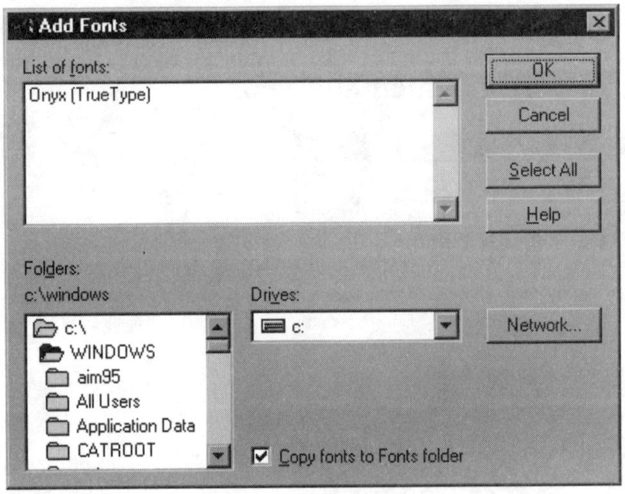

Figure 5-11 The Add Fonts dialog box.

2. **Locate and install the font.**

   Insert the fonts disk in the appropriate drive. In the Drives drop-down list box, select the drive containing the font files, and then select the file from the Folders list. Click OK to install the font. By default, fonts are copied to the Fonts folder.

Seven Important Things to Remember About Printing

1. Installing a printer means identifying it to Windows and giving Windows some information about it.
2. You can use the Printing Troubleshooter to locate the source of a printing problem.
3. Whether you print from the desktop or from an application, it is Windows that does the printing.
4. You can establish default settings for your printer using the printer's Properties dialog box.
5. To specify details about how a document prints, you must print from an application. Otherwise, Windows uses the default settings.
6. When shopping for a printer, remember to check specifications such as the dots per inch and the pages per minute. The more dots per inch, the slower that pages are printed. Also, color prints slower than only black ink.
7. Your printer manual may show you how to print some special types of documents such as photographs, two-sided sheets, and transparencies, but some applications for creating greeting cards, folded brochures, and so on will also include instructions.

Summary

In this chapter, we looked briefly at the types of printers and how they work, and then we looked at the specifics for setting up a printer and printing. You can refer to this chapter when you get ready to install a new printer or when you need the steps for taking care of printing tasks, but don't forget about the instruction manual that came with your printer. The features on printers vary by manufacturer and model, and the manual will be targeted to your particular printer.

Chapter 6

HOW TO GET ON THE INTERNET

Featuring:

- What Is the Internet?
- What Is the World Wide Web?
- Getting Connected
- Connecting Through a Modem
- Connecting Through a Cable Modem
- Connecting Through a DSL Modem
- Connecting Through ISDN

If you are not yet using your computer to get on the Internet, I predict that you soon will be. (Maybe that's one of the reasons you are reading this book?) At present, only 19 percent of those of us over the age of 50 are using the Internet, but our usage is growing faster than that of any other age group. And we are far more likely to make online purchases than any other age group. Researchers tell us that 43 percent of senior online shoppers are primarily buying software and books, compared with about 20 percent of the overall population of Internet shoppers.

But we aren't just shopping on the Internet. We're researching our family trees, exchanging e-mail with friends and family, investing, signing up for Social Security payments, participating in online groups with people who have similar interests, planning vacations and making reservations, contacting local, state, and federal government officials to express our opinions, and on and on.

In this chapter, I'll start with a brief explanation of the Internet and the World Wide Web, and I'll tell you how to connect to the Internet using various communications devices.

What Is the Internet?

The short answer is that the Internet is a worldwide network of networks, but what is a network? A computer network is a group of computers and devices such as printers and modems that are connected in some way so that their users can share the stuff that's on all the computers. For example, if you and I work on computers that are on the same network and we give each other permission, you can open the documents that I create and read them, and I can look at the photos of your most recent trip. Or we might play an electronic game of bridge.

The Internet, then, is a huge network of networks, but strangely enough no one owns the Internet, and no one runs the Internet. Nevertheless, it seems to run just fine. Of course, the Internet is composed of many smaller networks, and many of these networks are managed by corporations, governments, and all sorts of other organizations, but no one entity or person is in charge of the Internet.

Although the Internet evolved from technological innovations that began in the late 1960s, it became universally available in the early 1990s. We've come a long way in a very short time, and that's primarily because of the development of the World Wide Web.

What Is the World Wide Web?

You will hear the terms *Internet* and *Web* used interchangeably, but they are really two different things. The Web, which is short for World Wide Web (abbreviated WWW), is the total set of resources (files, documents, pictures, software, and so on) that are available on all the Internet servers around the world. A server is simply a computer that stores resources and then displays ("serves") them when you request them. To make your request, you use an application called a *Web browser.*

The Web browser that's included with Microsoft Windows is Microsoft Internet Explorer. To access a resource on the World Wide Web, you tell Internet Explorer its *address.* Internet Explorer then sends this address out over the Internet to the server that stores the resource, and then the server sends the resource back to you.

An Internet address is referred to as Uniform Resource Locator (abbreviated URL). Some people pronounce URL as a word, *earl,* and some say U-R-L. A URL is actually a representation for a string of numbers that identify a computer on the Internet. Since it's easier for us humans to remember names instead of numbers, we typically use URLs.

You've seen URLs all over the place—on TV, in magazines, on cereal boxes, on business cards, everywhere. The address of the Internet site for Microsoft Corporation is *http://www.microsoft.com.* Here is what each part of this URL means:

- The first part, *http*, is the *protocol.* You access Internet resources using various protocols, which are merely the rules connecting to certain kinds of resources. The http protocol (HyperText Transfer Protocol) is the most common.
- The second part, *www*, indicates that the resource is on the World Wide Web.

- The third part, *microsoft*, is the name of the server.
- The fourth part, *com*, is the *domain name.* Servers on the Internet are classified into domains, and a domain indicates the type of server. I'll show you how this works shortly.

When talking about a URL, you pronounce a period as "dot." So for short, you'd refer to *http://www.microsoft.com* as "microsoft dot com."

Although it's true, as I said, that no one is the "boss" of the Internet, there is an organization that manages domain names, and it is a non-profit corporation called the Internet Corporation for Assigned Names and Numbers (ICANN). In late 2000, this organization recognized seven domain types within the United States:

- *.com* is a commercial organization.
- *.edu* is an educational institution, for example, a university.
- *.gov* is a government, for example, an entity that is part of the U.S. government.
- *.int* is an international organization, such as the United Nations.
- *.mil* is a branch of the U.S. military.
- *.net* is a network organization.
- *.org* is a nonprofit organization.

By mid-2001, however, ICANN will begin issuing URLs that incorporate seven new domain types. These new suffixes were designed as alternatives to *.com*, which is currently crowded with 20 million registrations. Think of it as similar to adding area codes to the phone system to accommodate growth. Here are the new domain names you can expect to see:

- *.aero*, which will indicate airlines, airports, computer reservation systems, and related industries.
- *.biz*, which will be specifically for businesses.

- *.coop*, which will designate business cooperatives such as credit unions and rural electric co-ops.
- *.info*, which will be a more global identifier. Currently, most .com registrations are in the United States.
- *.museum*, which will indicate accredited museums worldwide.
- *.name*, which will be a category for individuals.
- *.pro*, which will indicate a professional status such as doctor or lawyer.

Getting Connected

Before you can connect to the Internet, you need two things: a communications device and an account with an Internet service provider (ISP). The most common communications device for home use today is a modem, but increasingly other, higher-speed devices are becoming available, including those that use the same wiring that brings cable TV into your home. An ISP is a business that, for a fee, provides Internet connectivity to homes, businesses, and other organizations.

In the following sections, I'll start by describing how to set up a modem, and then I'll discuss some high-speed connections that may be available to you. I'll also show you step-by-step how to acquire the services of an ISP and how to set up your Internet connection.

Connecting Through a Modem

If you acquired your computer system recently, it probably came with a modem that is on the inside of the system unit. A modem is a device that lets a computer transfer information over a telephone line. It is connected to a wire that looks just like the wire that connects your telephone to the jack in the wall. The wire is attached to your computer on one end and plugs into a phone jack on the other end.

A modem that sits inside the system unit is called an *internal modem;* but a modem can also be on the outside of your computer, and in that case it is called an *external modem.* Both internal and external modems work in exactly the same way: they convert the digital signals that your computer sends into analog signals that the phone system can understand, and vice versa when your computer is receiving information from over the Internet.

The Settings for Your Modem

When Windows was installed on your computer, it recognized the modem, installed it automatically, and established some settings for the modem to use, such as the speaker volume for the modem (the noise level at which you hear the modem dialing out and connecting to the computer at your ISP). Normally, you don't want to change these settings, but let's take a look at them so that you know what they are. Follow these steps:

1. **Open Control Panel, as shown in Figure 6-1.**

   Click the Start button, click Settings, and then click Control Panel.

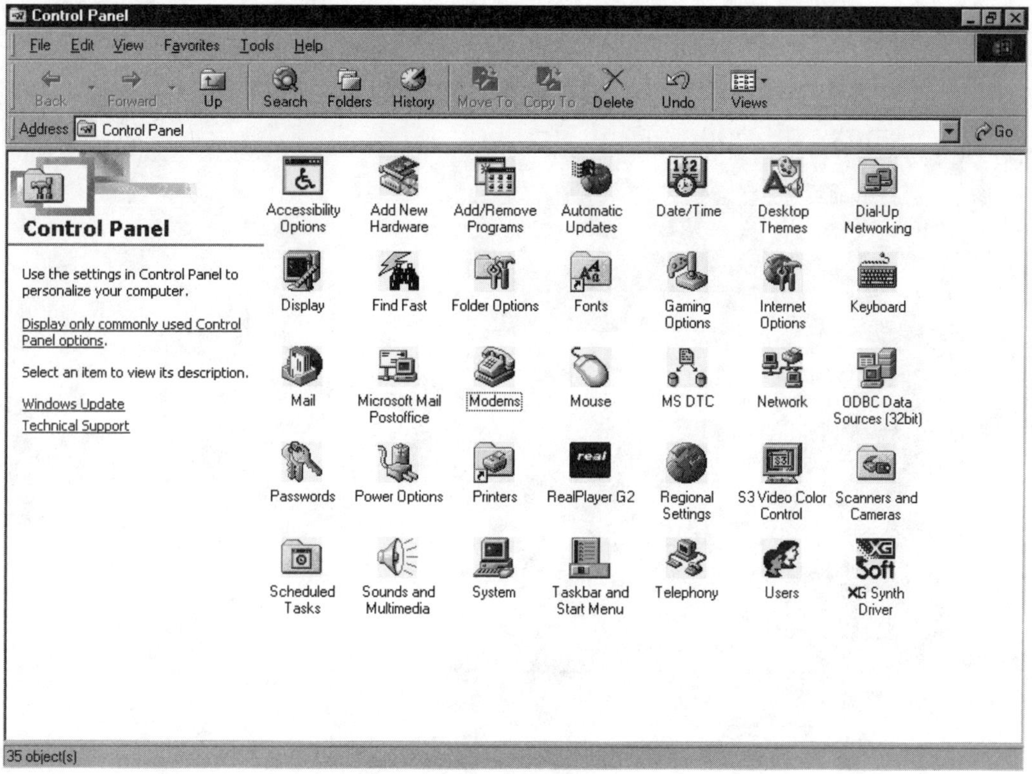

Figure 6-1 The Windows Control Panel.

2. **Open the Modems Properties dialog box, as shown in Figure 6-2.**

   Double-click the Modems icon. The Modems Properties dialog box will open at the General tab.

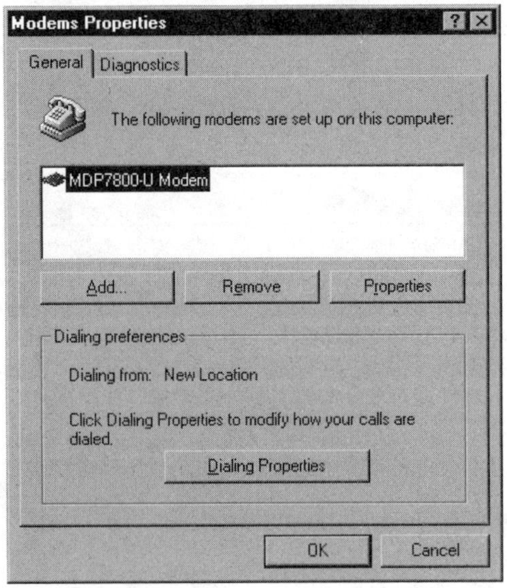

Figure 6-2 The Modems Properties dialog box.

NOTE *The* properties *of something in Windows are simply the characteristics of the item. You can use the Properties dialog box for an item to view and, sometimes, change these characteristics.*

3. **Open the Properties dialog box for your modem.**

   Click the Properties button in the General tab. Figure 6-3 shows the Properties dialog box for my modem.

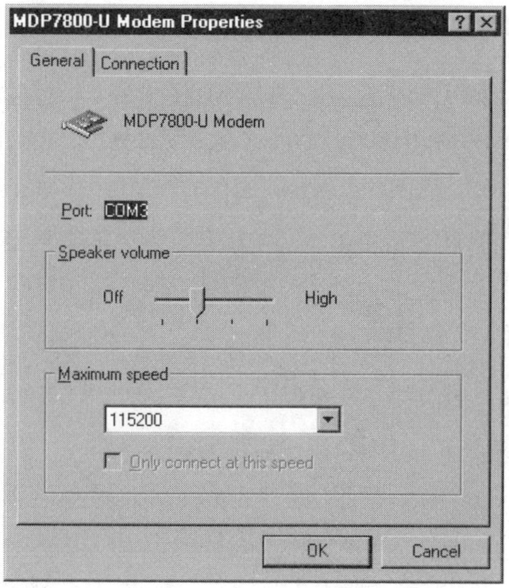

Figure 6-3 The Properties dialog box for my modem.

The Properties dialog box for your modem gives you the following information:

- The port on which your modem is installed. A *port* is the connecting point between a device such as a modem and your computer. It is usually identified by a name and a number.
- The speaker volume for your modem. Click the slider and move it to increase or decrease this volume.
- The maximum speed at which your modem connects. The number that Windows supplies here by default is about twice the actual speed of the fastest modem available today, so you don't need to change this.

Normally, the only change you should make in the Properties dialog box for your modem is to adjust the speaker volume. What you may well need to fiddle with, however, is the way your modem dials out.

TIP *If you just purchased a new computer and you can't get the modem to work, get in touch with a technical support person at the store where you bought the computer.*

Telling Your Modem How to Dial Out

Later in this chapter, we'll look at how to use the Internet Connection Wizard to tell Windows how you want to connect to the Internet, and in the process, you'll tell the wizard the phone number you want your modem to dial. For any number of reasons, you may need to change that phone number—your ISP may give you a different phone number, you may move to another location, your local phone system may implement 10-digit dialing, your area code may change, and so on.

To make any changes in how your modem dials out, you use the Dialing Properties dialog box. If you move to a new location, need to dial a special number for an outside line, or want to disable call waiting, follow these steps:

1. **Open the Dialing Properties dialog box, as shown in Figure 6-4.**

   Click the Start button, click Settings, and then click Control Panel to open Control Panel. Double-click the Modems icon to open the Modems Properties dialog box, and then click the Dialing Properties button.

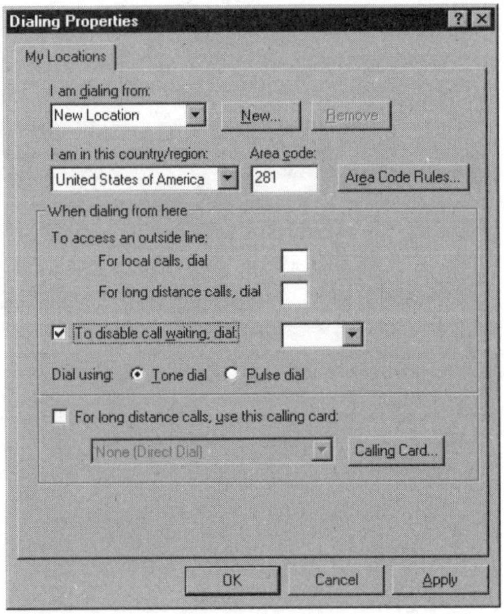

Figure 6-4 The Dialing Properties dialog box.

2. **Tell Windows your country of residence and your area code.**

   In the I Am In This Country/Region drop-down list box, click the down arrow and select where you will be dialing from. In the Area Code box, type your area code.

3. **Tell Windows whether you need to dial a special number for local or long distance calls.**

   If you need to dial a number to reach an outside line for local calls, enter it in the For Local Calls, Dial box. If you need to dial a number to reach an outside line for long distance calls, type it in the For Long Distance Calls, Dial box.

4. **Tell Windows to disable call waiting.**

   If you have call waiting and it is enabled while you are connected to the Internet, an incoming telephone call will disconnect you from the Internet if you use the same phone line for both voice and the modem. To disable call waiting, click the To Disable Call Waiting, Dial check box and then enter the correct numeric code or select it from the list that appears when you click the down arrow. You can find this numeric code in your local phone book.

5. **Tell Windows whether your phone is tone or pulse dial.**

   Click the appropriate option button, and then click Apply.

TIP *If you plan to spend a lot of time on the Internet, consider adding an extra phone line that is dedicated to your computer. In this way, you don't have to worry about such things as call waiting, missing phone calls, or listening to others in the household complain because they can't use the phone.*

As you can see in Figure 6-4, the Dialing Properties dialog box also contains buttons that you can click to set up area code rules and a calling card. Let's look first at how to specify area code rules, which you'll need to do if your phone system uses 10-digit dialing. Follow these steps:

1. **Open the Area Code Rules dialog box, as shown in Figure 6-5.**

   In the Dialing Properties dialog box, click the Area Code Rules button.

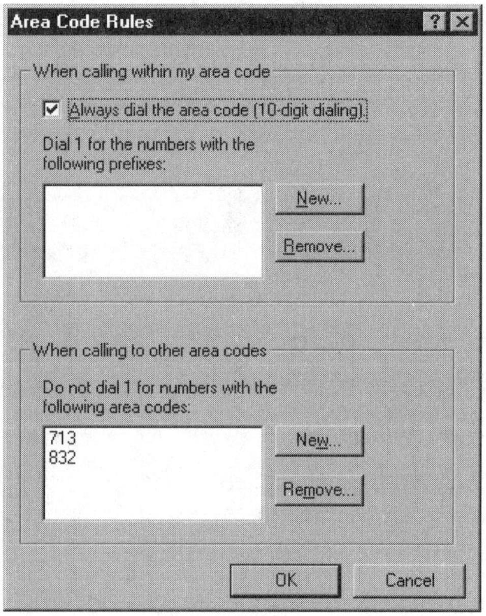

Figure 6-5 The Area Code Rules dialog box.

2. **Specify the rules.**

   Click the Always Dial The Area Code (10-Digit Dialing) check box. In the When Calling To Other Area Codes box, click New to open the New Area Code dialog box, as shown in Figure 6-6. Enter the area code that you call that does not need to be preceded by dialing 1, and click OK. If you need to enter several area codes, click New, and enter each one. When you've specified the rules, click OK to close the Area Code Rules dialog box.

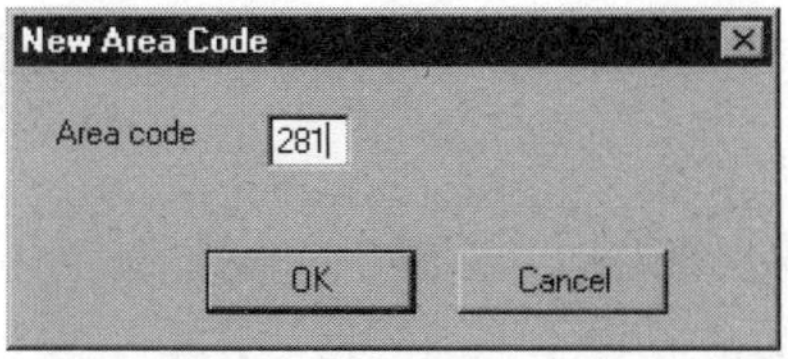

Figure 6-6 The New Area Code dialog box.

If you travel and take your computer along, you may find it handy to use a calling card if your ISP doesn't have an 800 number that you can access. To tell Windows about your calling card, follow these steps:

1. **Open the Calling Card dialog box, as shown in Figure 6-7.**

   In the Dialing Properties dialog box, click the Calling Card button.

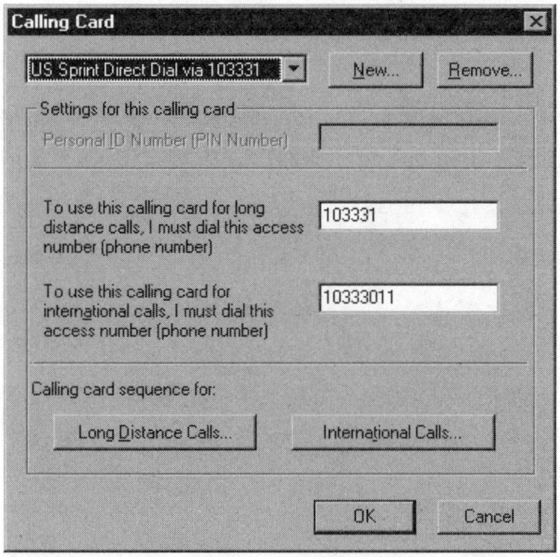

Figure 6-7 The Calling Card dialog box.

2. **Tell Windows which card you want to use.**

   In the drop-down box at the top of the dialog box, click the down arrow and select the name of your card. Windows will automatically enter the access number for long distance and international calls in the middle boxes in the dialog box.

3. **Tell Windows the calling card sequence for long distance and international calls.**

   Click the Long Distance Calls button to open the Calling Card Sequence dialog box. Click the down arrow in the Dial drop-down list for each step, and select the number to dial. If you must then wait for a response or for a period of time, select that from the Then Wait For drop-down list. Click OK when you're finished. Click the International Calls button to open the Calling Card Sequence dialog box again, and follow the same procedure. Click OK when you're finished. Click OK again in the Dialing Properties dialog box.

Finding an Internet Service Provider

As I mentioned earlier in this chapter, you will need an Internet service provider before you can connect to the Internet. Before I get into the various ways that you can find an ISP, I need to explain that there are a couple of different kinds of ISPs, and they are distinguished by what they provide. America Online (AOL), for example, is an ISP that provides e-mail, Internet access, chat rooms, personal home pages, instant messaging, photo delivery, and all sorts of content such as newspapers, magazines, and so on. Many ISPs, however, provide just e-mail and Internet access. As you will see in the next chapter, you can access many of the features that a service such as AOL provides from the World Wide Web itself. Which kind of service you select depends on your personal preferences. Many people start out by using a service such as AOL and later switch to a more generic provider.

You can find an ISP in a number of ways. Often you'll find a setup CD for a service included in your local newspaper or bound into a magazine. All you need to do is pop the CD into your computer and follow the onscreen instructions to get connected. When you buy a new computer, you'll often see an icon on the desktop that gives you easy access to an 800 number for various ISPs. You can then sign up online.

In addition, the Internet Connection Wizard can help you find an ISP. To use the wizard, follow these steps:

NOTE *A wizard is simply a guide that steps you through a process.*

1. **Start the wizard.**

   If you have an Internet Connection Wizard icon on your desktop, simply click it. Otherwise, click the Start button, click Programs, click Accessories, click Communications, and then click Internet Connection Wizard. You'll see the screen shown in Figure 6-8.

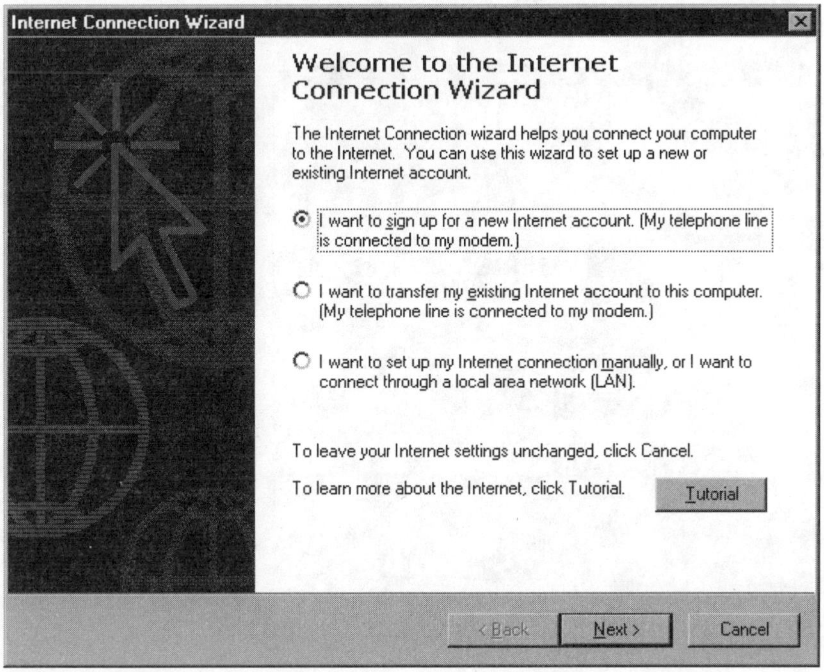

Figure 6-8 Starting the Internet Connection Wizard.

2. **Tell the wizard that you have a modem and want to sign up for a new account.**

   Click the first option button, and then click Next.

3. **Tell the wizard to dial a referral service.**

   Select one of the 800 phone numbers that the wizard displays, and then click Next.

4. **Check out the services.**

   When the wizard connects to the referral service, it displays the list shown in Figure 6-9. To see a description of a service, select it. If you find one that meets your needs, select it and click Next. On the next screen, you'll find instructions for how to connect and use that service. Click Finish to set up the service.

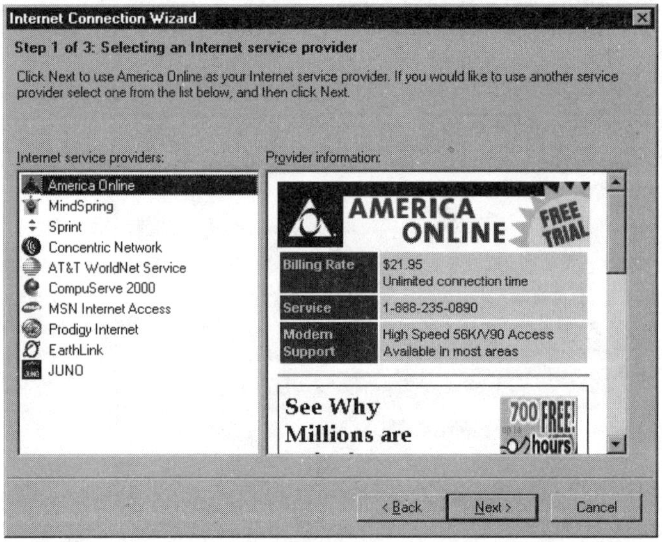

Figure 6-9 A list of ISPs that the wizard suggests.

Another way to find an ISP is to ask people in your area which ISP they use and if they are happy with the service. You can also check your local newspapers or phone books.

Basically, when you contact an ISP, you want to know how much a service costs and exactly what you're getting for your money. These days, most ISPs offer unlimited access to e-mail and the Web for one set fee. If you travel and take your computer on the road, be sure to find out if the ISP has a toll-free number that you can dial to check your e-mail.

Setting Up Your Internet Connection

If you acquire the services of a local or a regional ISP, you'll need to give Windows some information about the account. You do so using the Internet Connection Wizard. Before you start, be sure that you have the following information from your ISP:

- Your user name and your password
- The phone number to dial in to your ISP
- The name of your incoming mail server
- The name of your outgoing mail server

Start the wizard as you did in the previous section, and then follow these steps:

1. **Tell the wizard what you want to do.**

   In the first screen of the wizard, click the third option button, and then click Next to open the Setting Up Your Internet Connection screen, as shown in Figure 6-10.

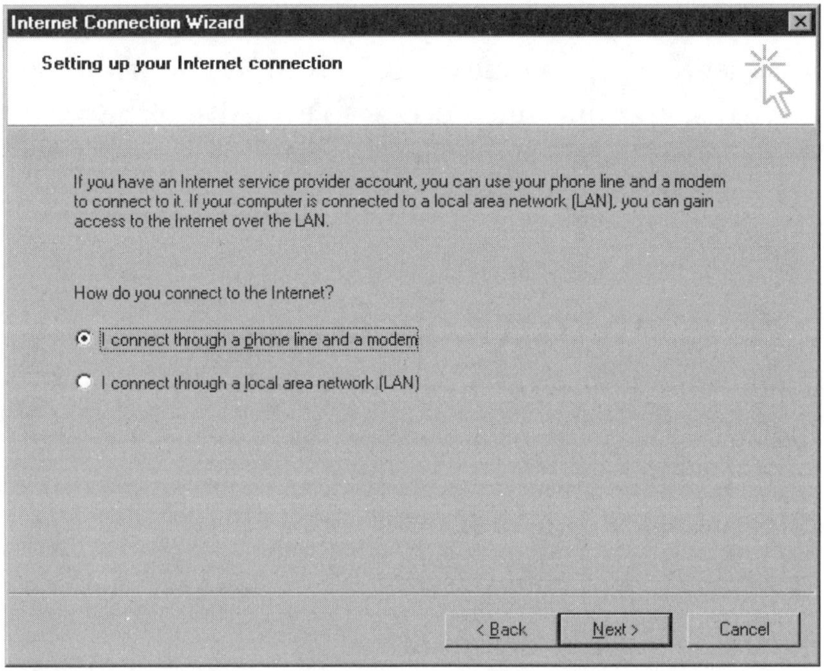

Figure 6-10 Tell the wizard how you connect to the Internet.

2. **Tell the wizard how you connect to the Internet.**

   Click the I Connect Through A Phone Line And A Modem option button, and then click Next.

3. **Give the wizard information about your account.**

   Enter the area code and phone number that your ISP gave you, and click the drop-down list to select your location. If you need to dial the area code and the country code (1 is the code for the United States), click that check box. Click Next.

4. **Give the wizard information about your logon.**

   In the User Name box, type the user name that your ISP assigned you. In the Password box, enter the password that you were assigned. Click Next.

5. **Enter a name for this Internet connection.**

   In the Connection Name box, type a name for this connection. It can be anything you want, but it's good to choose something that identifies the account, especially if you will have more than one account. This name will appear under an icon in the Dial-Up Networking folder. Click Next.

6. **Set up your e-mail account.**

   Click Yes, click Next, click Create A New Internet Mail Account, and then click Next. Enter the name that you want displayed in the From field when you send an e-mail message, and click Next. Enter your e-mail address (the one your ISP gave you), and click Next. You'll see the screen shown in Figure 6-11.

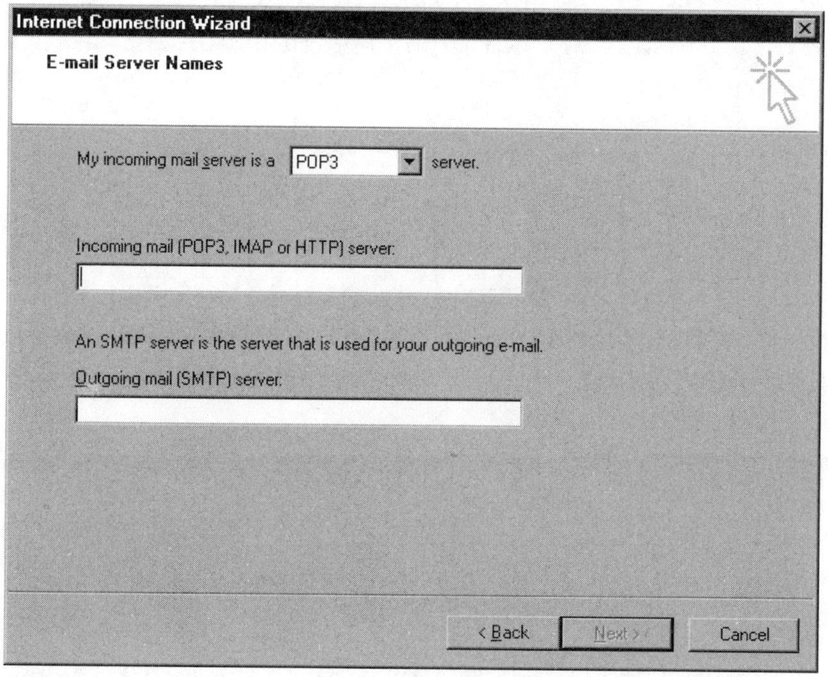

Figure 6-11 Tell the wizard about your e-mail servers.

NOTE *An e-mail server at your ISP is a computer or a program that sends or receives e-mail messages.*

7. **Describe the e-mail servers at your ISP.**

   Using the information you received from your ISP, enter the type of your incoming mail server (select from the drop-down list), enter the name of your incoming e-mail server, and enter the name of your outgoing e-mail server. Click Next.

8. **Tell the wizard your e-mail account name and your password.**

   In the Account Name box, type your account name, and enter your password in the Password box. If you want Windows to remember your password so that you don't have to type it every time you connect to your e-mail program, click the Remember Password check box. Click Next, and then click Finish in the last screen of the wizard.

If you don't want to connect to the Internet right now, clear the check box on the last screen of the wizard. But, of course, you want to connect to the Internet! When you do, you'll open a Microsoft Web site in Internet Explorer. If you're ready, skip to the next chapter for a tour of Internet Explorer and some information about sites that are especially useful for seniors and how to reach them.

Using High-Speed Connections

If you're new to the Internet, and you've just started connecting using a modem, you may think that all the talk about high-speed connections is just something for spoiled technical types. But as you use the Internet and especially if you have an opportunity to access the Web over a computer that has a high-speed connection, you'll become painfully aware of the difference. The modem is still the most common and popular Internet connection device, but it is also the slowest.

High-speed connections have been available in some areas of the United States for a long time (in computer years) but are still not widely available. One of my sons lives in Connecticut, and he's had a high-speed connection for a couple of years. I live in a suburb of Houston, and I'm still being told "wait 'til next year." Nevertheless, I want you to know what's out there so that you can make an informed choice when these technologies are available where you are. Some are no more expensive than a phone line and a modem and are simple to set up and use.

Connecting Through a Cable Modem

Today more than 100 million homes are wired for cable TV, so if your cable provider offers cable modem service, by all means check it out. When you access a Web site over the Internet, you are "downloading" that information to your computer from the server where it is stored. A cable modem downloads 30 to 100 times faster than the fastest modem.

A cable modem is a little box that is about 10 inches by 2 inches by 7 inches. It is external to your computer and connected to your computer. When a cable modem is installed, the coaxial cable that comes into your home from a pole is divided into two connections by a splitter. One connection goes to your TV, and the other goes to your cable modem. Data traveling to your computer from the Internet goes through the coaxial cable, through your cable modem, and into your computer. Data traveling from your computer to the Internet follows this path in reverse.

NOTE *A cable modem isn't a modem in the truest sense of the word. As I mentioned earlier in this chapter, a modem converts the digital signals that the computer sends to the analog signals that the phone system can use and vice versa. A so-called cable modem transmits and receives all data as digital signals.*

The most difficult part of getting connected via cable modem may be getting your cable company to actually come to your home in a timely fashion. That said, once a technician arrives on the premises, he or she will fiddle with the main cable a bit, attach the splitter, and then run the cable to the cable modem. If your computer already has a network card (and many new computers do), the technician will attach the cable modem to the network card (which is inside the system unit) with another cable. If your computer doesn't have a network card, the cable company will probably provide one and configure it—perhaps for an additional fee.

The technician should then configure your computer settings, and he or she may install some authentication software on your computer. And that's it. You can now do a couple of things—you can log on to the Internet, or you can call your telephone company and cancel the second line you've been using for Internet access, if you had one. You can also most likely cancel your ISP account, because in most cases your cable provider becomes your ISP.

WARNING *Cable modem is "always on." You don't need to dial up and connect as you do with an analog modem. When you turn on your computer, you are automatically connected to the Internet. Consequently, your computer system is vulnerable to the possibility of unauthorized access. You'll want to install firewall software. Firewall software lets you get out to the Internet but prevents unauthorized users from getting into your computer from the Internet. Check with your cable service provider about getting firewall software.*

Connecting Through a DSL Modem

Another popular high-speed option is a digital subscriber line (DSL) modem. Again, a DSL modem is not really a modem in the truest sense because it transmits all data as digital signals. Like a cable modem, a DSL modem is external to the computer, and it looks similar to a cable modem.

DSL uses your existing phone lines, but transmits data at higher frequencies than those used to transmit voice. Therefore, you can use your fax machine or your telephone at the same time you are accessing the Internet with your computer.

The DSL modem attached to your computer must be the same as the DSL modem at the telephone company office, and the telephone company office (also called a central office) must be within a certain distance of your home. Many ISPs offer DSL connections as well as dial-up (modem) connections, and if your central office is within the specified distance, the ISP will send a technician to your home to install a DSL modem. The process is almost identical to that of setting up a cable modem, but in this case, the technician uses the phone line instead of the coaxial cable.

As with cable modem, DSL modem is "always on," so you'll want to check with your ISP about installing firewall software to protect your computer from unauthorized access.

Connecting Through ISDN

Integrated Services Digital Network (ISDN) is not a new technology, but it is a popular high-speed alternative if cable modem or DSL is not available in your area. Many phone companies offer ISDN service.

ISDN uses existing telephone wires and requires an ISDN modem. Unlike the cable modem and the DSL modem, an ISDN modem is really a modem in the truest sense. It is an adapter that lets you send and receive digital signals over ISDN phone lines. Using ISDN, you can access the Internet while talking on the phone over the same connection; thus, you can disconnect the second phone line if you've been using one for Internet access.

After you contract with your phone company for ISDN service, you need to install your ISDN modem. The process is exactly the same as installing an analog modem; Windows recognizes the ISDN modem and installs it when you connect it to your computer. To set up ISDN, you use the ISDN Configuration Wizard. To find out more about this wizard, open Microsoft Help And Support (click the Start button and then click Help), click the Index tab, and search on ISDN.

Connecting to the Internet on a Budget

I assume you're reading this book because you have a computer or are in the process of getting one. But if you know someone who wants to use e-mail and browse the Internet but doesn't want the expense of purchasing a computer, tell them about WebTV. WebTV is a small boxlike appliance that turns a television screen into a computer monitor.

Slightly larger than a cable box, the WebTV unit sits on top of a TV. It ranges in cost from $99 to $199, and the monthly service charge is similar to that of an ISP—from $19.95 to $24.95. Setting up WebTV is easy. Simply follow the large diagrams, and connect the cables and phone lines. The kit even includes a double phone plug so you can share the unit with your telephone.

Once you're connected and registered, click the View button on the unit's remote to switch from watching TV to accessing the Internet. You can read e-mail by scrolling through an onscreen keyboard with the remote. In TV view, WebTV can download all the TV listings for the following day, and you can browse through the listing on the screen to select what you want to watch or videotape.

WebTV is no substitute for a real computer—you can't do word processing or any other standard computer task—but it's become popular among noncomputer users because it's so easy to learn and use. And it's not expensive.

Seven Important Things to Remember About the Internet

1. The Internet and the World Wide Web are not the same thing. The Internet is a worldwide network of networks, and the World Wide Web is the total set of resources that are available on the Internet.
2. An Internet address is called a Uniform Resource Locator (URL) and consists of names that represent a string of numbers that identifies a computer on the Internet. The period in a URL is pronounced as "dot."
3. To connect to the Internet, you need a communications device and an account with an ISP.
4. A modem is the most common device used to connect to the Internet, but it is also the slowest.
5. When you access a Web site, you are "downloading" it from the server on which it is stored. When you send e-mail, you are "uploading" a message that you've composed on your computer to the Internet.
6. If cable modem, DSL modem, or ISDN is available in your area, check out the service. These are high-speed connection devices and can be many, many times faster than an analog modem connection.
7. If you install a high-speed modem, check with the installer about adding firewall protection software because these devices are always on. Since you are always connected to the Internet when your computer is on, unauthorized users could access your computer.

Summary

In this chapter, I've given you an overview of the Internet and the World Wide Web and discussed the various ways you can connect to the Internet. You can follow the steps in this chapter to set up an analog modem, cable modem, DSL modem, and an ISDN modem.

Chapter 7

EXPLORING THE WORLD WIDE WEB

Featuring:

- Connecting to the Internet
- A Quick Tour of Internet Explorer
- Getting Around on the Web
- Finding Exactly What You Want on the Web
- Buying and Selling on the Web
- An Important Site for Seniors
- Important Sites for Citizens
- Safe Surfing

As an old joke goes, the preacher who has been waxing eloquent for well more than an hour, says, "And now I'm going to tell you what you've been waiting until 12:15 to hear." That's a bit how I feel about the information in this chapter. I know many of you are primarily interested in learning how to use your computer to access the vast resources that are on the Internet, and it may seem as if I've taken a long time to get to this point in the book. (And, hey, if you just skipped straight to this chapter, that's okay, too.)

Understanding how your computer works and how to use Microsoft Windows prepares you for using the Internet, and in this chapter, you'll get acquainted with the essential Internet tool—Microsoft Internet Explorer, the Web browser that's included with Windows. Along the way, I'll point you toward some great resources for seniors. It's a fabulous time to be over 50, doing Windows, and browsing the World Wide Web.

Connecting to the Internet

Before you can browse the Web, you need to connect to the Internet. If you have a cable modem or a DSL modem (I described both in the previous chapter), you're on the Internet as soon as you turn on your computer. If you have an analog modem, you need to tell it to connect to your ISP and, hence, to the Internet. You can do this in various ways. Here are the steps to connect using the Dial-Up Networking folder:

1. **Open the Dial-Up Networking folder, as shown in Figure 7-1.**

   Click the Start button, click Settings, and then click Dial-Up Networking.

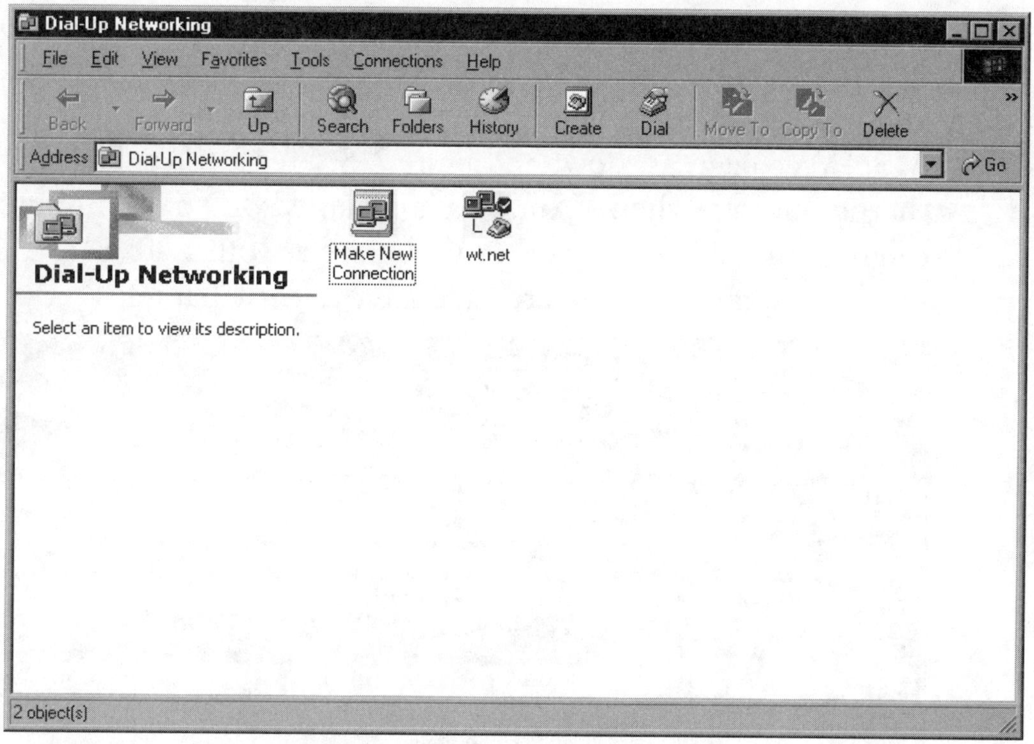

Figure 7-1 The Dial-Up Networking folder.

2. **Open the Connecting To dialog box, as shown in Figure 7-2.**

   Double-click the icon for the connection you created using the Internet Connection Wizard. You'll hear the modem dialing, and when you are connected, the Connecting To dialog box will disappear from the screen. Close the Dial-Up Networking folder, and then open Internet Explorer or Microsoft Outlook Express (the e-mail program that's included with Windows). In the next chapter, I'll discuss how to use Outlook Express. As you know from an earlier chapter, you can click the Launch Internet Explorer Browser on the Quick Launch bar to open Internet Explorer.

Figure 7-2 The Connecting To dialog box.

A quicker way to connect to the Internet is simply to open Internet Explorer. When you do so, you'll see the Connecting To dialog box and hear the modem dialing. When you're connected, you'll see the MSN Web page, as shown in Figure 7-3. This is the default start page that is selected when Windows is installed on your computer. You can retain it or select any other Web page as your start page. I'll show you how to change the start page later in this chapter.

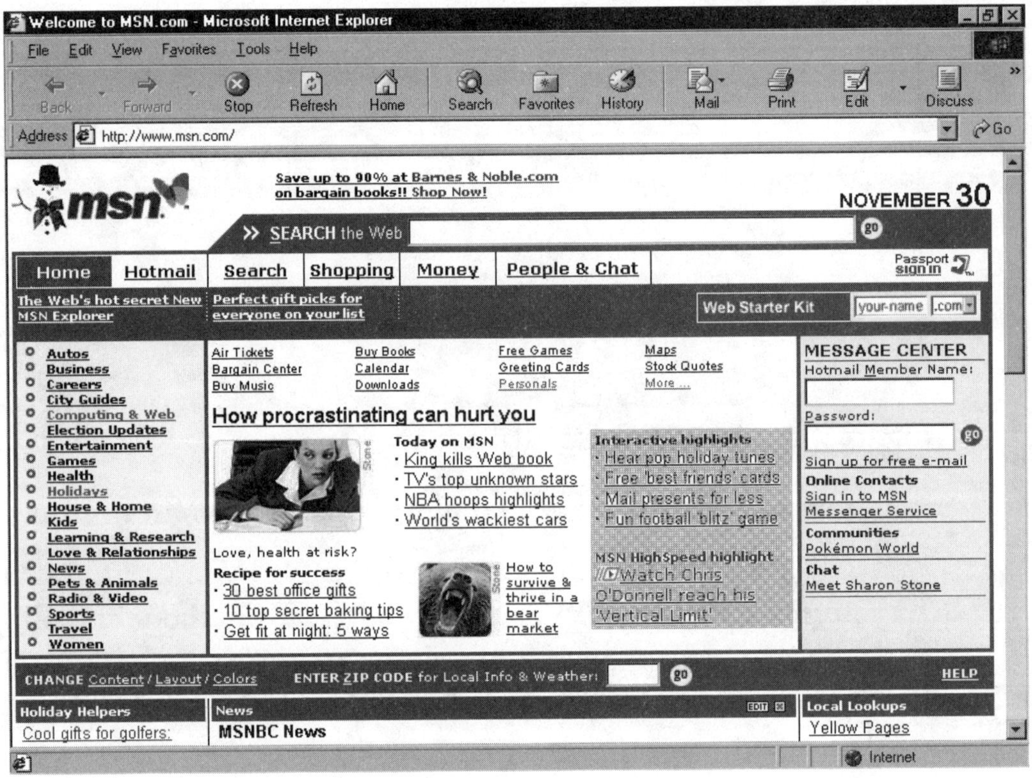

Figure 7-3 The default start page.

You can also open Internet Explorer from any document that contains a URL. Simply click the URL, and the page it refers to will open in Internet Explorer. In addition, in Windows Explorer, clicking a filename that ends in .htm or .html opens that file in Internet Explorer.

The Language of the Web

If you open any Web page in your Web browser, click the View menu, and then click Source, you'll see something similar to the following:

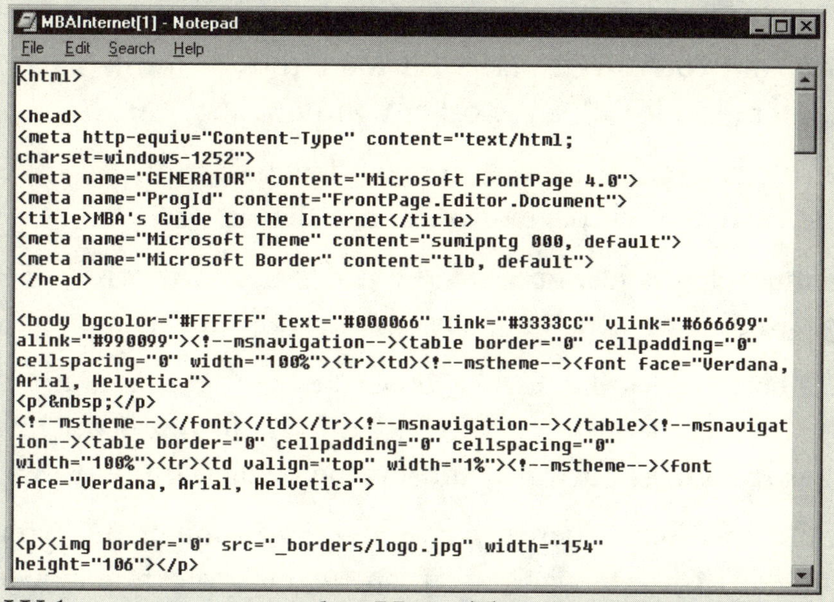


```
<html>

<head>
<meta http-equiv="Content-Type" content="text/html;
charset=windows-1252">
<meta name="GENERATOR" content="Microsoft FrontPage 4.0">
<meta name="ProgId" content="FrontPage.Editor.Document">
<title>MBA's Guide to the Internet</title>
<meta name="Microsoft Theme" content="sumipntg 000, default">
<meta name="Microsoft Border" content="tlb, default">
</head>

<body bgcolor="#FFFFFF" text="#000066" link="#3333CC" vlink="#666699"
alink="#990099"><!--msnavigation--><table border="0" cellpadding="0"
cellspacing="0" width="100%"><tr><td><!--mstheme--><font face="Verdana,
Arial, Helvetica">
<p> </p>
<!--mstheme--></font></td></tr><!--msnavigation--></table><!--msnavigat
ion--><table border="0" cellpadding="0" cellspacing="0"
width="100%"><tr><td valign="top" width="1%"><!--mstheme--><font
face="Verdana, Arial, Helvetica">


<p><img border="0" src="_borders/logo.jpg" width="154"
height="106"></p>
```

Web pages are created in HyperText Markup Language (HTML), and behind every Web page full of text, graphics, animations, and so on is a page that looks similar to this. The job of your Web browser is to render the HTML on the screen. For example, it looks at a <head> tag and displays what follows that tag in a special format.

As far as programming languages are concerned, HTML is not a difficult language to learn and use, but you can create pages in HTML without knowing anything about the language. For example, you can create simple Web pages using Microsoft Word, and you can use any of several software programs to create more complicated Web pages. Two of the most popular choices are Microsoft FrontPage and Allaire's HomeSite. Using these applications, you can create a Web page almost as easily as you create a document in a word processor, and each hides the HTML while you are working.

A Quick Tour of Internet Explorer

The components of the Internet Explorer window are much like those in other Windows applications. You'll see vertical and horizontal scroll bars as necessary, you can size portions of the window by clicking and dragging, and you can display a ScreenTip by pointing to a toolbar button. Here is a list of some other components:

- The **title bar** is at the top of the window, and it displays the name of the current Web page or other file that is open.
- The **menu bar** is just beneath the title bar, and it contains a set of menus, many of which appear in other Windows applications.
- The **Standard toolbar** is just beneath the menu bar, and it contains several buttons that correspond to items on the menu bar, as well as the Back, Forward, and Home navigation buttons.
- The **Address bar** is beneath the Standard toolbar, and you use it to enter a URL or filename. You can also click the drop-down arrow to select a URL.
- The **Activity Indicator** is at the far right of the menu bar and is animated when Internet Explorer is sending or receiving data.
- The **Main** window displays the resource you most recently accessed.
- The **status bar** is at the bottom of the screen. When you choose a menu command, the status bar displays a description of what it does. When you point to a link, the status bar displays its URL. When you click a link, the status bar displays a series of messages related to the progress of finding and opening that resource.
- The **Security zone** is at the far right of the status bar and displays the currently active Security zone. I'll discuss Internet security later in this chapter.

On a Web page, any word or phrase that is underlined is a hyperlink, or just link for short. A graphic can also be a link. If you see a hand with a pointing finger over a graphic when you point to it, the graphic is a link.

Getting Around on the Web

After you open Internet Explorer, you can start browsing the Web immediately. All you have to do is click a link or enter a URL in the Address bar. To see how this works, let's go to one of the premier sites for seniors on the Web, the American Association for Retired Persons (AARP) site at *http://www.aarp.org*. If you have the msn.com site open, simply select the msn.com/ portion of the URL in the Address bar, type *aarp.org*, and press the Enter key. You'll see a page similar to that shown in Figure 7-4.

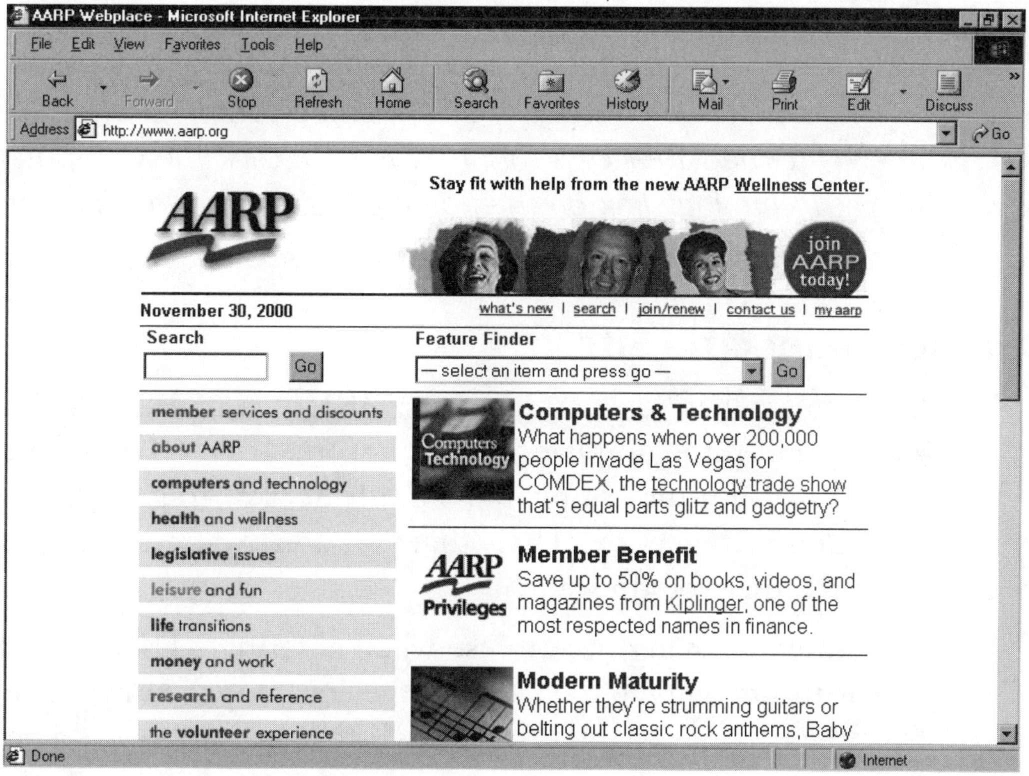

Figure 7-4 The AARP site.

Notice that in the previous paragraph I used the word *similar* to describe what you'll see when you open this page in Internet Explorer. Figure 7-4 shows the page as it was the day I opened it while writing this book. The best sites on the Web regularly update their content, and the AARP site is no exception to this rule. The World Wide Web is dynamic and constantly changing, which is a good thing. The downside to this, however, is that sites come and sites go. What's there this morning may not be there this afternoon or tomorrow. Therefore, as you go through the rest of this book, you may find that some sites I discuss are not where I said they would be or don't exist at all. The best sites will direct you to a new location if a site moves. When others disappear, you'll be presented with an annoying screen that says something like "Error 404: Site Not Found." When that happens, try the site again later or resign yourself to the fact that the page no longer exists.

TIP *The AARP site has a superb computer section that includes tips, how to's, a glossary of terms, and a tutorial that explores the Internet. To access this information, click the Computers And Technology link on the home page, as shown earlier in Figure 7-4, and then follow the links.*

Going to Specific Sites

Sometimes when you start to enter a URL, it completes itself for you. This is the AutoComplete feature at work. If AutoComplete enters the URL you want, simply press the Enter key to go to that site. If AutoComplete enters a URL that you don't want, continue typing the URL that you do want.

A handy timesaving trick to use when entering a URL that ends in *.com* is to simply type the name of the company. You may remember from the previous chapter that a URL that ends in *.com* is a business. For example, if you want to go to the General Electric site, simply type *general electric* in the Address bar and press the Enter key. Internet Explorer automatically finds and fills in the actual URL and goes to the site. Try it.

Using Links

To follow a link, you simply click it, and clicking links is part of the serendipitous experience of browsing the Internet. You may start out at the site of your local public library and end up at a site on the other side of the planet. It's a great deal of fun, but you'll find that you soon lose track of exactly where you are and where you've been. Three buttons on the Standard toolbar come to your rescue:

- Click the Home button to return to your start page, which is msn.com if you haven't changed it. (I'll show you how shortly.)
- Click the Back button to return to the page you last visited.
- Click the Forward button to return to the page you visited before you clicked the Back button.

Changing Your Start Page

Now that you've explored the Web a bit, you may have found a page you'd rather see when Internet Explorer starts. You can use the currently open page, any other page if you know its URL, or a blank page. To set a page other than msn.com as your start page, open Internet Explorer and follow these steps:

1. **Open the Internet Options dialog box at the General tab, as shown below.**

   Click the Tools menu, and then click Internet Options.

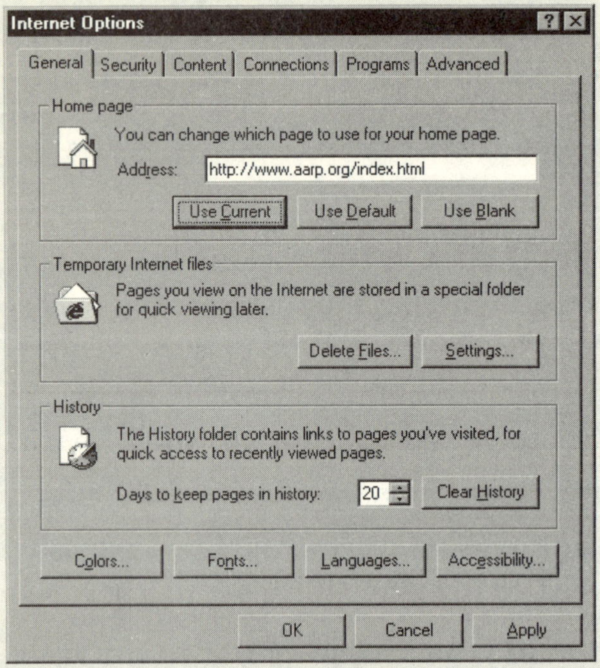

2. **Select your start page.**

If you want the currently open page to be your start page, click the Use Current button. If you want a different page and you know its URL, enter the URL in the Address box. If you want a blank page, click the Use Blank button. If you ever want to return to using the default start page, open this dialog box and click the Use Default button. Click OK when you've made your choice.

You can always come back to this dialog box and select a new page as your start page.

Keeping Track of Your Favorite Sites

When you come across a site that you know you'll want to revisit, you don't need to jot the URL down on a sticky note. Instead, you can add it to your Favorites list and then quickly click the link to go to that page. To add a site to your Favorites list, go to the page, and then follow these steps:

1. **Open the Add Favorite dialog box, as shown in Figure 7-5.**

   Click the Favorites menu, and then click Add To Favorites.

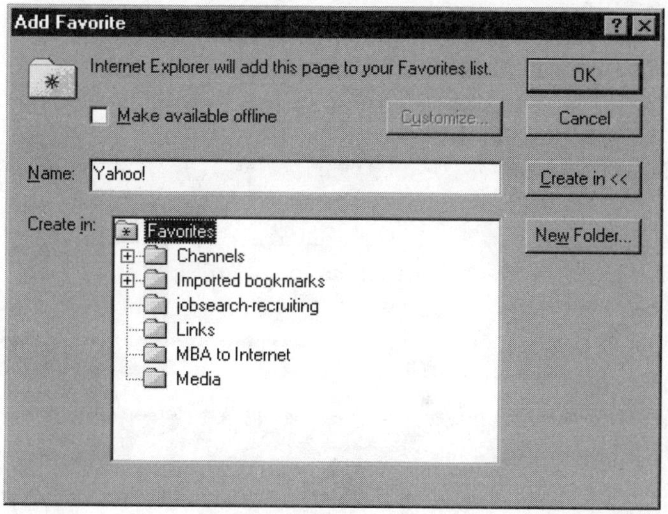

Figure 7-5 The Add Favorite dialog box.

2. **Add the site to your list.**

   In the Name box, accept the suggested name or type another. Select a folder in which to store the name from the Create In list, or click the New Folder button to create a new folder and then store the name in that folder. Click OK.

To use your Favorites list, click the Favorites menu to open the list, and then click a name, which is a link.

Returning to Where You Were

You have a couple of other ways to retrace your steps on the Web. For starters, you can click the down arrow in the Address bar. Internet Explorer keeps track of the last several sites you visited and displays them in this drop-down list.

You can also open the History list. By default, Internet Explorer keeps track of all the pages you visited for the last 20 days in the History list. You can retain more or fewer pages in this list, and I'll show you how shortly. To open and use the History list, follow these steps:

1. **Open the History list.**

   Click the History button on the Standard toolbar. Figure 7-6 shows my History list the day I was writing this chapter.

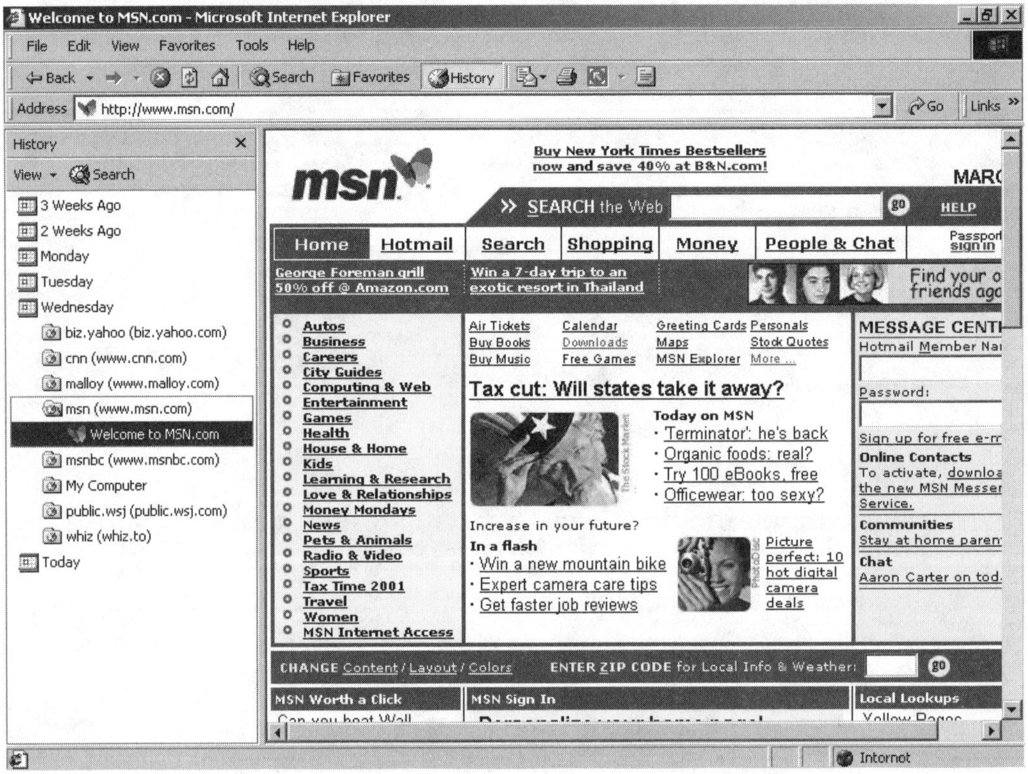

Figure 7-6 The History list in Internet Explorer.

2. **Go to a site on your History list.**

   Click one of the displayed links to go to the site. To display links to your earlier Web travels, click the calendar next to one of the other time periods. To close the History list, click its Close button (the X). You can also click the View button in the History list to display the list by date, site, most visited, or the order visited on the current day.

To change the number of days that pages are kept in the History list, open the Internet Options dialog box that was shown earlier in this chapter in the "Changing Your Start Page" sidebar, click the up or down arrow in the little box next to the Clear History button to select the number of days, and then click OK. If you ever want to empty the History list, click the Clear History button in this dialog box.

Saving and Printing Pages

If you want to make pages available so that you can view them when you are not connecting to the Internet (or *offline,* as this is frequently referred to), you can do so in a couple of ways. Remember, though, that when you view a page offline, you are seeing a static, not a dynamic, Web page. Its content will be the same as the last time you viewed it online (connected to the Internet). If you want to view new content or the page in its most current form, you'll need to connect to the Internet.

One way to make a page available when you aren't connected to the Internet is to click the Make Available Offline check box when you add a site to your Favorites list. When you then click that site in your Favorites list, Internet Explorer opens it from a storage place on your hard disk.

Another way to make a page available offline is to save it as a file on your hard disk. To do so, open the page and then follow these steps:

1. **Open the Save Web Page dialog box, as shown in Figure 7-7.**

   Click the File menu, and then click Save As.

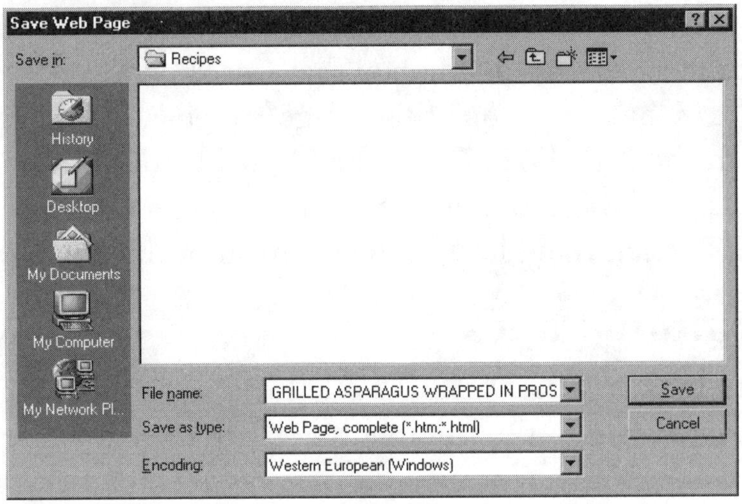

Figure 7-7 The Save Web Page dialog box.

2. **Select a folder, a filename, and a file type.**

   In the Save In box, select a folder in which to save your page. In the File Name box, accept the name that's suggested or type another name. In the Save As Type box, select a file type. (I'll explain these choices later in this section.) If you want to save the file with a character set other than Western European (Windows), click the drop-down Encoding list, and select a character set. If you click this list, you'll see that you can even save a Web page as Arabic (Windows) or Turkish (Windows)!

3. **Save the file.**

   Click the Save button.

Most Web pages contain a number of images and other files. When you save a Web page using the default type—Web Page, Complete—Internet Explorer creates a folder in which to store all those files and images. If you want to store everything on the page in one place, select the Web Archive, Single File type or select the Web Page, HTML Only type. I typically use the default type, but you can experiment to see which you prefer if you save a lot of Web pages.

Some Web pages oblige you by including a printer-friendly version on their site. The Food Network at *http://www.foodtv.com* is such a site. Figure 7-8 shows a recipe in the normal version of this page, and Figure 7-9 shows the page that is displayed when you click the Printer Friendly Version option on the home page.

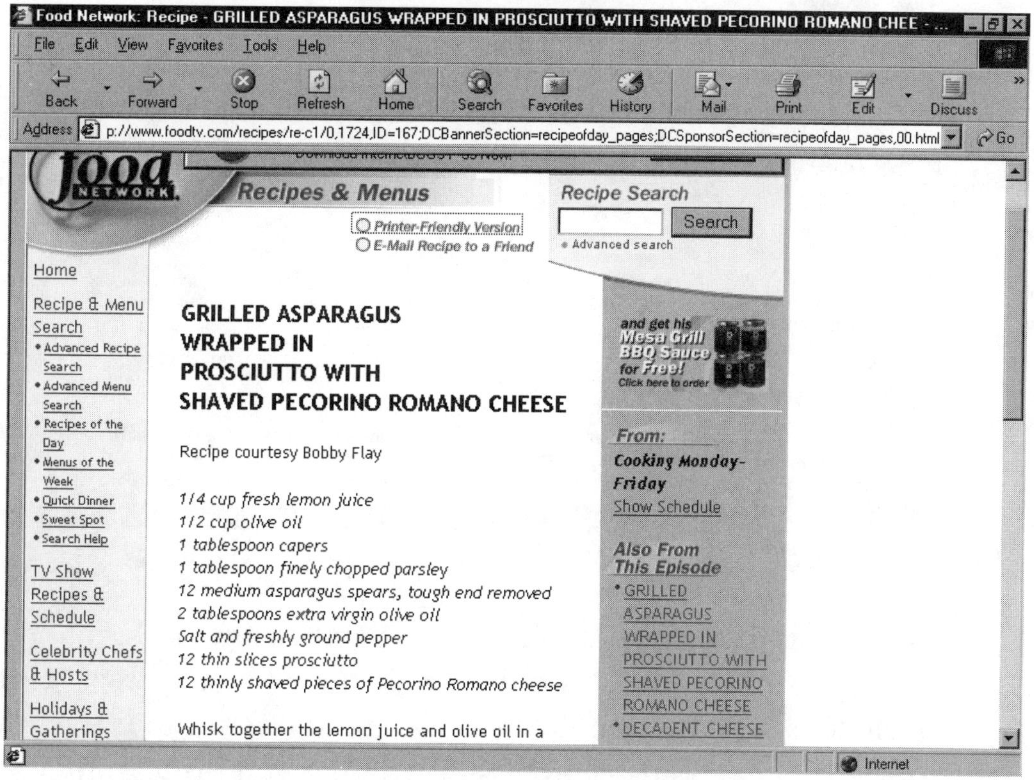

Figure 7-8 The home page at the Food Network site.

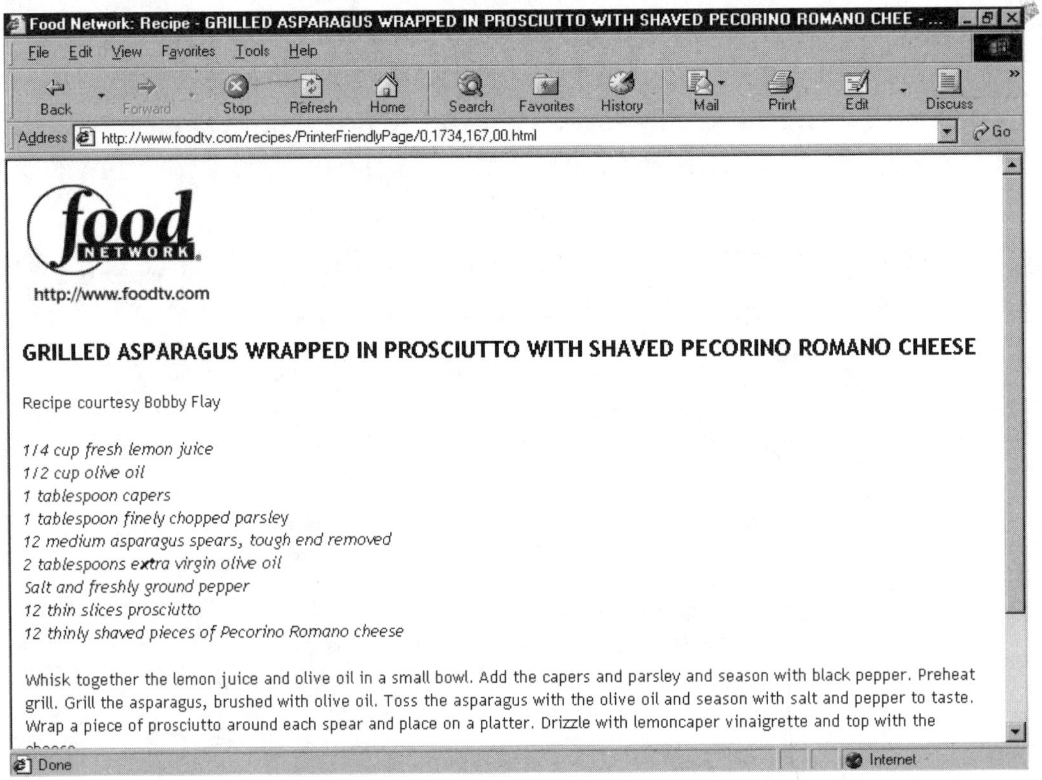

Figure 7-9 The printer-friendly version of a recipe at the Food Network site.

Most of the time you don't want to print all the background colors, images, banners, and so on that are included in a Web page. If a site includes a printer-friendly option, you can use this to extract the core of the content. But regardless of whether you print from a printer-friendly page or a normal page, you use the same procedure as you would to print from anywhere in Windows. Click the File menu, and then click Print to open the Print dialog box. If you have any questions about the options in this dialog box, check back in Chapter 5.

TIP *To see how your document will look on paper before it's printed, click the File menu and then click Print Preview.*

Finding Exactly What You Want on the Web

In mid-2000, it was estimated that there were some 2.1 billion unique, publicly available pages on the Internet, and it is estimated that within a few years this number will climb to 1 trillion. Although no one really knows for sure how many pages are on the Internet, there are lots and lots of pages. Finding any specific bit of information by browsing, clicking links, and so on is an exercise in futility. Fortunately, a much better solution is at your fingertips, and it's called a *search service.*

A search service is a site that uses devices called spiders, robots, or Web crawlers to locate and collect information about Web sites. When you use a search service, it looks in its collection of information, finds results that match what you're searching on, and delivers those results to you as a list of sites or categories.

Many search services are available on the Internet, but you can access several of them at once by searching in Internet Explorer. To see how this works, let's look on the Internet for health information that's related to seniors, a topic of interest to all of us. Follow these steps:

1. **Open the Search bar, as shown in Figure 7-10.**

   Click the Search button on the Standard toolbar. If you don't see all the categories shown in Figure 7-10, click the More link.

Figure 7-10

The Search bar in Internet Explorer.

2. Enter the search phrase.

Leave the Find A Web Page option selected. In the Find A Web Page Containing box, type *health information for seniors,* and then click the Search button. Figure 7-11 shows the results I got the day I searched on this phrase.

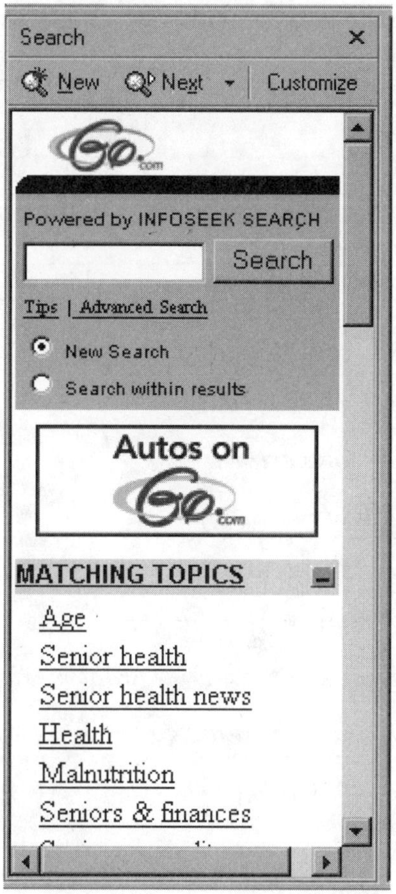

Figure 7-11

Health information resources for seniors.

3. **Explore the results.**

   You can click a category in the first part of the list to open links to sites in that category, or you can scroll down the list to see links to specific pages. Simply click a link to go to that site.

The Web is a virtual gold mine of health-related resources for seniors. You can research the safety of new medications, chat with others who have similar conditions, join online support groups, investigate alternative therapies, learn about health insurance benefits, and even consult with a physician online. Table 7-1 lists some of these valuable resources.

RESOURCE	URL
Alzheimer's Association	*http://www.alz.org*
American Cancer Society	*http://www.cancer.org*
American Diabetes Association	*http://www.diabetes.org*
American Heart Association	*http://www.americanheart.org*
American Lung Association	*http://www.lungusa.org*
Arthritis Foundation	*http://www.arthritis.org*
Centers for Disease Control	*http://www.cdc.gov*
Healthfinder	*http://www.healthfinder.gov*
Mayo Clinic	*http://www.mayohealth.org*
Medicaid	*http://www.hcfa.gov/medicaid/medicaid.htm*
Medicare	*http://www.medicare.gov*
National Institutes of Health's Age Pages	*http://www.nih.gov/nia*

Table 7-1 Health-related information for seniors.

You can customize how you search in Internet Explorer, and I'll show you how to do that shortly, but first I want to show you how to search really fast. As I was browsing some of the sites I found for health-related information for seniors, I found a comment that the Internet has numerous sites that provide information about cataracts. Since my mother has this eye condition, I thought I'd see what was available. Here's what I did: in the Address bar I typed *cataracts,* and then I pressed the Enter key. Figure 7-12 shows the results I got in a flash. Try it.

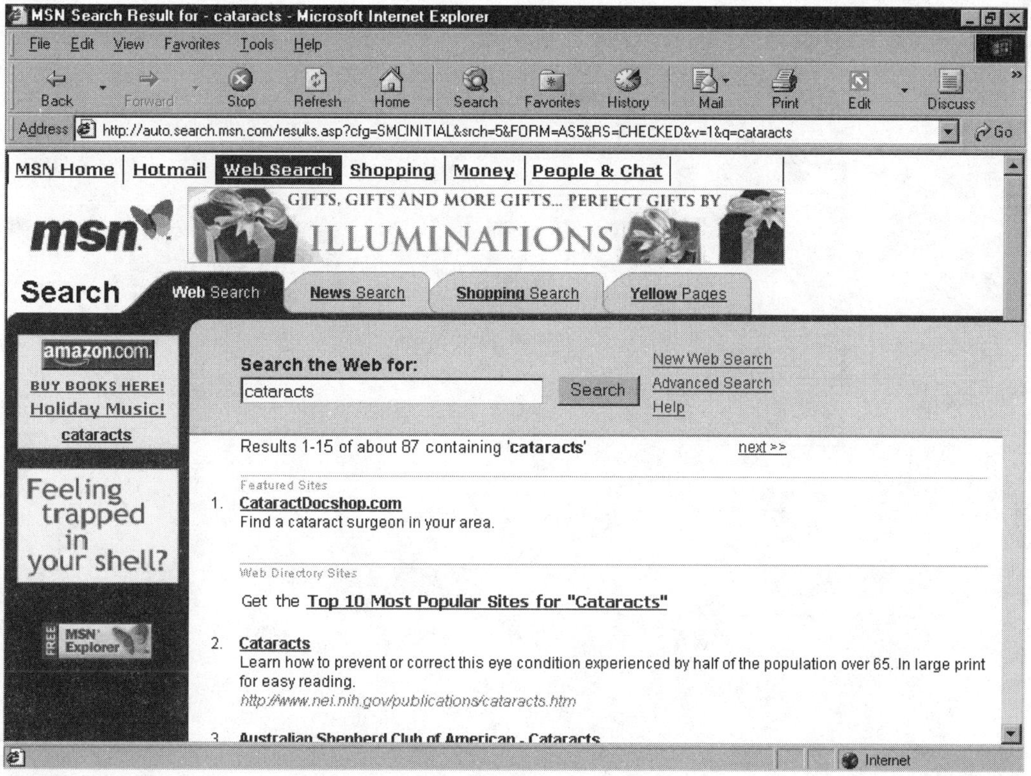

Figure 7-12 Information on the Internet about cataracts.

As you can see on the Search bar, in addition to a Web page, you can search for a person's address, a map, a picture, and so on. You can also specify which search service to use. To customize a search, open the Customize Search Settings dialog box, as shown in Figure 7-13. To do so, click the Customize button in the upper lefthand corner of the Search bar (see Figure 7-10). Click to clear or select options in this dialog box to specify your preferences.

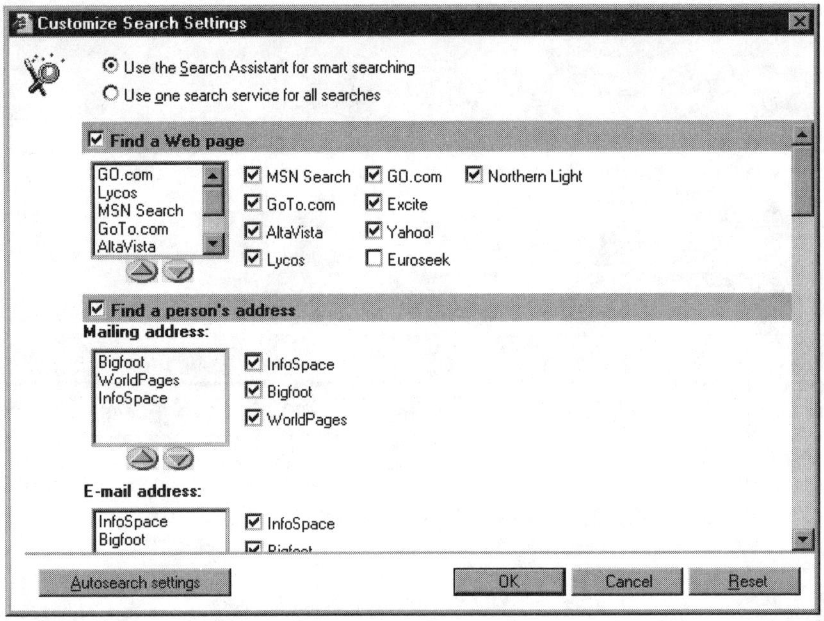

Figure 7-13 The Customize Search Settings dialog box.

Researching Your Family Tree

Genealogy has recently become a passion for seniors and other age groups. My 80-year-old cousin has been using the Internet to research our family tree for several years now, and recently my 30-something niece has joined her in this quest. Genealogy research and the Internet are a match made in heaven. Here I can only point you toward some of the hundreds and hundreds of sites that you can use to get information about your ancestors.

The place to start if you're a novice genealogist is Genealogy.com:

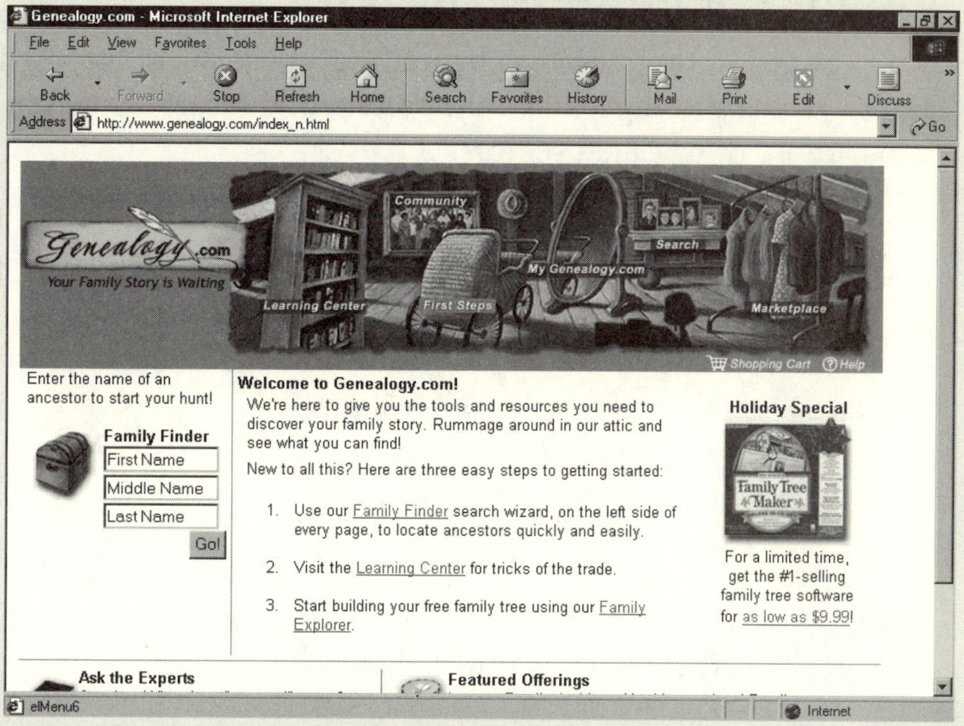

As you use the Internet to collect information about your family tree, you can enter that information and organize it using any of a number of excellent software programs. Family Tree Maker, which you can obtain from the Genealogy.com Web site, is one of the most popular. You can include comments and photographs and sort information in several formats.

The day I visited this page, the section "Ask the Experts" was explaining "removed" cousins. I found out that once-removed cousins are simply cousins that are separated by a generation. For example, my father's first cousin is my first cousin, once removed, because my father's first cousin is one generation younger than my grandparents. As the site suggests, this is easier understood when you chart the relationships, and instructions for doing this were provided.

Buying and Selling on the Web

I mentioned in the previous chapter that those of us over 50 are the fastest growing user group on the Internet. Here are some other facts about those of us called seniors:

- Today 35 million Americans are aged 65 and older, and this age group outnumbers the teenage group. By the year 2010, our number will swell to 50 million, and to 70 million by 2030.
- Those over age 65 control 70 percent of the assets in the United States, which equals about $7 trillion.
- We are avid newspaper readers, we watch a lot of television, and we are not brand loyal.
- We are shopping, investing, banking, and taking care of all sorts of financial transactions over the Internet, and we view ourselves as if we were 20 years younger than we are.

(Advertisers, pay attention!)

In this part of the chapter, I want to point you to some sites on the Internet where you can spend, save, and make some money, and I'll also talk about some precautions you should take when making Internet transactions. Sitting in the comfort of your home and letting your mouse do the walking is a great way to take care of business and pleasure.

Shopping

Before I get into the details of how and where you can shop on the Internet, I want to address a topic that's always uppermost when we deal with electronic transactions, and that is the security of your credit card. Many of us who blithely hand our credit card to the waiter at the pizza parlor become extraordinarily anxious at the thought of sending credit card information over the Internet. And, of course, using a credit card is the most efficient way to shop on the Web.

As usual, I think that when we understand how something works, we can decide much more intelligently whether we want to use it. Here is what happens when you use your credit card to buy something over the Internet:

- Once you indicate to a Web site that you want to make a purchase using your credit card, you are sent to a secure section of the site. You'll know that the area is secure when you see the *https* suffix in the Address bar rather than *http*. (The added "s" stands for "secure.") If you are not sent to a secure section of the site, just forget about making the purchase. Don't use a credit card to buy anything from a site that is not secure.
- Assuming the site is secure, you'll usually fill out a form that includes your contact information and your credit card name and number. You'll then need to click a Submit button or something similar. At that point, your credit card information moves from your computer to the site's secure server in a scrambled form so that it can't be read in transit. If a site claims that this information does not need to be scrambled, again, just forget about making a credit card purchase at this site.
- The scrambled information then goes out over the Internet to a transaction server that unscrambles it and then validates the information with your credit card company.
- If the card is validated, the transaction server informs the site, and your order is processed. You'll usually see a page that contains confirmation information.

I'm not saying that I can guarantee you 1000 percent that you should never be concerned about the security of credit card purchases over the Internet, but now that you know how the process works, you should be able to sleep a little better when you make virtual shopping trips.

Many sites mimic the shopping process in the nondigital world, using features such as shopping carts and checkout lines. One example is the BabiesRUs.com site. If you're a grandparent as I am and you have grandchildren who don't live near you, you'll probably find this site helpful.

When you find something you want to buy at this site, click the Add To Cart button, and then click the Your Shopping Cart link. You'll then see something similar to the screen in Figure 7-14. If that's all you want to buy, you can proceed to the checkout; if you still want to shop, click the Return To Shopping button.

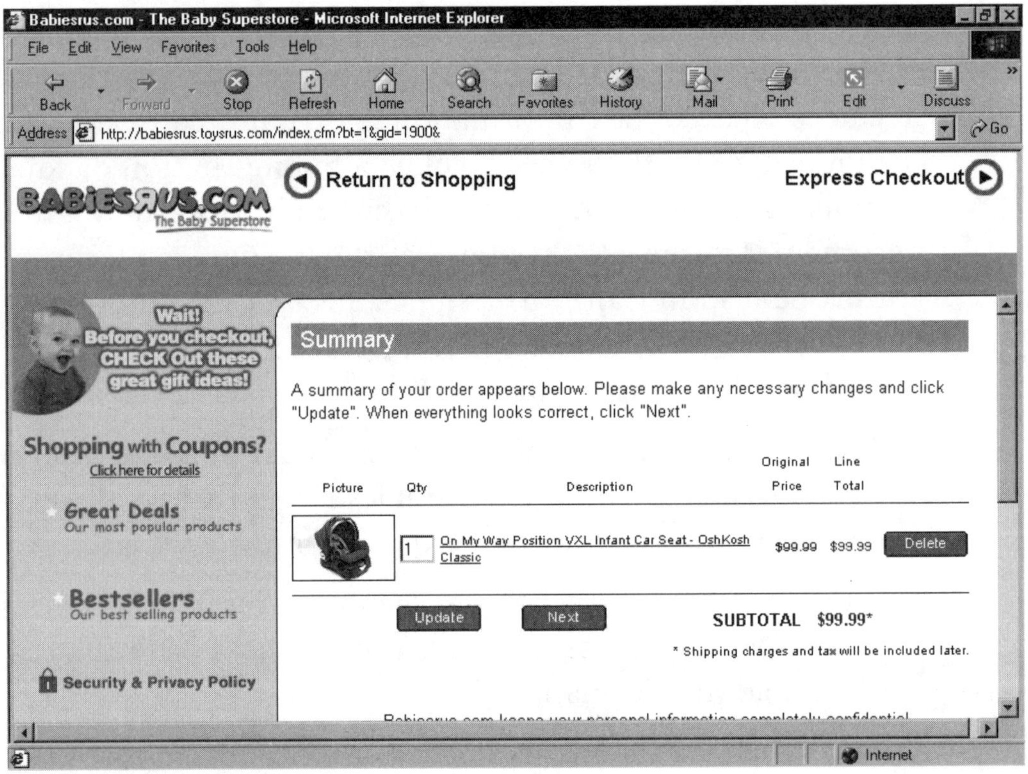

Figure 7-14 My shopping cart at BabiesRUs.com.

Click the Express Checkout button. If this is your first time to shop at BabiesRUs.com, you'll need to follow the instructions on the screen to enter your contact and credit card information and complete your purchase.

Other sites may have slightly different procedures, but most work in a similar manner. To find out if your favorite stores have sites on the Internet (and most will), use the technique I showed you earlier and type their name in the Address bar. Many retail establishments now have elaborate Web sites from which you can make purchases, send gifts, order from a bridal registry, and so on. The Internet equivalent of catalog shopping makes it even easier to do your holiday gift buying, search for hard-to-find items, have items sent to others directly from a Web site, and so on.

Investing

Investing online is not as easy as shopping online, but it has become extremely popular because online brokerage services offer low commissions to investors and easy access to investment information and resources. In this section, I'll introduce you to the process, but if you're interested in investing online, you'll want to check out a book that gets into much more detail. Try searching for such a book at any of the online bookstores, including these:

- Amazon.com is at *http://www.amazon.com*.
- Barnes & Noble is at *http://www.bn.com*.
- Borders is at *http://www.borders.com*.
- Powell's Bookstore is at *http://www.powells.com*.

When you invest online, you use your Web browser and an Internet connection to give buy or sell instructions to a broker. Before you can do so, you need an account with an online brokerage service. Many of the major business newspapers and magazines regularly review the advantages and disadvantages of working with various online brokers. In selecting an online broker, you need to first determine the range of services you need and then what you are willing to pay for those services. Compare this with the information you obtain from print sources and perhaps the advice of a financial professional before making a decision about which broker to use.

Once you've chosen an online brokerage service, you'll need to set up an account following their instructions. Typically, you'll fill out an application, and then you'll get an account name, an account number, and a password. This process usually takes several days. During this time, you'll also need to provide your initial investment of funds.

When you're ready to begin your investment activities, connect to the Internet, open Internet Explorer, and enter the URL of your brokerage in the Address bar. (Once the page is open, add it to your Favorites list.) You'll then typically need to click a Log In link that takes you to a page where you can enter your account name and password or login information. Figure 7-15 shows the login page at Fidelity.com. In this case, logging in involves entering your Social Security number and a PIN.

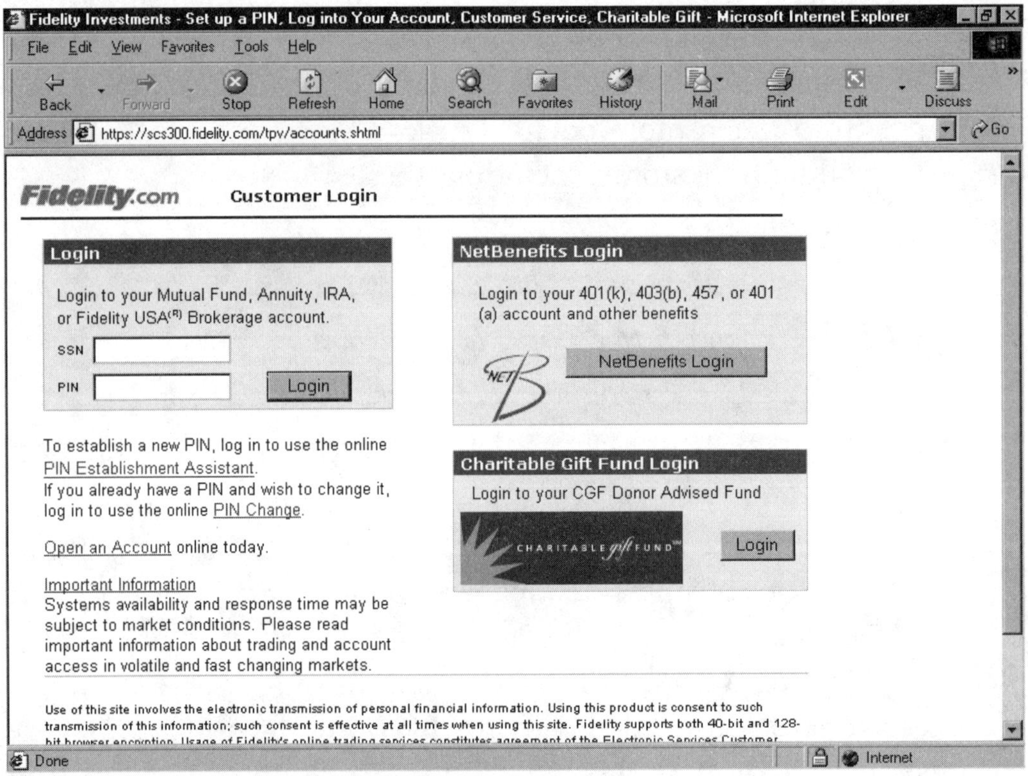

Figure 7-15 The login screen at Fidelity.com.

You'll typically find instructions for how to use the site's services online, and the most popular sites provide a rich set of tools and resources for investors, such as analysts' research and historical price and volume information about securities. All of these vary with the site, of course, and so once you are logged in for the first time, you'll do yourself a favor if you spend some time exploring the site.

At the Auction

Another extremely poplar online activity these days is buying and selling at online auctions. Figure 7-16 shows a page of antique, art, and collectible items being offered for sale at the Yahoo! auction site (*http://list.auctions.yahoo.com*). Another popular auction site is Ebay (*http://www.ebay.com*). Typically, along with the individual items, you'll see the current bid, the number of bids, and the time left to bid on the item. If you click the seller's link, you can usually find a listing of other items the seller has posted, pictures of the items, and information about them. You'll find instructions for how to bid and how to sell at each site. Sellers also get feedback ratings from their customers, and these are also posted at the site.

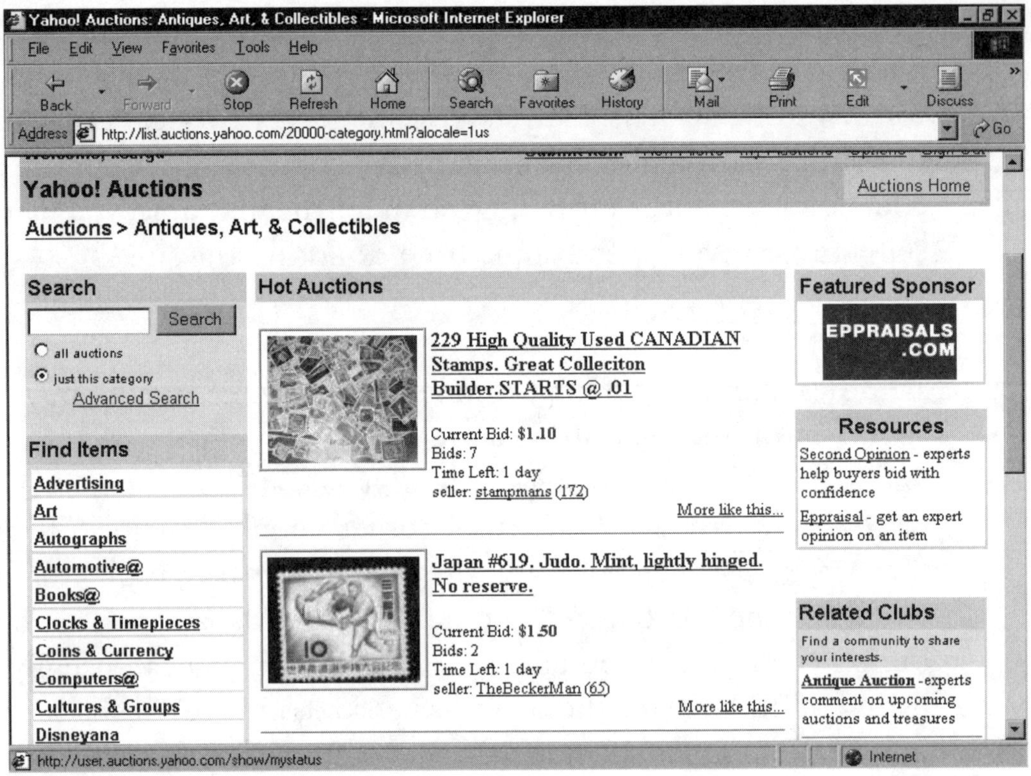

Figure 7-16 Items up for bid at the Yahoo! auction site.

I have friends and relatives who've been quite successful with their online auction transactions. They meet people with similar interests from all over the country while cultivating their hobby of collecting and trading. If you're thinking of buying at an online auction, here are some tips to consider before you buy:

- Always check a seller's feedback ratings. Customers who've had a bad experience are usually not shy about publicizing their feelings. But be aware that feedback ratings can be faked. A scam artist can stage a phony auction for the purpose of gaining positive feedback.
- Pay by credit card if you can. Credit card companies can give you a refund if you don't get what you pay for.
- Don't send a lot of money for an item, especially cash, if the seller has no feedback ratings.

- Get the seller's name and phone number, and obtain a commitment about when and how your item will be shipped.
- Stick with the sites that offer automatic insurance on fraudulent auctions. Both Ebay and Yahoo! do so.
- Become an informed purchaser, but have fun at the auction!

An Important Site for Seniors

Whether you are about to retire, already retired, plan to work forever, or are wishing you could retire, you need to know about the Social Security site at *http://www.ssa.gov*. At this site you can calculate how much you will receive in future Social Security payments, and you can even apply for them online.

To calculate your benefits, click the Benefits Planner link on the opening page, and then scroll down the next page and click Calculators. As you can see from the page in Figure 7-17, you can get a quick estimate and a more complete estimate using the calculators online. To get the most precise estimate, you'll need to download the Detailed calculator and install it on your home computer.

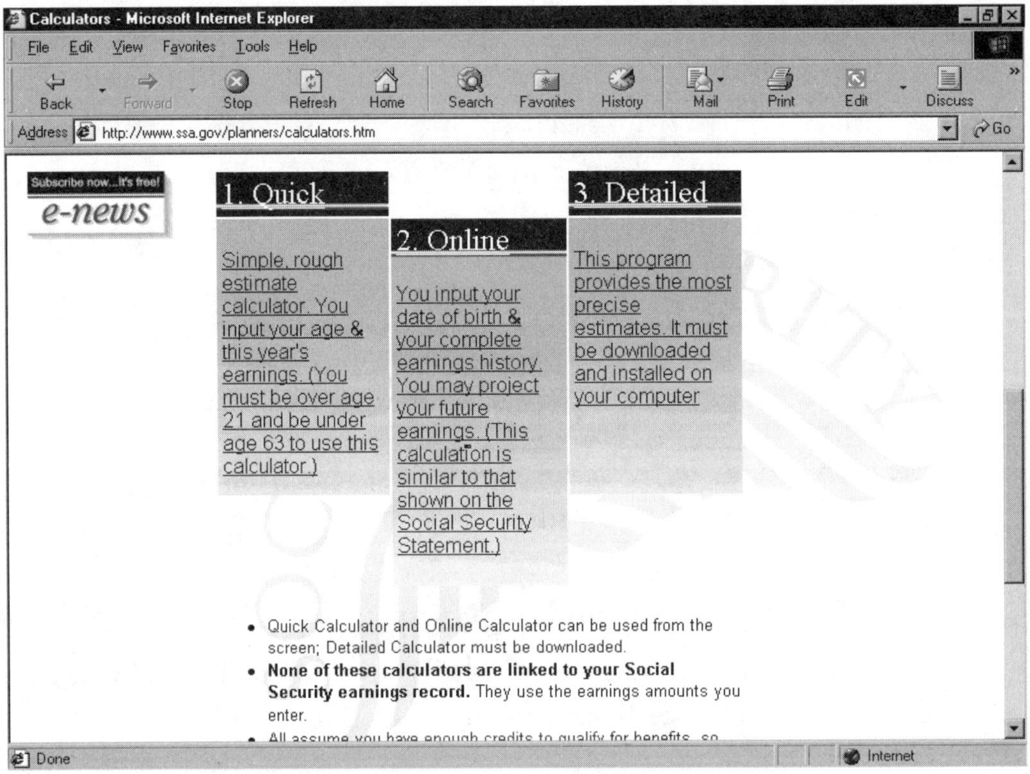

Figure 7-17 You can calculate your potential Social Security benefits payments online.

To actually apply for your Social Security retirement benefits online, you must be 61 years and 9 months or older and plan to start getting your benefits within four months. At the home page of the Social Security site, click the Apply To Retire Here link, and then on the next page click the Apply For Retirement Benefits link to open the page shown in Figure 7-18. Follow the onscreen instructions to complete the application.

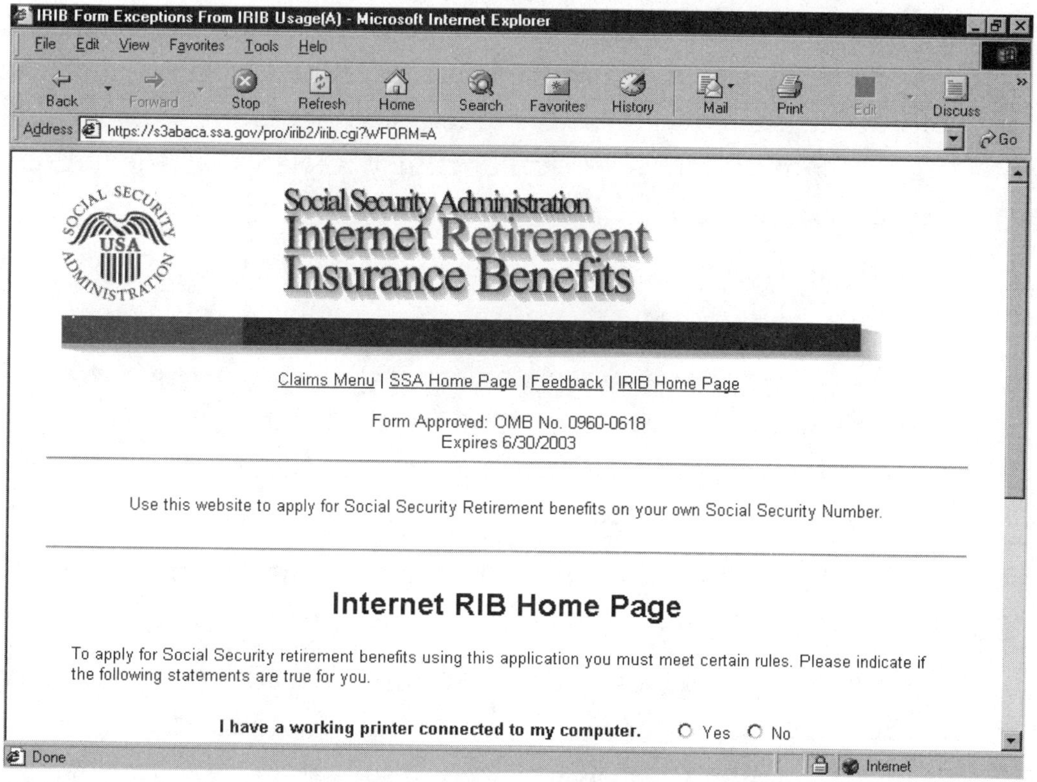

Figure 7-18 Applying for Social Security benefits online.

Important Sites for Citizens

In the United States, the election of 2000 was referred to as a "mess" by many political observers and media commentators. It nevertheless piqued our curiosity about the electoral process and caused many of us to ask and answer questions we hadn't thought about since our high-school civics classes. I recently attended a party at which a discussion of the events surrounding this election led to a search of the U.S. Constitution for the number of senate votes needed to approve a Cabinet appointment.

Much of this information is, of course, available on the Internet. Here are some sites to check out:

- To read the U.S. Constitution, go to *http://www.usconstitution.net*. At this site, you'll also find a copy of the Declaration of Independence, the Articles of Confederation, the Gettysburg Address, and other important historical documents relating to the United States government.
- To download a form that lets you register to vote from anywhere in the United States, go to *http://www.fec.gov/votregis/vr.htm*.
- The League of Women Voters is a nonpartisan organization whose mission is to encourage the informed and active participation of citizens in government. At their site (*http://www.lwv.org*), you'll find voter information as well as information about election reform.
- For a list of sites that provide polling locations in various cities and states throughout the United States, search on "voting locations."
- Go to the Federal Election Commission site at *http://www.fec.gov* to access campaign finance reports, party fund-raising data, information about political action committees, and all sorts of other information about federal elections past and present.
- Project Vote Smart at *http://www.vote-smart.org* is a comprehensive source for information on candidates and the issues.

Safe Surfing

You probably already know that you can find anything about anything on the Internet, and that some of it is stuff that you'd just as soon not see and not know about. You can, for example, inadvertently type the wrong suffix for a URL and end up staring at a page that is personally offensive and has nothing to do with the page you thought you were accessing. In such a case, click the Back button, or close Internet Explorer.

Most of the time, there isn't a lot you can do about this sort of thing. You can, however, use the Content Advisor in Internet Explorer to eliminate some of it. The Content Advisor uses a rating system established by the Recreational Software Advisory Council, which goes by the abbreviation RSACi. RSACi is an organization whose goal is to protect children from potentially harmful material on the Internet. When the Content Advisor finds a page rated at a level that exceeds the limit you've established, Internet Explorer does not open the page. The problem is that not all pages are rated. If a site wants to get a rating, it gets in touch with RSACi. Consequently, even if you have established the most conservative rating, you can still find yourself staring at offensive material because it isn't rated.

In my opinion, I would only enable Content Advisor if you have children using your computer and are concerned about their seeing age-inappropriate material. Even then, other software applications are available that do a better job than Content Advisor. You can find a list of some of these at the Family Resources PsychPage (*http://www.psychpage.com/family/soft.html*).

All that said, if you want to use Content Advisor, follow these steps:

1. **Open the Internet Options dialog box at the Content tab, as shown in Figure 7-19.**

   In Internet Explorer, click the Tools menu, click Internet Options to open the Internet Options dialog box, and then click the Content tab.

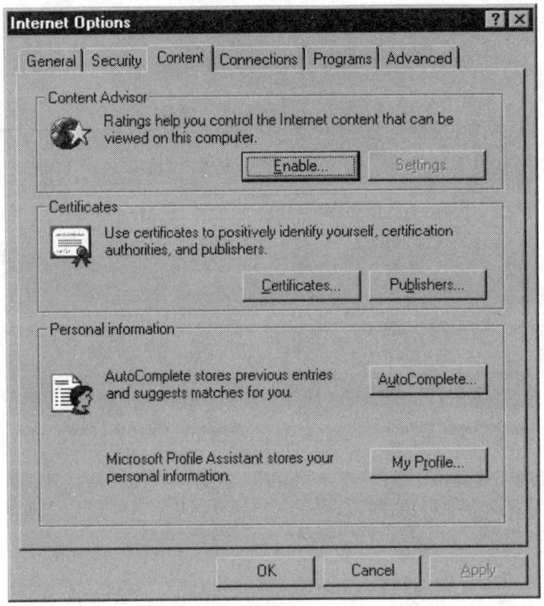

Figure 7-19 The Internet Options dialog box open at the Content tab.

2. **Open the Content Advisor dialog box, as shown in Figure 7-20.**

   Click the Enable button.

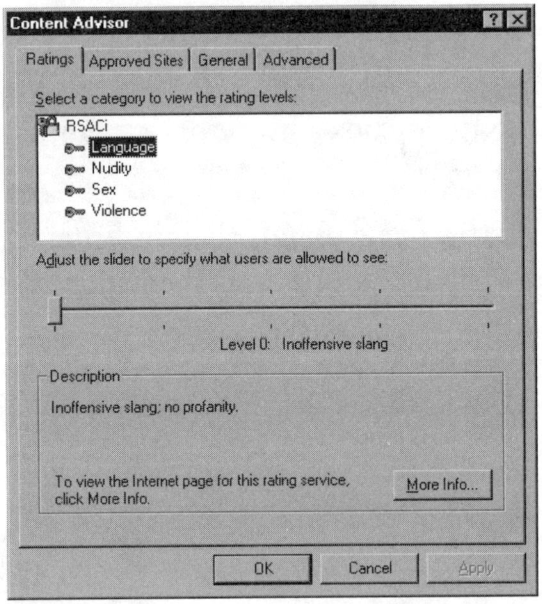

Figure 7-20 The Content Advisor dialog box.

3. **Establish the rating levels you want.**

   On the Rating tab, select a category and then move the slider to establish the level you want for that category. When you're finished, click Apply. Click the Approved Sites tab to create a list of Web sites that can always or never be viewed regardless of the rating level you set. Use the options on the General and Advanced tabs to further clarify what can be viewed on your computer. When you're finished, click OK. You'll see the Create Supervisor Password dialog box, as shown in Figure 7-21.

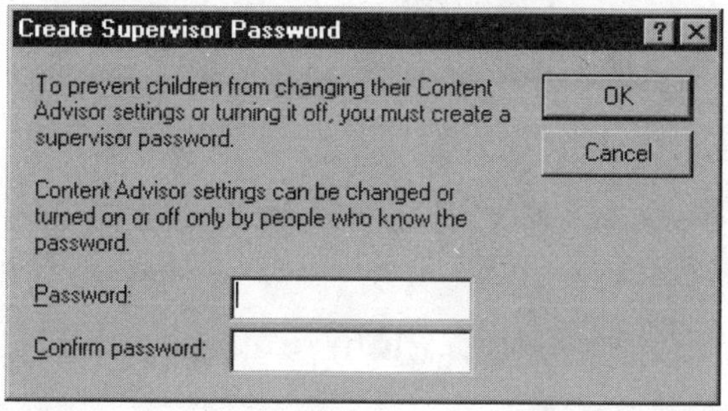

Figure 7-21 The Create Supervisor Password dialog box.

4. **Enter a supervisor password.**

   In the Password dialog box, enter a password, and then confirm it by entering it again in the Confirm Password dialog box. When you now click OK, the rating levels you've established can be changed only by someone who knows this password. Back in the Content tab on the Internet Options dialog box, the Enable button changed to the Disable button. To change the password or disable Content Advisor, you'll need to click the Disable button, supply the password you established, and then change the ratings or disable Content Advisor.

Seven Important Things to Remember About Using the World Wide Web

1. If you know the name of a business or a corporation but don't know the URL, enter the name in the Address bar and press the Enter key. Internet Explorer will find the URL and open the site.
2. To search quickly for a phrase or a term, enter it in the Address bar and press the Enter key.
3. When you've followed lots of links and feel that you're lost in cyberspace, click the Home button on the Standard toolbar to go to your start page.
4. When you find a page you know you'll want to revisit, add it to your Favorites list.
5. To search for other sites that have important information for seniors, search on "seniors."
6. Never use your credit card to make a purchase at an Internet site if the site doesn't have a secure section and scramble this information when it's transmitted over the Internet.
7. You can find anything about anything on the Internet, and some of it is highly offensive to a lot of people. When you land in the midst of such a site, simply click the Back button or close Internet Explorer.

Summary

In this chapter, we've looked at how to connect to the Internet and use Internet Explorer to browse the World Wide Web. I've discussed how to go to specific sites and how to search the Internet, and along the way I've pointed out some great sites for seniors. You'll find a lot more as you continue exploring the vast resources of the Internet.

Chapter 8

SENDING AND RECEIVING E-MAIL

Featuring:

- What Is Outlook Express?
- Retrieving Your Mail
- Handling Messages
- Creating and Sending Mail
- Creating Mail with HTML
- Sending a File with Your Message
- Filtering Out Unwanted Mail
- Setting Up Mail for Multiple Users
- About Newsgroups
- Personalizing Outlook Express

Among my family and friends, e-mail is indispensable. Some live close by, but most are spread all over the United States, and some live overseas. These days it's become fashionable to lament the lost art of writing letters by hand. I see nothing lamentable about how convenient it now is to stay in touch so easily and so much more often. Recently, I even had e-mail from a childhood boyfriend. He found me at an Internet site that provides directories of high-school classmates (*http://www.classmates.com*) and sent me a note. I hadn't seen or heard from him or about him in more than 45 years! We've been sharing life experience stories about our children and grandchildren and catching up by exchanging photos. It's been delightful, and it would never have happened but for e-mail.

And, if it weren't for e-mail, I wouldn't be sitting here in the comfort and quiet of my home office, making a living by writing. I stay in constant touch with publishers, co-authors, editors, and technical consultants and transfer all my work back and forth over the Internet via e-mail. I doubt that anything has changed the way we live and work as much as e-mail.

What Is Outlook Express?

Microsoft Outlook Express is the e-mail application that's included with Microsoft Windows. You can use it to send and receive e-mail if you have an e-mail account with an Internet service provider (ISP). Other e-mail applications are available, such as Qualcomm Eudora and Netscape Messenger, and if you have an account with an online information service such as America Online (AOL), you can also send and receive e-mail using their program.

NOTE *You can also use Outlook Express to read newsgroups, which I'll explain briefly toward the end of this chapter.*

In this chapter, I'll deal with Outlook Express, which you can open in the following ways:

- Click the Launch Outlook Express button on the Quick Launch toolbar (the fastest and easiest way).
- Click the Start button, click Programs, and then click Outlook Express.

- In Internet Explorer, click the Mail button on the Standard toolbar, and then click Read Mail or Read News.

Figure 8-1 shows the main Outlook Express screen.

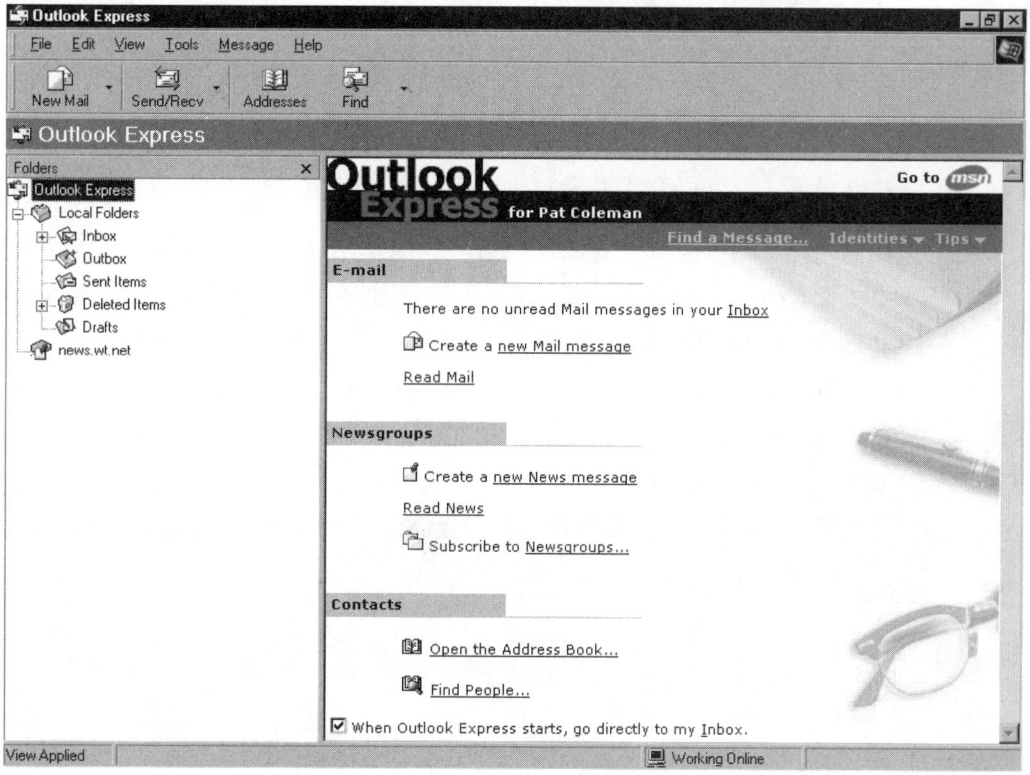

Figure 8-1 The main screen in Outlook Express.

At the top of this window is the menu bar, and below that is the toolbar. The Folders list, which is on the left side of the window, is a tool for organizing messages. You can add your own folders to this list (I'll show you how later in this chapter), but by default the Folders list contains the following folders:

- The **Inbox folder** stores newly received messages and messages that you haven't disposed of in some way.
- The **Outbox folder** contains messages that are ready to be sent.
- The **Sent Items** folder contains copies of messages that you have sent.

- The **Deleted Items folder** contains copies of messages that you have deleted. In other words, it is similar to the Recycle Bin folder. When you delete a message, it isn't deleted immediately but goes to the Deleted Items folder.
- The **Drafts folder** contains messages that you are working on but that aren't yet ready to send.

Retrieving Your Mail

If you are connected to the Internet and you have Outlook Express open (whether maximized or minimized), you'll hear a sound when you have new messages. By default, Outlook Express opens at your Inbox folder. Figure 8-2 shows my Inbox folder in Preview Pane view. Message headers appear in the upper pane, and you select a message to open it in the lower pane.

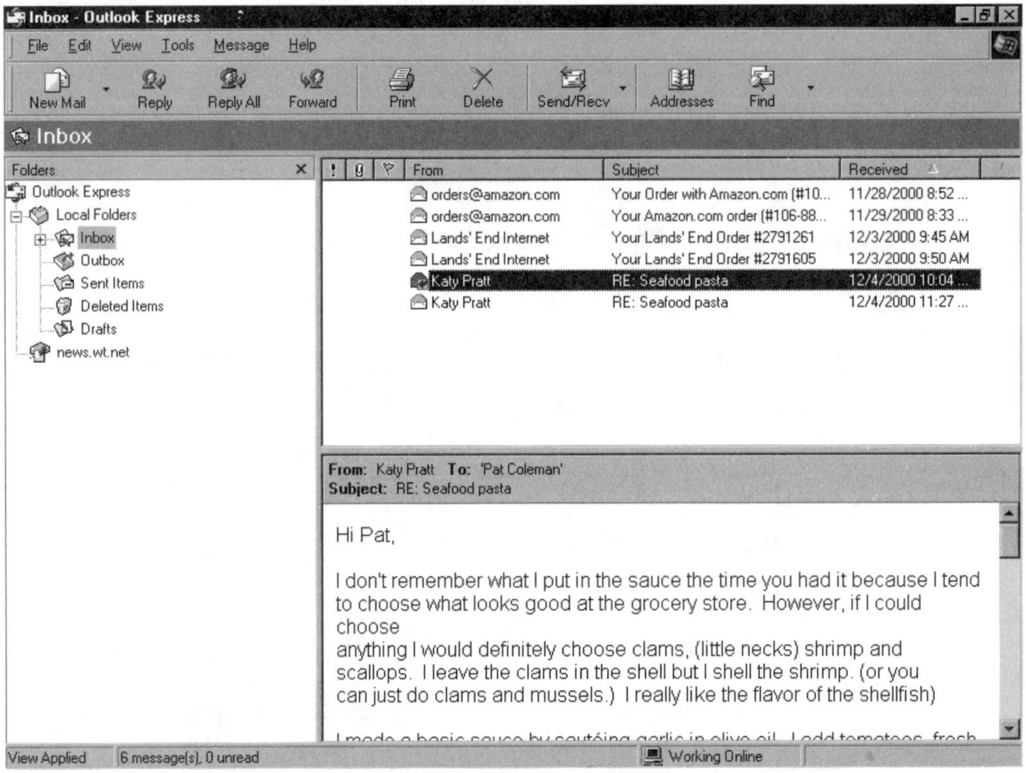

Figure 8-2 Reading a message in Preview Pane view.

I prefer not to use the Preview pane and view messages in a separate window. To change the layout, follow these steps:

1. **Open the Window Layout Properties dialog box, as shown in Figure 8-3.**

   Click the View menu, and then click Layout.

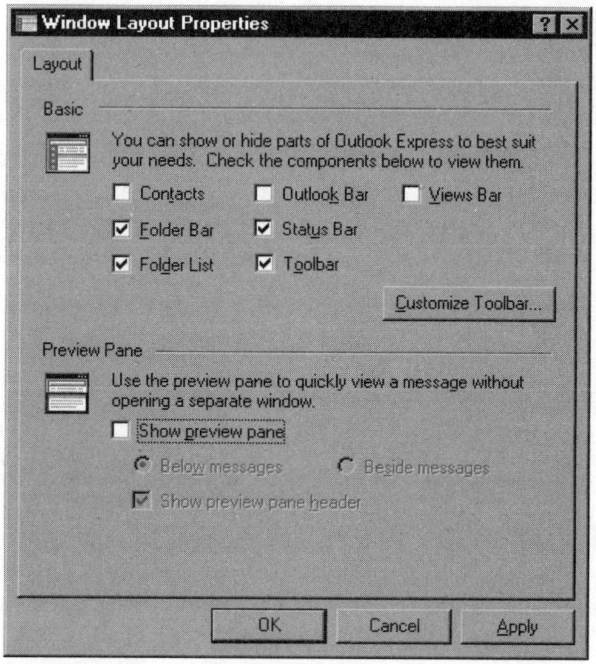

Figure 8-3 The Window Layout Properties dialog box.

2. **Tell Windows not to use the Preview pane.**

   Click the Show Preview Pane check box to clear it, and then click OK.

Now when you click a message header, the message will open in its own window, as shown in Figure 8-4. (My daughter-in-law and I are planning the menu for a holiday dinner.)

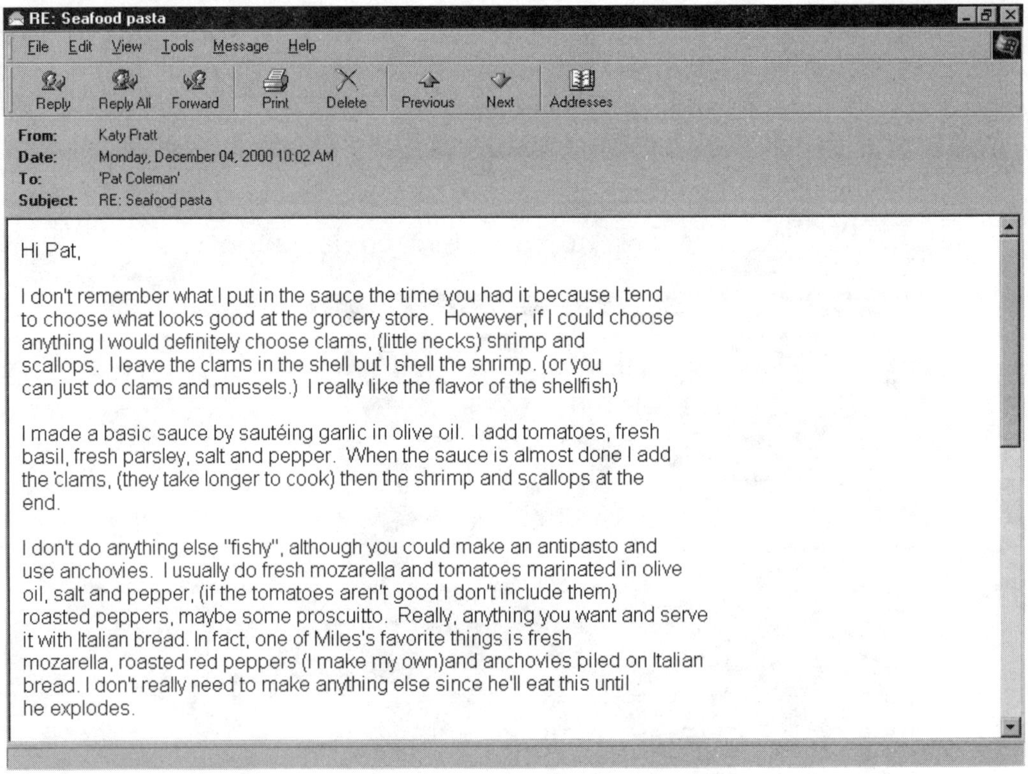

Figure 8-4 Opening a message in its own window.

Handling Messages

After you read a message, you can click its Close button to close it, and you can handle it in a number of other ways. You can save it, delete it, print it, move it to a folder, mark it in some way, and so on.

Saving

You can save a message as a file if you want to, or you can save it to a folder in your Folders list. To save it as a file, select the message header or open the message, click the File menu, and then click Save As to open the Save Message As dialog box. This dialog box works just the same as any Save As dialog box in Windows.

To save the message to a folder, follow these steps:

1. **Open the Move dialog box, as shown in Figure 8-5.**

   Select the message header or open the message, click the Edit menu, and then click Move To Folder.

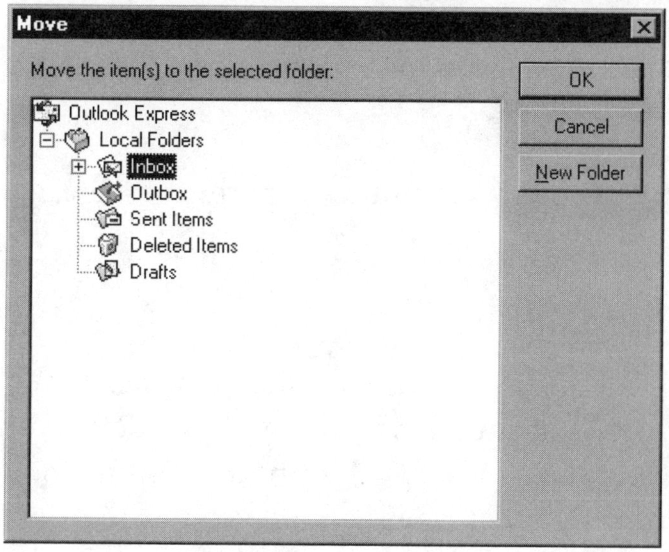

Figure 8-5 The Move dialog box.

2. **Create a new folder for your message.**

   You can move a message to any of the default folders, but that doesn't make a lot of sense. What you probably want to do is create some folders for people with whom you regularly correspond, projects you're working on, and the like. To create a new folder, click the default folder inside which you want to create a new folder. (I create folders in the Inbox folder, but you can use any default folder.) Now, click the New Folder button in the Move dialog box to open the New Folder dialog box, as shown in Figure 8-6. In the Folder Name box, type a name for the folder, and then click OK. You'll now see your newly created folder in the list.

Figure 8-6 The New Folder dialog box.

3. **Move the message to the folder.**

   Select the folder in which you want to store the message, and click OK.

Printing

Printing in Outlook Express works just like printing in any other Windows application. To print quickly and with the default settings, open the message, and then click the Print button on the toolbar. To specify your own settings (such as how many copies to print), click the File menu and then click Print to open the Print dialog box. You already know how to use this dialog box. If you have any questions, check back in Chapter 5.

Marking

If you want to keep your messages in your Inbox until you decide what to do with them, you can mark them in a couple of ways. When you haven't read a message, the message header is displayed in boldface. After you read the message, the header is in normal type. I indicate to myself that I haven't yet disposed of this message and that I need to reply to it or take some other action by marking it as unread. To mark a message as unread, select it, click the Edit menu, and then click Mark As Unread.

You can also flag a message, that is, literally place a little red flag to the left of the message header. To flag a message, select it, click the Message menu, and then click Flag Message.

Replying

To reply to a message, open it, and then click the Reply button in the message window. You can either include the message in the reply or not. If you want to include the message in all replies, click the Tools menu, and then click Options to open the Options dialog box, as shown in Figure 8-7. Click the Send tab, verify that the Include Message In Reply check box is checked (click it if it is not selected), and click OK.

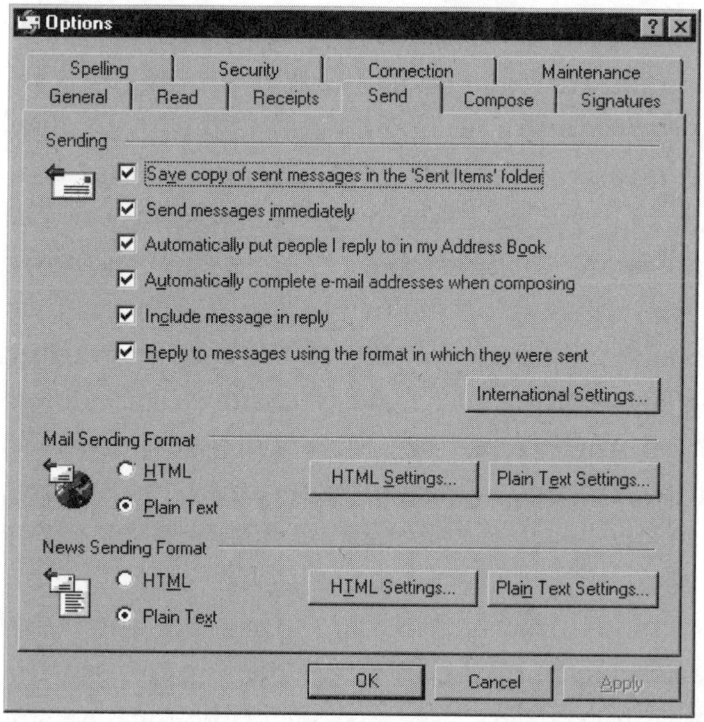

Figure 8-7 The Options dialog box open at the Send tab.

Now, when you reply to a message, the original message appears in the message window. If you don't want to include the message in the reply, click the Edit menu, click Select All, and then press the Delete key. You'll notice that the reply window includes the original sender's name in the From field and that the Subject line is filled in.

It's customary not to include the original message in a reply unless it's necessary for the sense of the correspondence. I'm showing you how, though, because there is no way to selectively include the reply. The reason that including the reply is not customary is that it wastes transmission time; that is, the message becomes overly long and takes longer to send and to receive. But don't hesitate to include the original message if you have any doubt that the original sender will be confused about your reply.

Forwarding

Forwarding an e-mail message is really easy: simply open the message, click the Forward button to open the message in a new window, fill in the e-mail address of the person to whom you want to forward the message, and click the Send button. You'll want to exercise some discretion when forwarding messages. First, be sure that forwarding the message will not infringe on the original sender. Second, and this is one of my big personal pet peeves, don't just keep forwarding messages that have been forwarded to you without at least deleting the header information in the messages. I receive jokes, urban legends, and the like that have been forwarded to tons of people many, many times. Getting to the heart of the matter usually takes a long time, and when I get there, it's often something I've seen before or something I don't care about anyway. Most annoying! For the most part, I can identify the sender from the message header and see that it's a message that's been forwarded. So, I just select the message and press the Delete key.

WARNING *You can easily pick up computer viruses from e-mail messages, especially those that have been forwarded through a lot of people. A good rule of thumb is not to open an e-mail message if you don't know the source. A computer virus is a program that you can unwittingly open on your system and that can render your system useless. You've probably read and heard about such viruses that attach themselves to business computer systems and do a great deal of damage. Though you may not have millions of dollars of proprietary data on your computer system, you still want to protect it. Be cautious, then, about opening an e-mail message that has been forwarded any number of times, and especially be wary of such e-mail if a file is attached. We'll look at attached files in a later section in this chapter.*

Deleting

You can delete e-mail messages in a couple of ways:

- Select the message header, and press the Delete key.
- Open the message, and press the Delete key.

As I mentioned earlier in this chapter, when you delete a message, it goes to the Deleted Items folder, and it stays there until you manually delete it. To do so, select the Deleted Items folder, click the Edit menu, click Empty 'Deleted Items' Folder, and click Yes when you're asked if you want to delete these items.

You can, however, specify that you want to delete the items in the Deleted Items folder whenever you close Outlook Express. To do so, follow these steps:

1. **Open the Options dialog box.**

   Click the Tools menu, and then click Options.

2. **Tell Outlook Express to delete the items when you close Outlook Express.**

   Click the Maintenance tab, as shown in Figure 8-8, and then click the Empty Messages From The 'Deleted Items' Folder On Exit check box. Click OK.

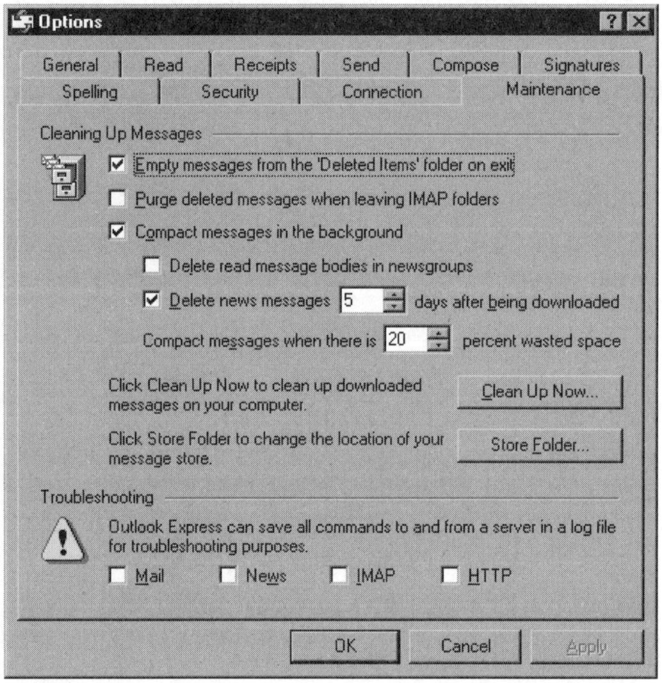

Figure 8-8 The Options dialog box open at the Maintenance tab.

Creating and Sending Mail

In Outlook Express, you can send e-mail messages in two formats: plain text and HTML. Not all e-mail programs can deal with HTML messages, including AOL and the free version of Eudora. Before you send a message in HTML, which is essentially a Web page, send the person a plain text message and ask if he or she can read HTML messages.

To compose and send a message in plain text, follow these steps:

1. **Open the New Message window, as shown in Figure 8-9.**

   Click the New Mail button on the toolbar.

Figure 8-9 The New Message window.

2. **Verify that you are working in plain text.**

   Click the Format menu, and be sure that the Plain Text item has a black button to its left.

3. **Address and compose your message.**

   In the To line, enter an e-mail address, or click the icon to open your Address Book and select an address. (In Chapter 13, I'll explain how to set up and use your Address Book.) Follow the same procedure to copy someone on the message using the Cc line. To send a blind carbon copy of the message, click the Cc icon to open the Select Recipients dialog box. You can then type a name, click the Bcc button, and click OK, or you can select the name from your Address Book if you have one set up. In the Subject line, enter a subject for your message, and then click in the message body and type your message.

TIP *You don't have to enter anything in the Subject line, but it's a courtesy to your recipient. He or she can then see the subject in the message header.*

4. **Send the message.**

   Click the Send button.

By default, messages are sent immediately if you are connected to the Internet. If you want to wait and send a message later, click the File menu, and click Send Later. Doing so places your message in the Outbox folder, and it is sent when you click the Send/Recv button.

Creating Mail with HTML

To compose a message in HTML format, open the New Message window, click the Format menu, and then click Rich Text (HTML). As you can see in Figure 8-10, the New Message window contains a Formatting toolbar that includes many of the tools you use in your word processor.

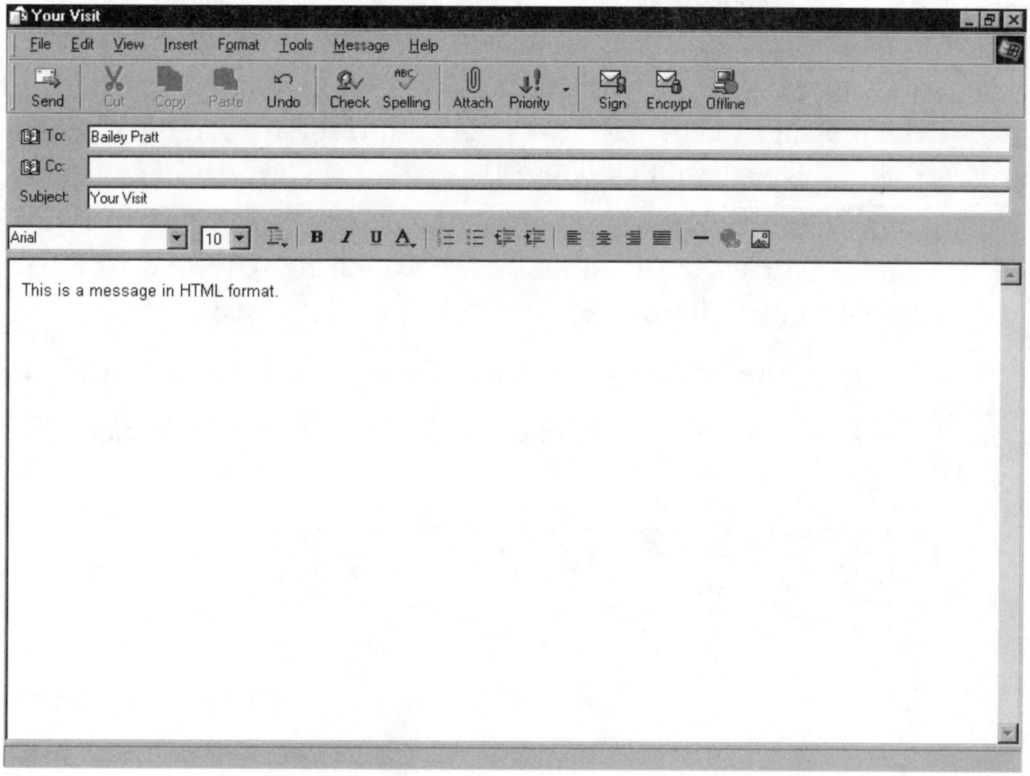

Figure 8-10 Creating a message in HTML.

When you create a message in HTML, you can add the following to your message:

- A bulleted list (like this one).
- Effects such as boldface, italics, underline, and font color.
- A numbered list.
- Paragraphs that are flush left, flush right, or centered.
- A horizontal line.
- A picture.

Sending a File with Your Message

When you receive a message that has a little paper-clip icon next to the message header, a file is attached to the message. When you open the message, you'll see the filename of the attachment in the Attach line. If the file is in a format that your computer can read, simply double-click the filename of the attachment to open it. To save an attachment that you receive, follow these steps:

1. **Open the Save Attachments dialog box, as shown in Figure 8-11.**

   Open the message, click the File menu, and then click Save Attachments.

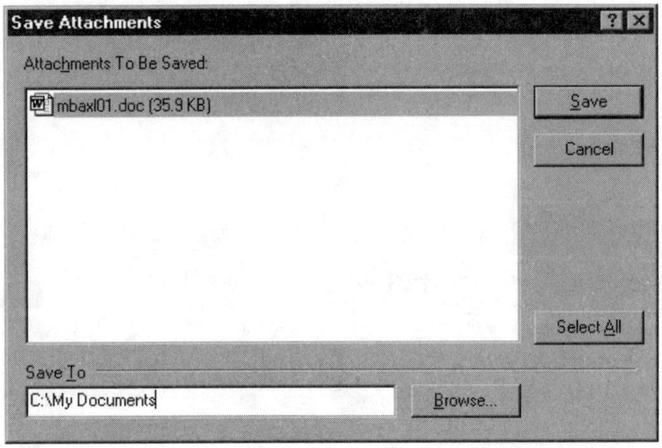

Figure 8-11 The Save Attachments dialog box.

2. **Save the file.**

   In the Save To box, enter or browse to the folder in which you want to save the file, and then click Save.

You can attach any file that you have stored on your computer to an e-mail message. Remember, though, that some people won't be able to open some attachments. For example, if you attach a picture file to a message, a recipient who has an AOL account won't be able to open those pictures. Also, you need to be considerate of your recipient's Internet connection when sending big files. Those who have a slow connection, that is, those who connect with an analog modem rather than a cable modem or DSL, may have to wait a long time for such files to download (as in 15 to 20 minutes or more). You can compress big files (make them smaller) to make upload and download time faster, which I'll show you how to do later in this section.

To attach a file to a message you are composing, follow these steps:

1. **Open the Insert Attachment dialog box, as shown in Figure 8-12.**

   In the New Message window, click the Insert menu, and then click File Attachment.

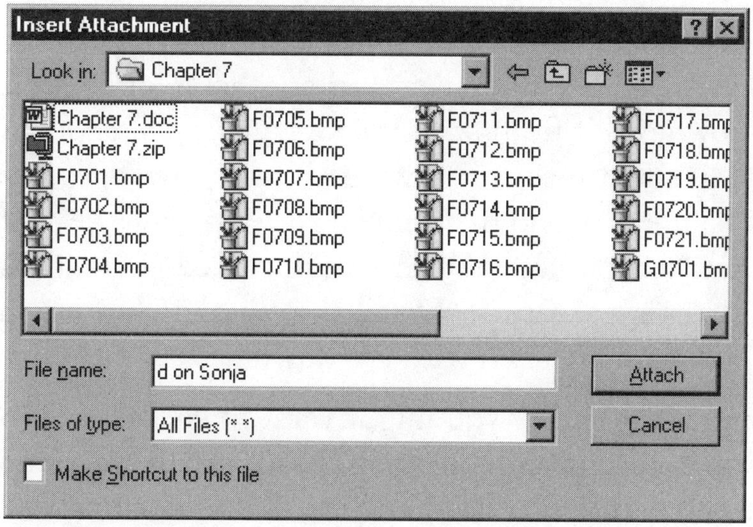

Figure 8-12 The Insert Attachment dialog box.

2. **Attach the file.**

   Enter the filename in the File Name box, or browse to find the file, and then click the Attach button.

Back in the New Message window, you'll see the filename in the Attach line.

TIP *When you want to send photos as attachments to your e-mail, you simply follow these same two steps. If you have a digital camera, you load the pictures of, say, your grandchildren, onto your computer, and then you send them as files, just as you would send any file. You can also send scanned photos if you have a scanner. Once the photo is scanned, it is stored as a file on your computer. To send it along with an e-mail message, just insert it as an attachment.*

Digital images, including photographs, are usually rather large files. As I mentioned, you can compress a big file to make it smaller so that it uploads and downloads faster. One application that you can use to do this is called WinZip. It's a popular program that a lot of people use, and you can download it from *http://www.winzip.com*. Follow the instructions at this site. Once you download the program, you can "zip up" large files before you send them, and your recipient, if he or she also has WinZip, can "unzip" them. When a file is "zipped," it transfers much faster than in its original format. Detailed, easy-to-follow instructions for using WinZip are included with the download.

Another compression utility you might want to check out is StuffIt, especially if you exchange large files with Mac users. If you send them a file compressed with WinZip, they'll be able to uncompress it and read it, but if they send you a file compressed with StuffIt, you won't be able to uncompress it and read it unless you also have StuffIt on your computer. To download StuffIt, go to
http://www.aladdinsys.com/stuffitwin/index.html.

Filtering Out Unwanted Mail

If you start getting messages from a person, a business, an organization, or any other source and you don't want to get these messages, you have a couple of alternatives. Often when you get e-mail from a business or an organization, it will include a line that says something to the effect "if you don't want to receive future mailings, go to *http://www.xxx.xxx* and let us know." But, of course, not all senders are this professional.

You can choose to block mail from certain senders and send it straight to the Deleted Items folder. To do so, follow these steps:

1. **Open the Message Rules dialog box at the Blocked Senders tab, as shown in Figure 8-13.**

   In the main Outlook Express window, click the Tools menu, click Message Rules, and then click Blocked Senders List.

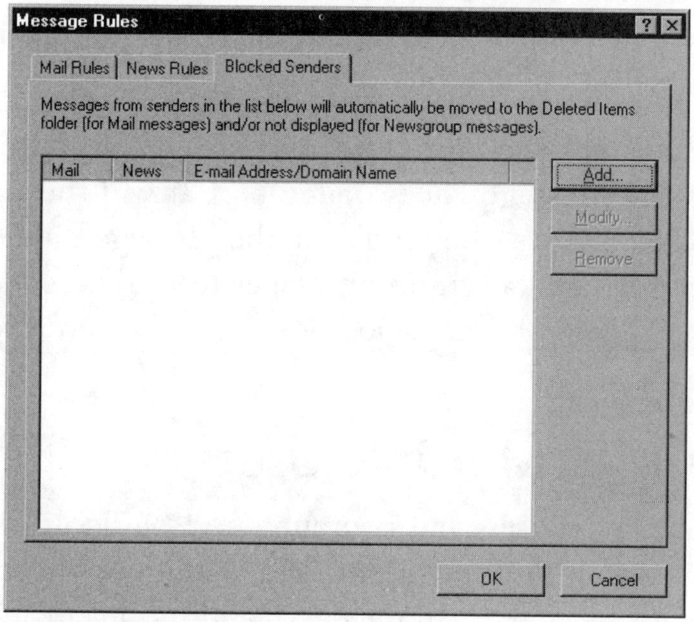

Figure 8-13 Blocking messages.

2. **Open the Add Sender dialog box, as shown in Figure 8-14.**

   Click the Add button.

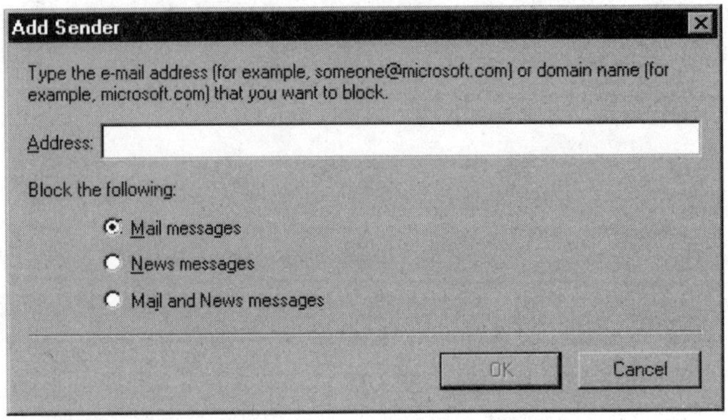

Figure 8-14 The Add Sender dialog box.

3. **Tell Outlook Express the e-mail address you want to block.**

   In the Address box, enter the e-mail address of the sender you want to block, and then select whether you want to block mail messages, news messages, or both. Click OK, and then click OK again back in the Message Rules dialog box.

You can also select a message from the sender that you want to block before you open the Message Rules dialog box. It will then appear on the list of blocked senders when you open the Message Rules dialog box. Simply click OK, and all future messages from this sender will go straight to the Deleted Items dialog box when they download to your computer.

Setting Up Mail for Multiple Users

If more than one person uses your computer and Outlook Express, you may want to set up multiple identities. When you do so, each person sees only his or her e-mail messages and has his or her own Address Book. Even though you can assign passwords to identities, it is still possible for another identity to see your files; so you may want to keep that in mind.

When Windows is installed on your computer, one identity is established—the Main Identity. To set up other identities, follow these steps:

1. **Open the Manage Identities dialog box and the New Identity dialog box.**

   In the main Outlook Express window, click the File menu, click Identities, and then click Add New Identity. The Add New Identity dialog box opens on top of the Manage Identities dialog box, as shown in Figure 8-15.

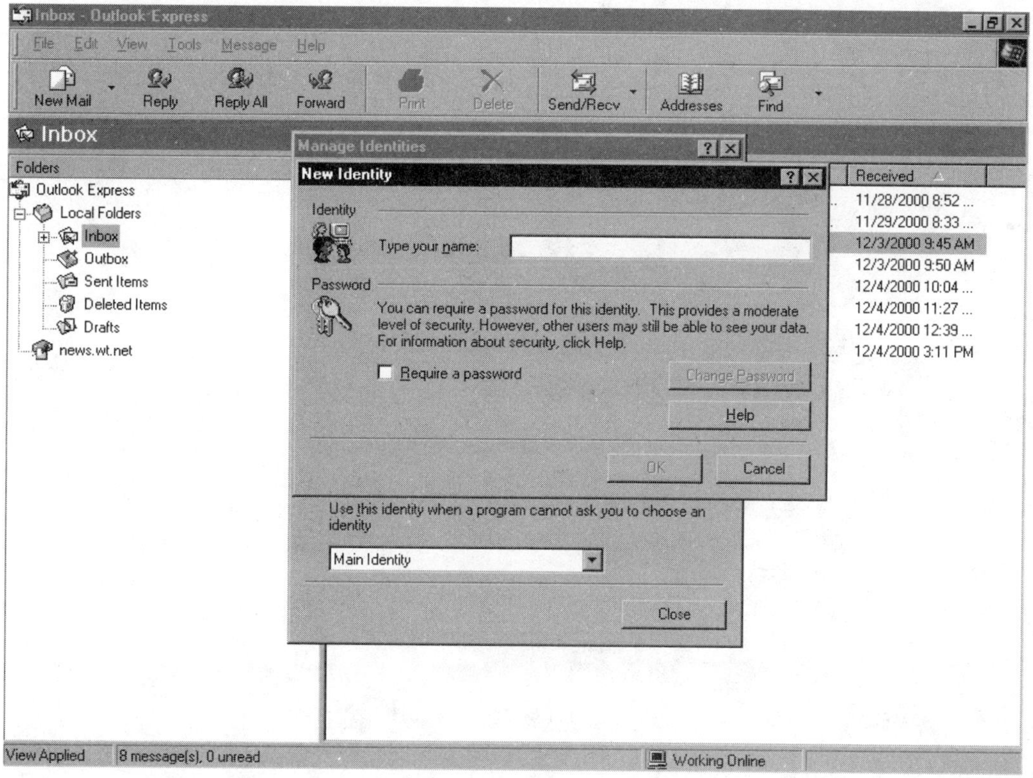

Figure 8-15 Setting up a new identity.

2. **Tell Outlook Express the name the identity will use and, optionally, specify a password for the identity.**

   In the Type Your Name box, enter a name for the identity. If you want to specify a password for the identity, click the Require A

Password check box, which will open the Enter Password dialog box. In the New Password box, type a password, and then type it again in the Confirm New Password box and click OK. Click OK again in the New Identity dialog box. You'll be asked whether you want to switch to the new identity now. If you do, click Yes; otherwise, click No and then close the Manage Identities dialog box.

The name of the new identity will appear in the Identities list in the Manage Identities dialog box.

To switch from one identity to another, follow these steps:

1. **Open the Switch Identities dialog box, as shown in Figure 8-16.**

   Click the File menu, and then click Switch Identity.

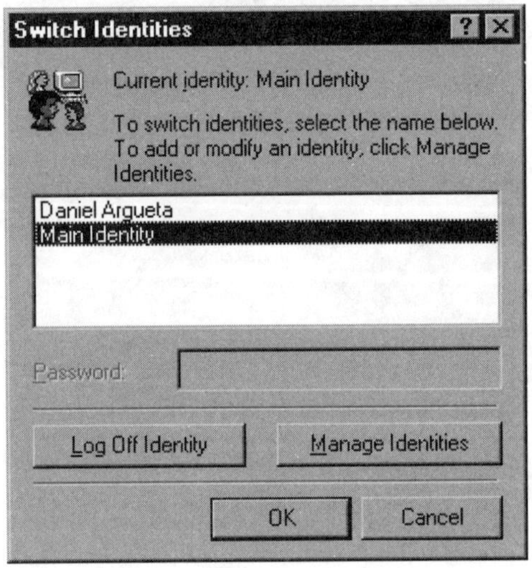

Figure 8-16 The Switch Identities dialog box.

2. **Switch to a different identity.**

   Select the identity from the list, enter the password, and click OK. If this is the first time the new identity is being used, the Internet Connection Wizard will start. Follow the instructions on the screen to set up e-mail for the new identity. When you click Finish, you can use Outlook Express as the new identity.

NOTE *When you use more than one identity with Outlook Express, you'll be asked which identity to use whenever you open Outlook Express.*

About Newsgroups

A newsgroup is not an electronic gathering of people who meet to discuss current events, but a collection of articles about a specific topic, or at least that's what a newsgroup is supposed to be. You can find newsgroups on every conceivable topic from quilting to artificial intelligence to religion to whatever. A problem arises in that you can find anything about anything at any time in any newsgroup, and you will probably be offended by some of it.

That said, you can use Outlook Express to set up and use newsgroups. Newsgroups are stored on a server at your ISP, and you need to set up a news account to access them. To do so, click Outlook Express in the Folders list, and then in the pane on the right of the screen, click Set Up A Newsgroups Account to start the Internet Connection Wizard. As you did when establishing an Internet connection for e-mail, follow the instructions on the screen and supply the needed information. You'll need to get the name of the news server from your ISP.

When you've established an account, you can download the list of newsgroups from the server at your ISP. To do so, click Yes when Outlook Express asks you about this. Downloading could take some time, depending on the speed of your Internet connection—newsgroups number in the tens of thousands. But only the names are downloaded; the contents remain on the news server until you specifically access a newsgroup. When the list has downloaded, you'll see the Newsgroup Subscriptions dialog box, as shown in Figure 8-17.

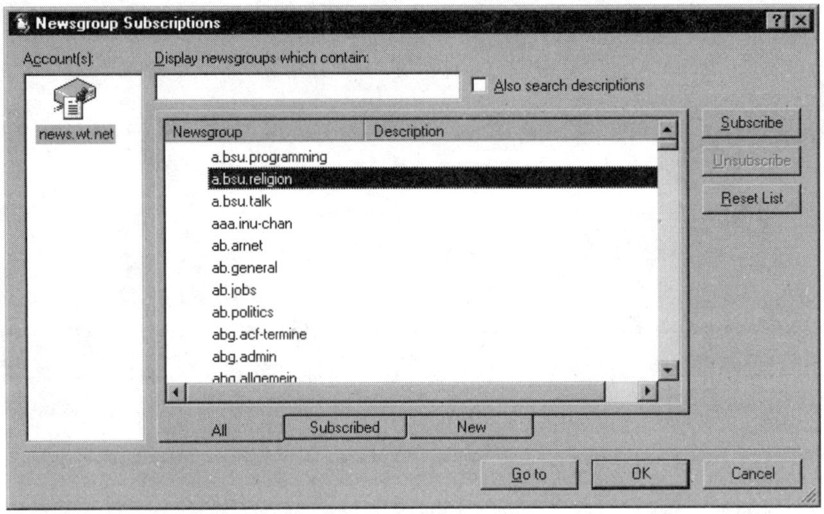

Figure 8-17 The Newsgroup Subscriptions dialog box.

Finding a Newsgroup That Interests You

You can select a newsgroup to read by scrolling this list (a time-consuming task) or by searching on a term. To search, enter the word or phrase and then just wait a bit. Soon you'll see a list of newsgroups whose names contain your search term. Figure 8-18 shows the list of newsgroups I found when searching on "genealogy."

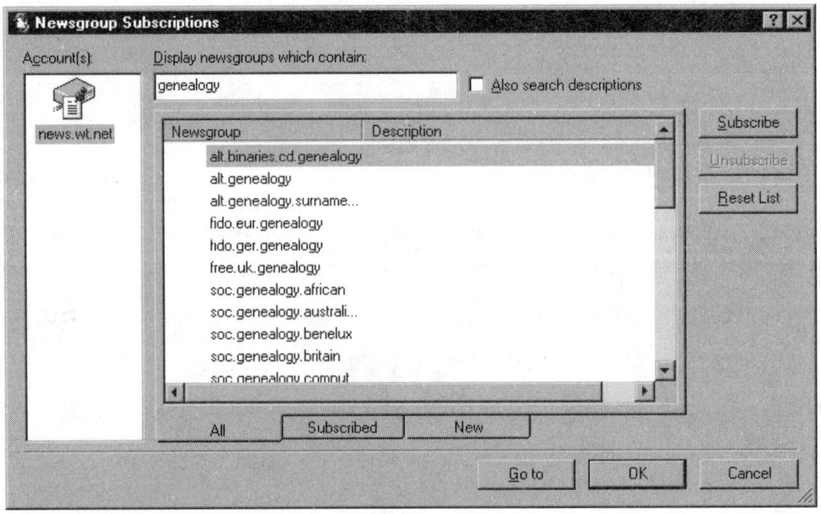

Figure 8-18 A list of genealogy newsgroups.

To read a newsgroup, select its name from the list and click the Go To button. If you find a group that seems to have value to you, you can subscribe to it. Subscribing doesn't involve money, as with a daily printed newspaper, but means creating a subfolder for a particular newsgroup in your news folder. Your newsgroup folder was created when you set up a newsgroup account, as we did earlier in this section. After you subscribe, you can click the folder to display a list of messages in the newsgroup. Simply double-click the message header to open it in a separate window and read it.

Replying to a Newsgroup

Replying to a newsgroup is known as posting. To send an original message to a newsgroup, open the newsgroup and then click the New Post button on the toolbar to open the New Message window. The name of the newsgroup will appear in the Newsgroups line. Now simply type your message in the body of the window, and when you're finished, click the Send button. To reply to an individual article, click the Reply button, and to reply to the entire newsgroup, click the Reply Group button.

TIP *Before you post to a newsgroup, it's a good idea to "lurk," that is, to read lots of the current postings and get a sense of the group's culture.*

When you're finished reading newsgroups, click the Inbox folder to check your recent mail or to compose a new e-mail message.

Personalizing Outlook Express

You can personalize, or customize, Outlook Express in several ways, and to do so you use the Options dialog box, which we've looked at earlier in this chapter. To open the Options dialog box, click the Tools menu and then click Options. Here, I'm not going to get into all the many choices you'll find there. You can explore the tabs in this dialog box to get a sense of what you might want to do. If you have a question, click the Help button (the button with the question mark that's right next to the Close button) and then click an option to see an explanation or description.

I do want to point out how to take care of some of the most obvious tasks.

- If you'd rather not hear a sound when new messages arrive, click the General tab, and clear the Play Sound When New Messages Arrive check box.
- If you want Outlook Express to check for new messages more or less frequently, click the General tab, be sure that the Check For New Message Every check box is checked, and then change the number of minutes by clicking the arrows in the Minute(s) spin box.
- If you want to send messages immediately when you click the Send button rather than their being placed in your Outbox folder, click the Send tab, and click the Send Messages Immediately check box.
- If you want to retain a copy of all the messages you send, click the Send tab, and click the Save Copy Of Sent Messages In The 'Sent Items' Folder check box.

The Seven Most Important Things to Remember About E-Mail

1. Remember, you're talking to a real human being, not a computer. Follow all the rules of social interaction that you would in nondigital communication.
2. DON'T TYPE IN ALL CAPITAL LETTERS. This is perceived as shouting.
3. You can use emoticons (smileys) to express a tone of voice. For example, :-) is a smile. (Turn this page sideways if you can't see the smile.) You'll find a long list of emoticons at *http://members.aol.com/bearpage/smileys.htm*.
4. Always include a subject line. Busy people (and who isn't?) may not open your message if they don't know what it's about.
5. Read over your e-mail message before you send it. A message full of typos won't communicate you or your topic well.
6. Don't include an original message in a reply unless it's really necessary for the context of your reply.
7. Your message can get forwarded, printed, and otherwise distributed in ways that you never considered; so give some thought to the content of your messages.

Summary

This chapter has focused on how to use Outlook Express, the e-mail application that is included with Windows. We've looked at how to read, send, reply, forward, print, save, delete, and otherwise process messages. I've given you some guidelines about what you might and might not want to include in an e-mail message. My main point, however, is that e-mail is a great communications tool, and I encourage you to master the really rather simple skills involved in using it and to use it to keep in touch with friends, family, business associates, and other contacts, wherever they may be located.

Chapter 9

MAINTAINING WINDOWS AND YOUR COMPUTER

Featuring:

- Using the Windows System Tools
- What You Need to Know About Computer Viruses

Your computer is not as maintenance-free as some of the other electronic gadgets you use, but it doesn't take a lot of time to fine-tune some adjustments that will make your computer run smoother and faster. Although the tools you use have some technical-sounding names and the tasks that these tools perform sound a little complicated, you can easily learn to use them.

In this chapter, I'll introduce these tools and show you how to use them. I'll also talk about another topic that is important in maintaining your computer system—avoiding viruses (malevolent programs that can wreak havoc with your system).

Using the Windows System Tools

Most of the tools that you'll typically use to maintain your computer system come with Microsoft Windows and are called system tools. To see a list of them, which is shown in Figure 9-1, click the Start button, click Programs, click Accessories, and then click System Tools.

Figure 9-1 The Windows System Tools.

In this chapter, I'm not going to discuss every single one of these tools, but only those that you'll need to use rather regularly. Some tools apply to a computer network, and others are used primarily by technicians. I'll skip those.

Protecting Your Hard Drive

As you know by now, the hard drive on your computer is the device on which you store information. To keep it running smoothly, you need to periodically get rid of unnecessary files, reorganize information so that Windows can find it quickly, and look for spots on your hard disk that might cause a problem. These days, hard drives are really quite reliable, though not totally foolproof, so to be on the safe side, you need to occasionally "clean house."

Cleaning Up Your Hard Drive

In the process of managing your computer, Windows creates a number of files on your computer that aren't really necessary and that just take up space. Even if you have tons of space on your hard drive, it's just tidier and neater to get rid of stuff that you don't need. To do this, you run the Disk Cleanup tool. Follow these steps:

1. **Open the Select Drive dialog box, as shown in Figure 9-2.**

   Click the Start button, click Programs, click Accessories, click System Tools, and then click Disk Cleanup.

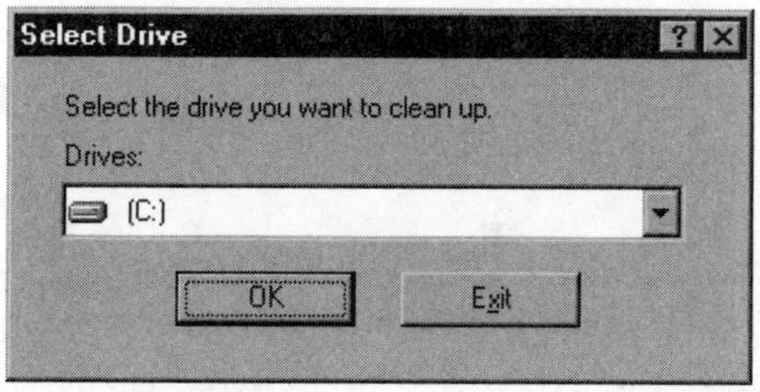

Figure 9-2 The Select Drive dialog box.

2. **Tell Windows which drive to clean up.**

   In the Drives drop-down list, select the drive you want to clean up, and then click OK. (If you have only one hard drive, it will be drive C, which will be selected by default.)

3. **Open the Disk Cleanup dialog box, as shown in Figure 9-3.**

   Click OK in the Select Drive dialog box. After Windows calculates the amount of space you will save, the Disk Cleanup dialog box is displayed.

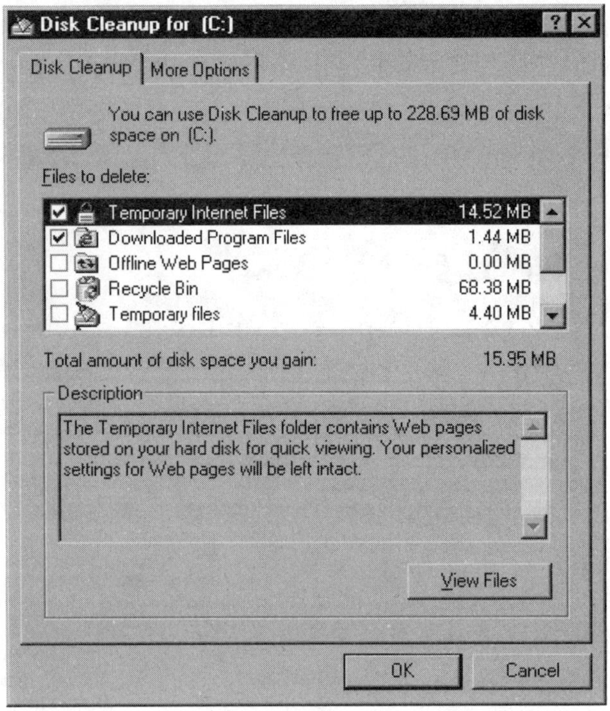

Figure 9-3 The Disk Cleanup dialog box.

4. **Tell Windows which files to delete.**

   In the Disk Cleanup dialog box, you'll see a list of files that can be deleted and the amount of space that you will save by doing so. To decide whether you want to delete these files, you need to know what they are, which you can find out by selecting a type of file and then looking in the Description box. All these explanations are quite clear, so I won't repeat them. To select a group of files to delete, click the category to place a check in the check box. If you don't want to delete files that Windows has checked, click the check box to clear the check mark. When you've made your selections, click OK. When Windows asks whether you're sure you want to delete these files, click OK, and Windows will delete them.

You can free additional space by getting rid of Windows components and applications you don't use and by reducing the space that System Restore uses.

NOTE *System Restore is a program that you can use to reinstate settings that you established at an earlier time. About the only time you would ever need to use System Restore is before you make changes to the Registry. The Registry is a database of configuration information for your computer. I'm not even going to tell you where to find it or how to open it, because you should never, ever use it. Unless you really know what you're doing, you can do some serious damage to your system if you mess around with the Registry. Consequently, you don't need to worry about the System Restore program either. The only reason I'm explaining either is that you'll see the System Restore option on the More Options tab in the Disk Cleanup dialog box.*

If you want to free more space by deleting Windows components that you don't use, click the More Options tab in the Disk Cleanup dialog box, and then click the Clean Up button in the Windows Components box to open the Add/Remove Programs Properties dialog box at the Windows Setup tab, which is shown in Figure 9-4. To find out what a component does, select it from the Components list and then check the description at the bottom of this tab. To delete a component, select it and then click OK.

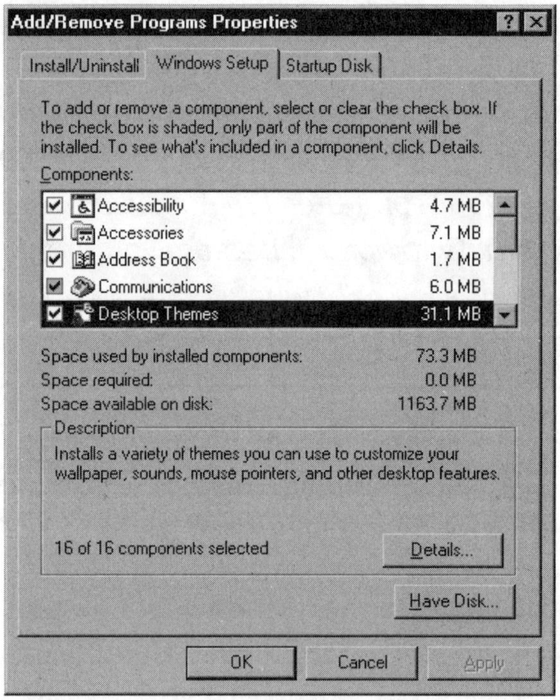

Figure 9-4 The Add/Remove Programs Properties dialog box open at the Windows Setup tab.

You can also free up some hard disk space by removing applications that you don't use. To do so click the Clean Up button in the Installed Programs dialog box to open the Add/Remove Programs Properties dialog box at the Install/Uninstall tab. Select the program in the list, and click the Add/Remove button. When Windows asks if you really want to delete the program click Yes.

TIP *When you buy a new computer, the manufacturer has installed Windows on it as well as some applications. You may find that you never use some of these, so you might as well get rid of them. You can easily do so using the procedure I described in the preceding paragraph.*

Reorganizing Your Hard Drive

When you tell Windows to save a file on your hard drive, Windows puts the file wherever it finds room. Over time, any one file can have a piece here, a piece there, a piece somewhere else, and so on. Windows always knows the location of these pieces, called fragments, but because Windows has to go to several locations to pick up the fragments, the time to open files can get slower and slower.

Consequently, about once a month it's a good idea to tell Windows to collect all these fragments, a process known as *defragmenting*. No surprise, to do this you use the Disk Defragmenter tool. Follow these steps:

1. **Tell Windows which drive you want to defragment.**

   Click the Start button, click Programs, click Accessories, click System Tools, and then click Disk Defragmenter to open the Select Drive dialog box. (This is the same dialog box you saw earlier in this chapter in Figure 9-2.) Select the drive, and click OK to open the Defragment Drive dialog box, as shown in Figure 9-5.

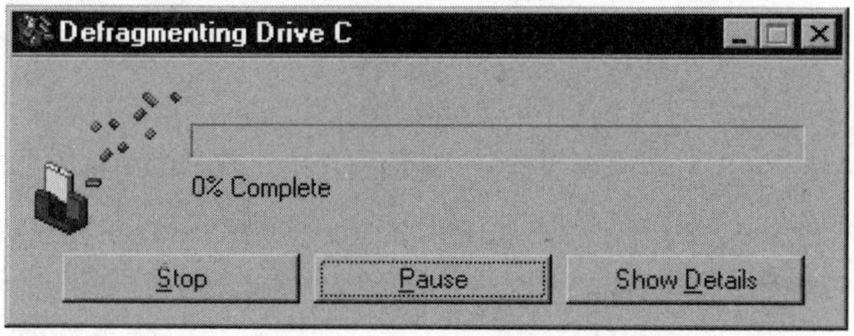

Figure 9-5 Starting to defragment a hard drive.

2. **Check the progress of the Disk Defragmenter.**

   As you can see in Figure 9-5, a progress bar indicates the percentage of the defragmenting process that is complete. If for whatever reason you want to halt the process, click the Stop button. (Doing so won't hurt a thing.) You can also click the Pause button to halt the process for a while and then resume it. To see a graphical representation (which is rather colorful but complicated) of what's going on, click the Show Details button. To return to a nongraphical view, click the Hide Details button. You'll be notified when the defragmenting process is complete.

TIP *Defragmenting a hard disk can take some time if you haven't done so in a while, so it's a good idea to take care of this task when you don't need to use your computer for anything else. If you attempt to use your computer during the process, Disk Defragment will stop and then start over from the beginning.*

Scanning Your Hard Drive for Trouble Spots

ScanDisk is a tool that checks your hard disk for errors and repairs any damaged areas it finds. You might have seen Scan Disk run even though you didn't tell it to do so. If Windows shuts down and the proper sign-off procedure (which I described in Chapter 2) is not followed, ScanDisk will run when you restart the system. This sometimes occurs if Windows shuts down as the result of a power glitch.

You can also run ScanDisk yourself. To start ScanDisk, click the Start button, click Programs, click Accessories, click System Tools, and then click ScanDisk. You'll see the dialog box shown in Figure 9-6. Run the Standard check about once a week (click the Standard option in the Type Of Test box), and run the Thorough check about once a month (click the Thorough option button in the Type Of Test section). In this way, an accumulation of little trouble spots doesn't turn into a serious problem. Click the Start button to begin scanning your disk. During the process, a progress bar at the bottom of the ScanDisk dialog box will indicate what's going on. You'll be notified when ScanDisk is finished. Unlike Disk Defragmenter, ScanDisk does its work quickly.

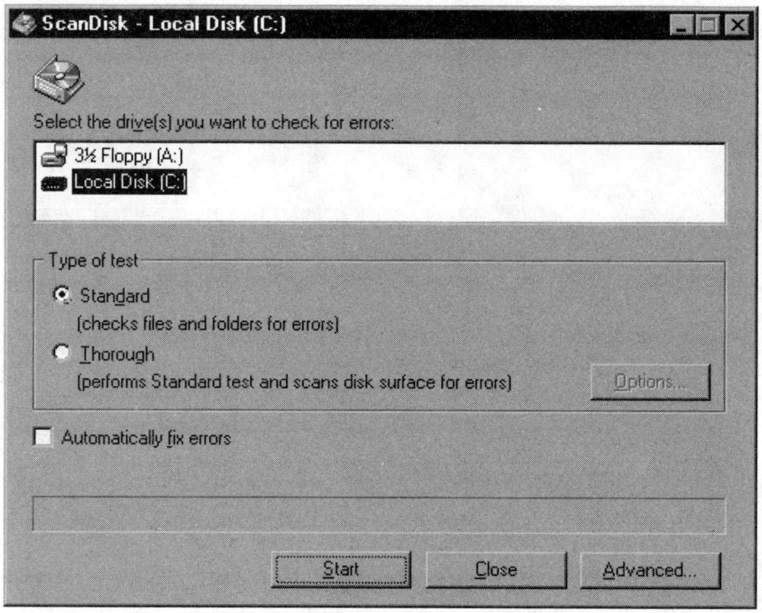

Figure 9-6 The ScanDisk dialog box.

Getting Maintenance Help from Windows

Although I've just shown you how to take care of some maintenance tasks yourself, you can also tell Windows to take care of these tasks for you.

Using the Maintenance Wizard

A wizard, as you know, is a guide that steps you through a process. The Maintenance Wizard, however, really just does the process for you. It deletes unnecessary files from your hard disk, runs the Disk Defragmenter, and configures your most frequently used programs so that they run faster.

You can choose to run the Maintenance Wizard on a schedule that you set, or you can run the wizard manually whenever you want. To start the Maintenance Wizard, click the Start button, click Programs, click Accessories, click System Tools, and then click Maintenance Wizard. You'll see the screen shown in Figure 9-7.

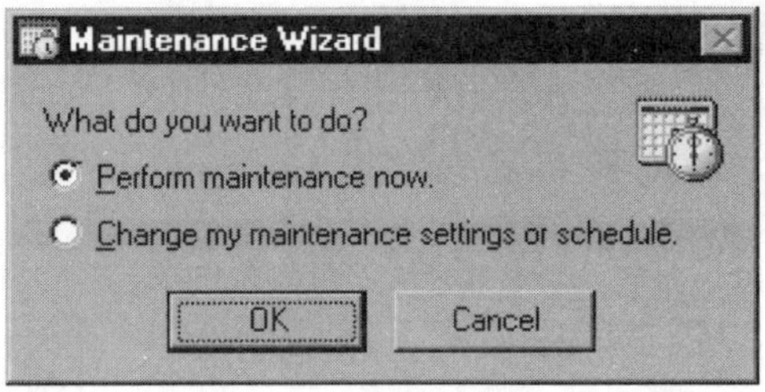

Figure 9-7 Selecting how to start the Maintenance Wizard.

To start the Maintence Wizard immediately, click the Perform Maintenance Now option button and click OK. Without your intervention, the Maintenance Wizard will take care of the tasks described in the previous section. If you want to schedule when the Maintenance Wizard takes care of these tasks, click the Change My Maintenance Settings Or Schedule option button, and then click OK. You'll see the screen shown in Figure 9-8.

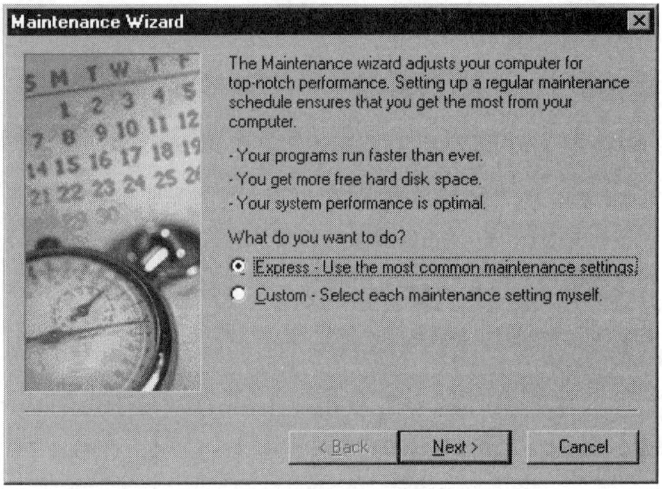

Figure 9-8 Setting up a schedule with the Maintenance Wizard.

To use the Maintenance Wizard, follow these steps:

1. **Tell the wizard which kind of settings to use.**

   In the first screen (see Figure 9-8), you can select Express or Custom. Using Express is the easiest, and I suggest you use it. Leave the Express option selected, and click Next to open the screen shown in Figure 9-9.

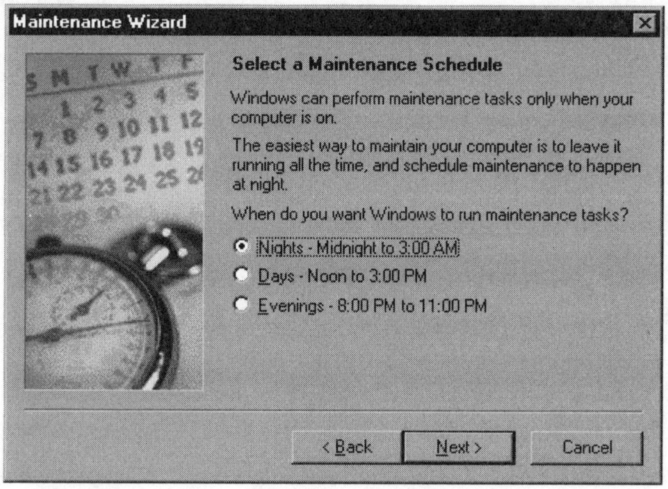

Figure 9-9 Telling the wizard when to run.

2. **Tell the wizard when to run.**

   Select a time period when you won't be needing to use your computer, and click Next. Remember, Windows can take care of maintenance tasks only when your computer is on, so if you decide to run the Maintenance Wizard in the middle of the night, leave your computer on when you go to bed.

3. **Complete the wizard.**

   In the final screen of the wizard, as shown in Figure 9-10, click the check box at the bottom if you want to perform each scheduled task when you click Finish. If you want to stick to the schedule you just established, simply click Finish.

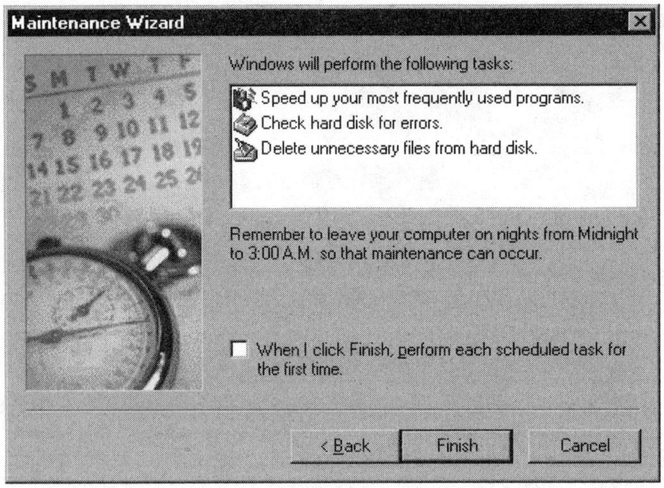

Figure 9-10 The final screen of the Maintenance Wizard.

Using Task Scheduler

Another way to schedule maintenance tasks is to use the Scheduled Task Wizard. In addition, you can use this wizard to schedule other programs to run at a time you select. For example, if you are using AOL, you can use the Scheduled Task Wizard to start AOL whenever you start your computer. To use the Scheduled Task Wizard, follow these steps:

1. **Open the wizard.**

   Click the Start button, click Programs, click Accessories, click System Tools, and then click Scheduled Tasks to open the Scheduled Tasks folder, as shown in Figure 9-11.

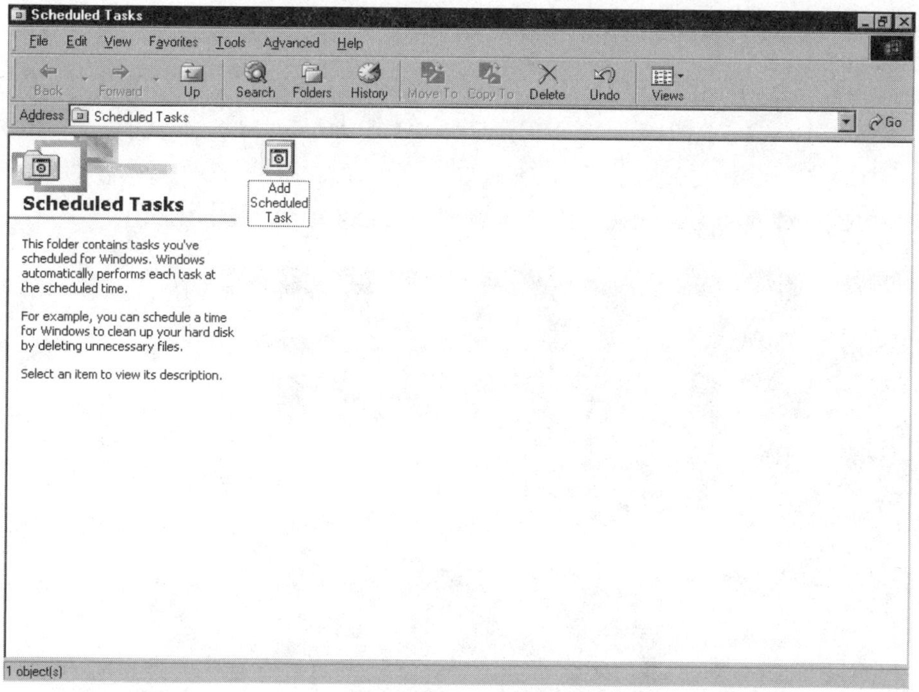

Figure 9-11 The Scheduled Tasks folder.

2. **Start the Scheduled Task Wizard.**

   Double-click Add Scheduled Task to open the first screen of the wizard, which is shown in Figure 9-12.

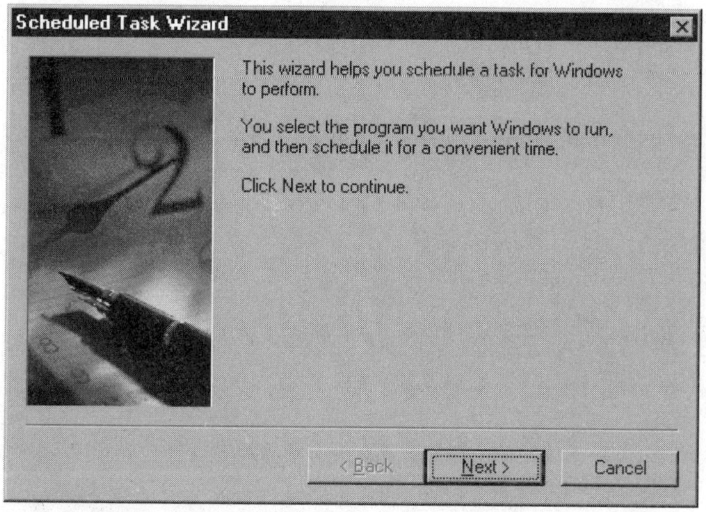

Figure 9-12 Starting the Scheduled Task Wizard.

3. **Select a program you want to schedule.**

   Click Next to open the list of programs shown in Figure 9-13. Select a program to schedule, and click Next to open the screen shown in Figure 9-14. Select a time when you want to start the selected program, click Next, and then click Finish.

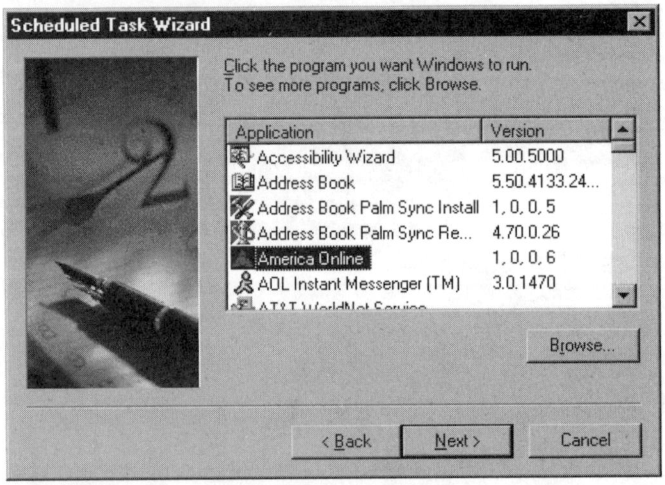

Figure 9-13 Selecting a program.

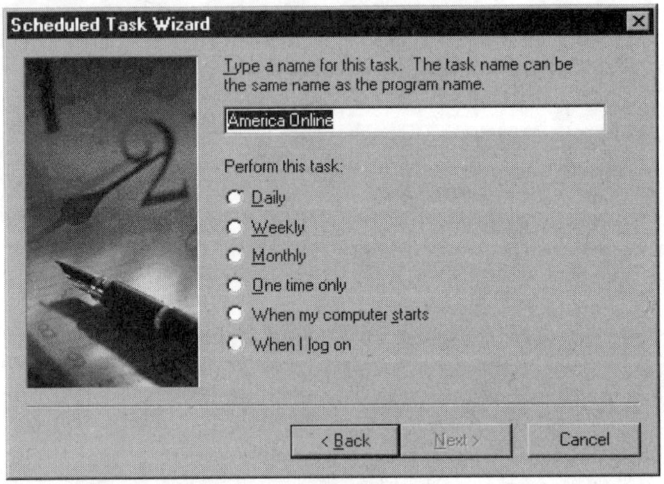

Figure 9-14 Selecting a time.

What You Need to Know About Computer Viruses

In Chapter 8, I mentioned that you can catch a computer virus from an e-mail attachment. Here I want to give you some more details about viruses and tell you about other ways you can protect your system from them.

A computer virus is a malevolent program that can attach itself to your computer system without your knowledge or permission and cause damage that can range from a minor annoyance to the complete destruction of your system. These programs are created and distributed in unscrupulous ways by computer users who have various motives. Some just want to see whether they can do it; others are really intent on causing destruction.

Computer viruses travel from one system to another via infected diskettes, e-mail, files that are downloaded from the Internet, and even shrink-wrapped software that you buy at a retail store. After a virus attaches itself to your system, it is triggered into action by a specific date or when you run a particular program.

To protect your computer system, you need to acquire and run antivirus software regularly. Sometimes a new computer will come with an antivirus program, but normally this program will include only a couple of free upgrades to a database of known viruses. This won't be enough protection because new viruses are being discovered all the time, and your antivirus software needs to know about them.

The best advice I can give you is to buy a full-featured antivirus program and keep it upgraded. The two most popular such programs are McAfee's VirusScan and Norton Antivirus. To find out more about these programs and how you can acquire and use them, go to *http://www.mcafee.com* and to *http://www.symantec.com*.

Seven Other Important Ways to Protect the Health of Your Computer

In addition to using antivirus software, here are some other ways you can protect your computer from viruses. I've mentioned some of these techniques already in this book, but they are worth repeating.

1. If you have any question about what an e-mail message that you receive might contain, be ultra-careful and delete it without opening it.
2. Keep your antivirus software current by updating it to detect the latest known viruses.
3. Weigh the cost of downloading free software from the Internet with the possible cost if it should contain a virus.
4. Do not give out important personal information unless you are certain you can trust the recipient and that it is necessary for a transaction.
5. If someone gives you a floppy disk that contains a neat game or a special font or anything else, scan it with your antivirus software before you put it on your computer.
6. Never give out your password online or over the phone.
7. Don't believe everything you hear about computer viruses. There are as many hoaxes as there are viruses. Check out information on one of the antivirus software vendor's sites, and check out the information at *http://www.mcafee.com.*

Summary

In this short chapter, I've given you the most practical ways to maintain the health and security of your computer system. These days, computers are more reliable, and operating systems are certainly more robust than in the past. But don't become complacent. Regularly run the system tools that come with Windows, and acquire and use antivirus software. In addition, don't forget about the other guidelines I've included for guarding against computer viruses. The information you have on your computer is important to you, or it wouldn't be there in the first place. Don't take chances with it.

Chapter 10

MAKING YOUR VERSION OF WINDOWS SPECIAL

Featuring:

- What Is Control Panel?
- Choosing Between the Active and the Classic Desktop
- Making Windows More Accessible for You
- Making the Keyboard Work More to Your Liking
- Taking Charge of the Mouse
- Customizing the Display

In earlier chapters in this book, I've walked you through some of the steps you can take to change how Microsoft Windows looks and works. For example, in Chapter 2 we looked at how to change the date and time, and in Chapter 3, we looked at how to create shortcuts on the desktop.

But you can customize Windows in many other ways. You can change the mouse from a right-handed to a left-handed device, you can specify a color scheme for dialog boxes and other parts of Windows, and you can make Windows more accessible if you have difficulty using the keyboard or viewing the screen.

In this chapter, we'll look at how to use the Windows Control Panel to make your version of Windows special for you and the way you need and want it to work.

What Is Control Panel?

You used Control Panel earlier in this book, and in those chapters I promised that I'd give you a lot more information about Control Panel in this chapter. Control Panel is a folder of applets, small applications that you can use to modify the settings in Windows and in devices on your computer system such as the keyboard, mouse, modem, and so on. To open Control Panel, click the Start button, click Settings, and then click Control Panel. You'll see something similar to Figure 10-1.

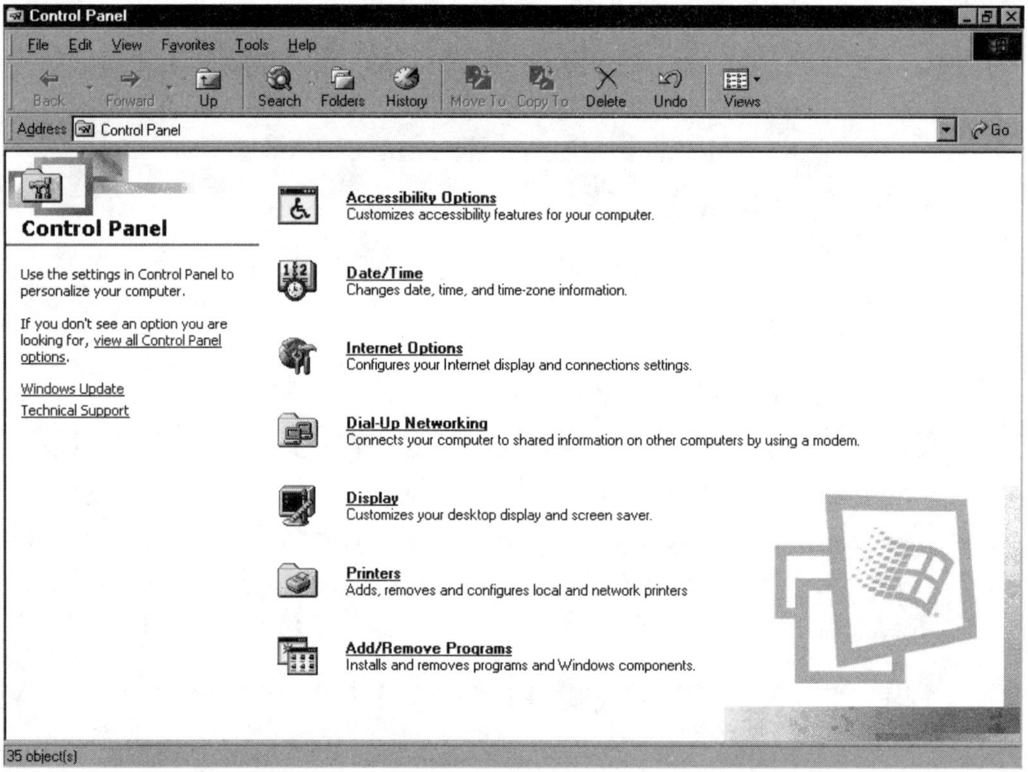

Figure 10-1 The Windows Control Panel.

By default, the Control Panel folder displays only those items most commonly used. To display all the items available in Control Panel, click the View All Control Panel Options link. Now you'll see something similar to Figure 10-2, which shows Control Panel in Large Icons view. You can also display Control Panel in Small Icons, List, and Details view. Click the View menu, and then click these other options to see how the display changes.

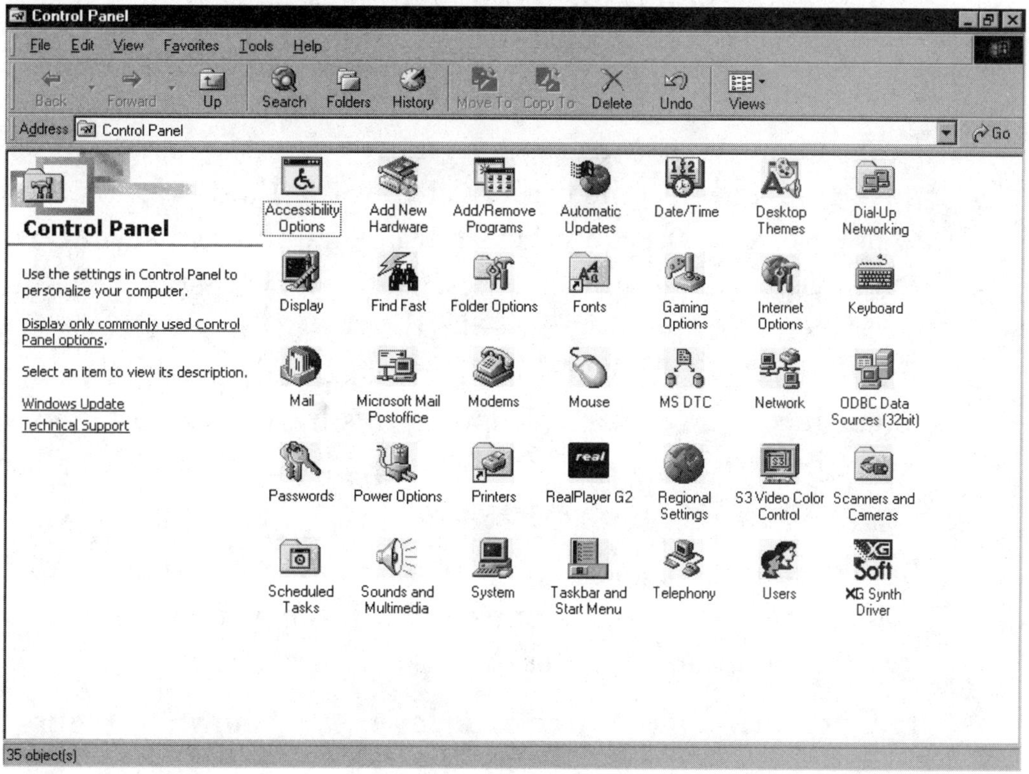

Figure 10-2 The Windows Control Panel in Large Icons view and displaying all the options.

Notice that on the left are links to Windows Update and to Technical Support. When you click either of these links and you are connected to the Internet, you'll be taken to that Web site. To use an applet in Control Panel, you double-click its icon.

Choosing Between the Active and the Classic Desktop

As you know well by now, you can do almost anything in Windows in several ways. This characteristic of Windows applies to how you view and use the desktop and to how you use and view folders. You may have heard people refer to the "user interface." The user interface, or UI, is simply the portion of the system with which you, the user, interacts. As you know from Chapter 1, a lot goes on behind the scenes that you never actually see.

In Windows Me, which is the version of Windows I'm using as I write this book, and in some earlier versions of Windows, you can choose to use a Classic user interface, a Web-like (or Active) interface, or a combination. And, in fact, when Windows is first installed, the user interface is sort of a hybrid—the desktop uses the Classic interface, and folders use the Web-like interface. Unless you've changed the setup since you got your computer, this hybrid user interface is what you've been using, and if you look back at Chapter 2, you'll see how the desktop looks in Classic view.

In this section, I'll show you how to view the desktop as a Web page. You can then decide for yourself which one you prefer. Follow these steps to configure your desktop as a Web page:

1. **Open the Folder Options dialog box, as shown in Figure 10-3.**

   Open the My Computer window or start Windows Explorer. Click the Tools menu, and then click Folder Options.

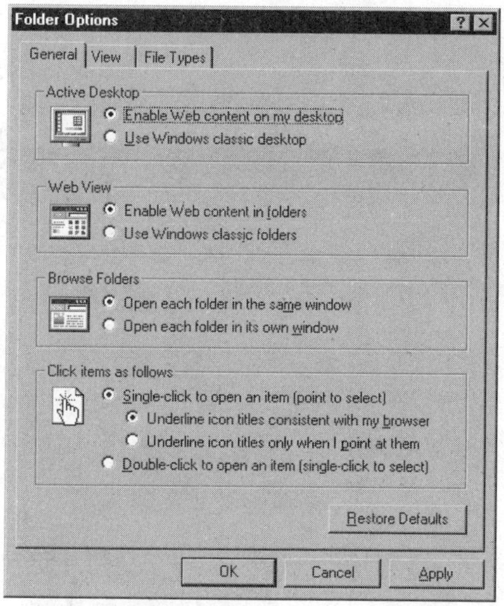

Figure 10-3 The Folder Options dialog box.

2. **Turn on Web view.**

   In the General tab, click the Enable Web Content On My Desktop option button in the Active Desktop section. In the Click Items As Follows section, click the Single-Click To Open An Item option button, and then click OK.

3. **Display your start page on the desktop.**

   Right-click an empty area of the desktop, choose Active Desktop from the shortcut menu, and then click My Current Home Page. Figure 10-4 shows my Active desktop and my current home page.

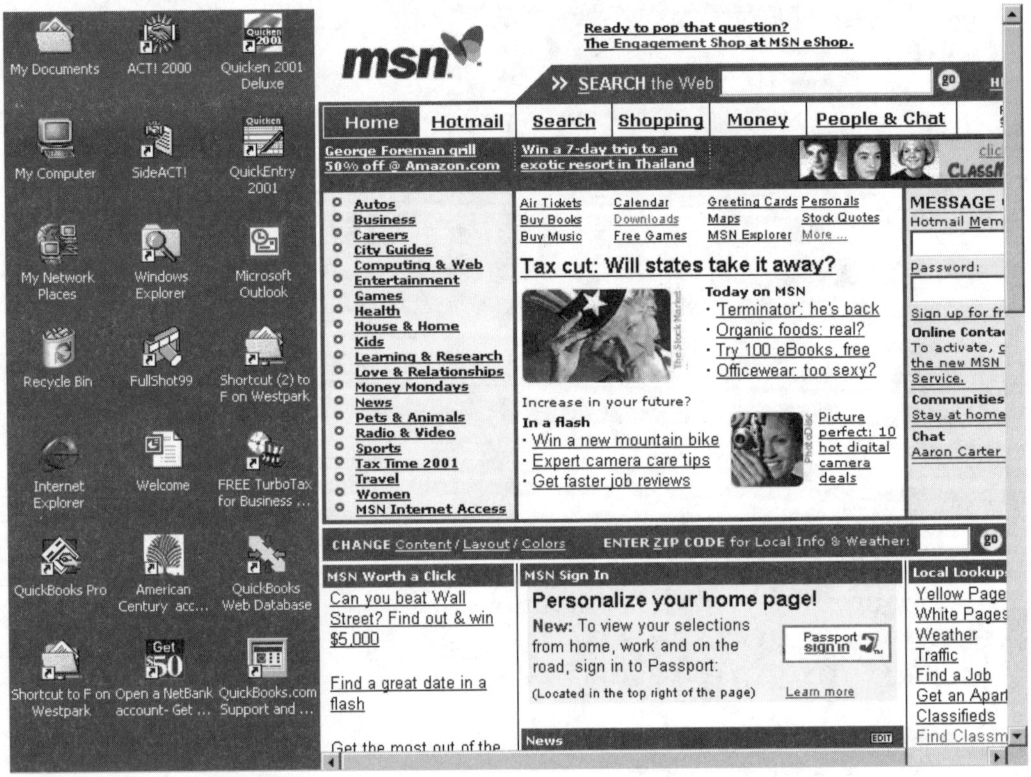

Figure 10-4 My Active desktop.

If you want to return to the default desktop, open the Folder Options dialog box again, and in the General tab, click the Restore Defaults button and then click OK.

Making Windows More Accessible for You

Using a computer is sometimes challenging for all of us, but it can be especially challenging if you have a disability such as a visual impairment, a mobility impairment, a hearing impairment, or cognitive or language impairments. In the United States, more than 30 million people are estimated to have a disability that makes using a computer difficult.

In its development of the Windows family of operating systems, Microsoft has considered assistive technology a key issue and, with each new version, enhances the accessibility features. We'll look at those features and how to use them in this section. If you'd like more information than is presented here or if you need assistive technology in addition to the options in Windows, go to the Microsoft Accessibility site (*http://www.microsoft.com/enable*). Figure 10-5 shows the home page at this site, from which you can access a newsletter, documentation, links to other products, and resources that are specific to individual impairments.

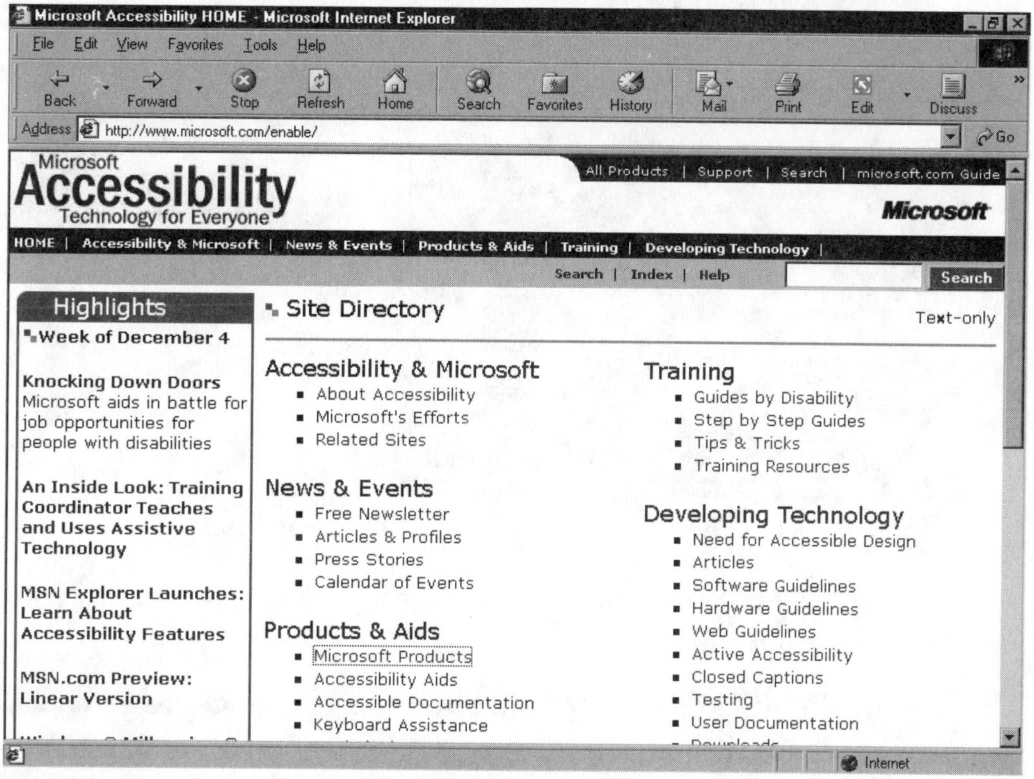

Figure 10-5 The Microsoft Accessibility site.

To customize the accessibility options in Windows, you can use the Accessibility Options applet in Control Panel, or you can use the Accessibility accessories.

Using the Accessibility Options Applet

Double-clicking Accessibility Options in Control Panel opens the Accessibility Properties dialog box at the Keyboard tab, as shown in Figure 10-6.

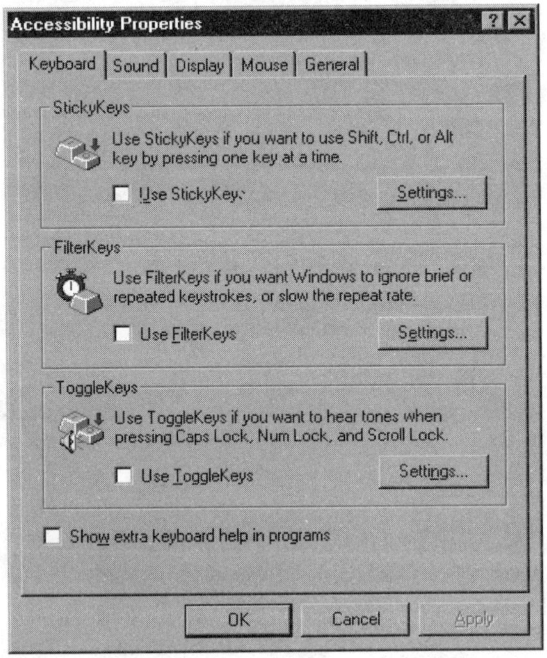

Figure 10-6 The Accessibility Properties dialog box.

On the Keyboard tab, you can customize your keyboard in the following ways:

- In the StickyKeys section, click the Use StickyKeys check box if you have difficulty pressing two keys at once, such as Ctrl+A. To specify options for how StickyKeys are treated, click the Settings button and use the Settings For StickyKeys dialog box.
- In the FilterKeys section, click the Use FilterKeys check box if you want Windows to ignore short or repeated keystrokes or to slow the repeat rate. To specify options for how FilterKeys are treated, click the Settings button and use the Settings For FilterKeys dialog box.

- In the ToggleKeys section, click the Use ToggleKeys check box if you want to hear a sound when you press Caps Lock, Num Lock, and Scroll Lock. To specify options for how ToggleKeys are treated, click the Settings button and use the Settings For ToggleKeys dialog box.
- If you want to display extra help for using the keyboard in an application (if such help is available), click the Show Extra Keyboard Help In Programs check box.

When you've finished selecting options in the Keyboard tab, click Apply if you want to continue setting options in the other tabs in the Accessibility Properties dialog box. Otherwise, click OK.

You use the other tabs to adjust the sound, the display, and the mouse:

- Click the Sound tab, and then click the Use SoundSentry check box if you want a visual cue when your system generates a sound. To specify options for how the SoundSentry works, click the Settings button and use the Settings For SoundSentry dialog box. Click the Use ShowSounds if you want captions for speech and sounds in an application.
- Click the Display tab, and the click the Use High Contrast check box if you want a display that's easier to read. You can also adjust the cursor blink rate and the width of the cursor using the slider bars on this tab.
- Click the Mouse tab, and then click the Use MouseKeys check box if you want to control the mouse pointer from the numeric keypad. Click the Settings button to open the Settings For MouseKeys dialog box to make finer mouse adjustments.
- Click the General tab to specify an idle time interval after which accessibility features are turned off, to enable warning message or sounds that signal the turning on or off of a feature, and to enable an alternative mouse or keyboard device.

Using the Accessibility Accessories

As you know, accessories are applications that are included with Windows. To open the Accessibility accessories, click the Start button, click Programs, click Accessories, and then click Accessibility.

Running the Accessibility Wizard

Stepping through the Accessibility Wizard is an easy way to set up accessibility options, including some that you can also set in the Accessibility Options dialog box. (Once again, there's more than one way to do something in Windows.) To start the wizard, click Accessibility Wizard in the Accessibility submenu. At the welcome screen, click Next. You'll see the screen in Figure 10-7, on which you can select the size of the text used on your screen.

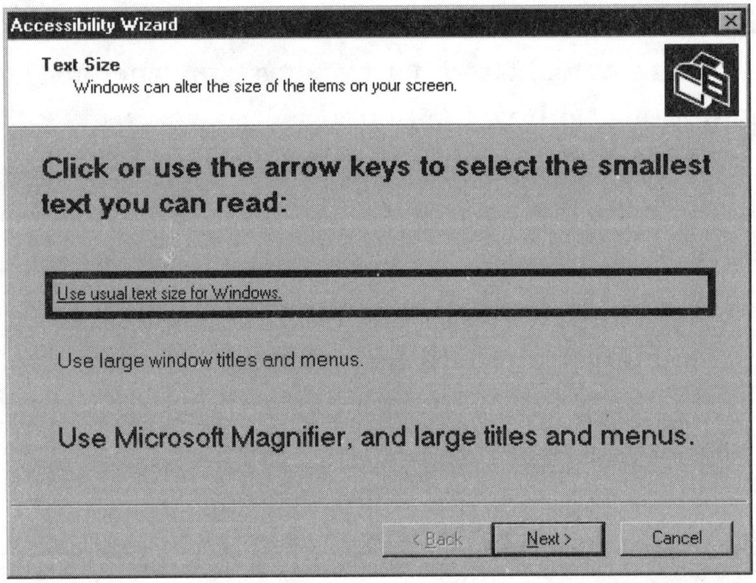

Figure 10-7 Specify text size with the Accessibility Wizard.

When you've made your choice, click Next. On the next screen, which is shown in Figure 10-8, you can tell the wizard to change the font size in title bars, menus, and so on, to use Magnifier (we'll look at this closely in a minute), and to disable personalized menus. Click Next when you've made these choices.

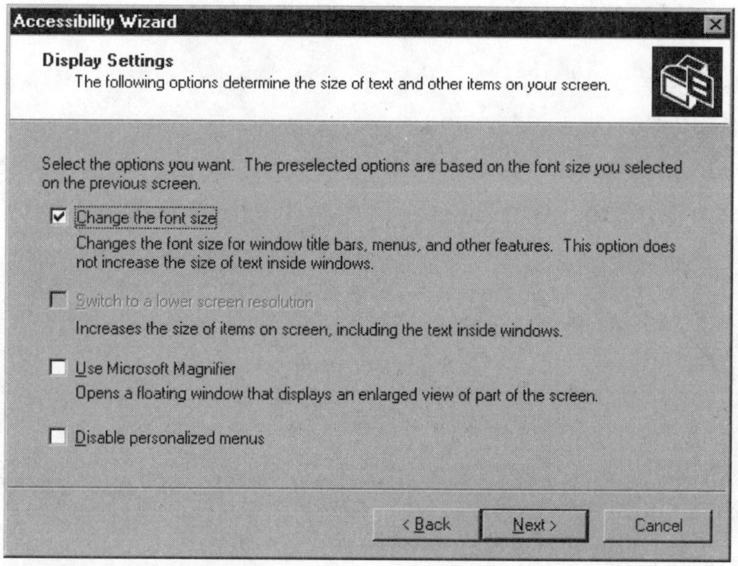

Figure 10-8 Select display settings on this screen.

On the next screen, which is shown in Figure 10-9, you can describe your particular difficulty. When you do so and click Next, the wizard then walks you through the steps for selecting accessibility options that apply to that difficulty. Follow the instructions on the screen, and when you're finished, click Finish.

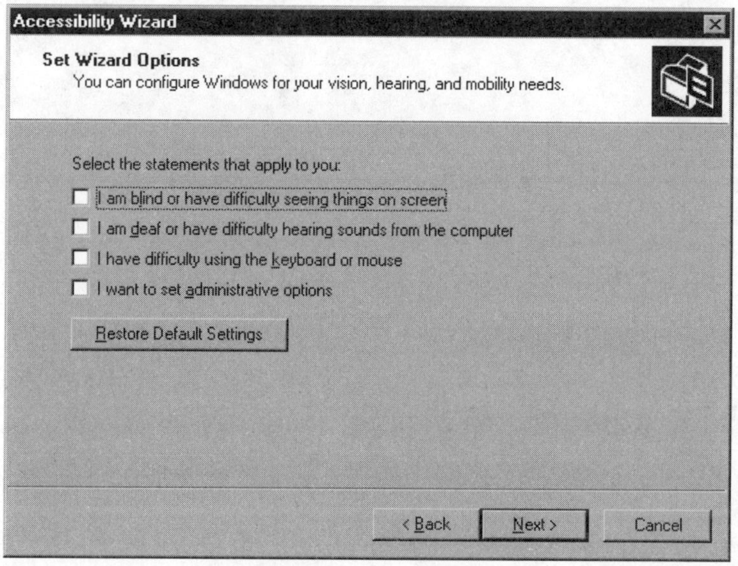

Figure 10-9 Tell the wizard about your particular difficulty.

Using Magnifier

When you run the Accessibility Wizard, you can specify that you want to use Magnifier, but you can also open Magnifier from the Accessibility submenu. Magnifier displays a portion of your screen in a separate window on the desktop, as shown in Figure 10-10.

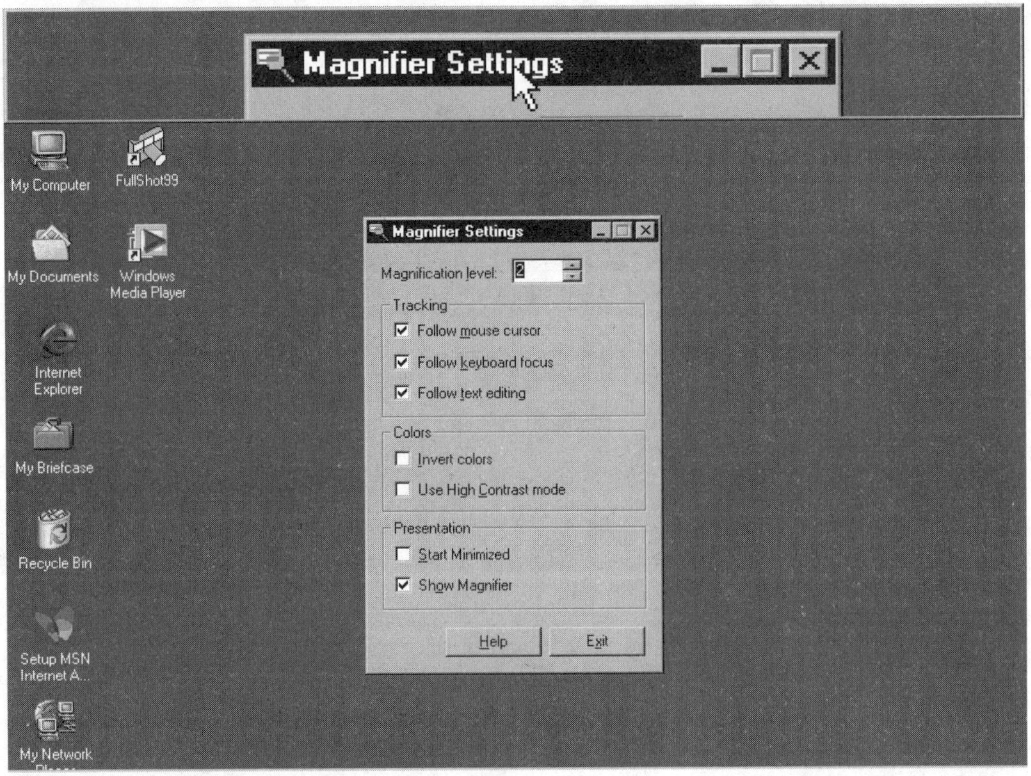

Figure 10-10 Setting up Magnifier.

In the Magnifier dialog box, you can tell Magnifier to follow the mouse, the keyboard, or the text editing focus. You can also specify how colors are displayed and the size at which to start Magnifier. To select an option, click its check box. When you want to close Magnifier, click the Exit button. As long as Magnifier is displayed, you'll need to work in the magnified portion of the screen. It's a little tricky, but you can soon get the hang of it.

Using the On-Screen Keyboard

If you have a disability that makes typing difficult, you might want to check out the On-Screen Keyboard. The first time you open the keyboard, you'll see a message saying that this feature provides only a minimal level of functionality and that you can find a more fully featured program at the Microsoft Accessibility site (*http://www.microsoft.com/enable/*). To see how the On-Screen Keyboard works and consider whether such a program might work well for you, follow these steps:

1. **Open Notepad (a little word-processing program that's included with Windows).**

   Click the Start button, click Programs, click Accessories, and click Notepad. When Notepad opens, maximize it.

2. **Open the On-Screen Keyboard.**

   Click the Start button, click Programs, click Accessories, click Accessibility, and then click On-Screen Keyboard. Your screen will look like the one in Figure 10-11.

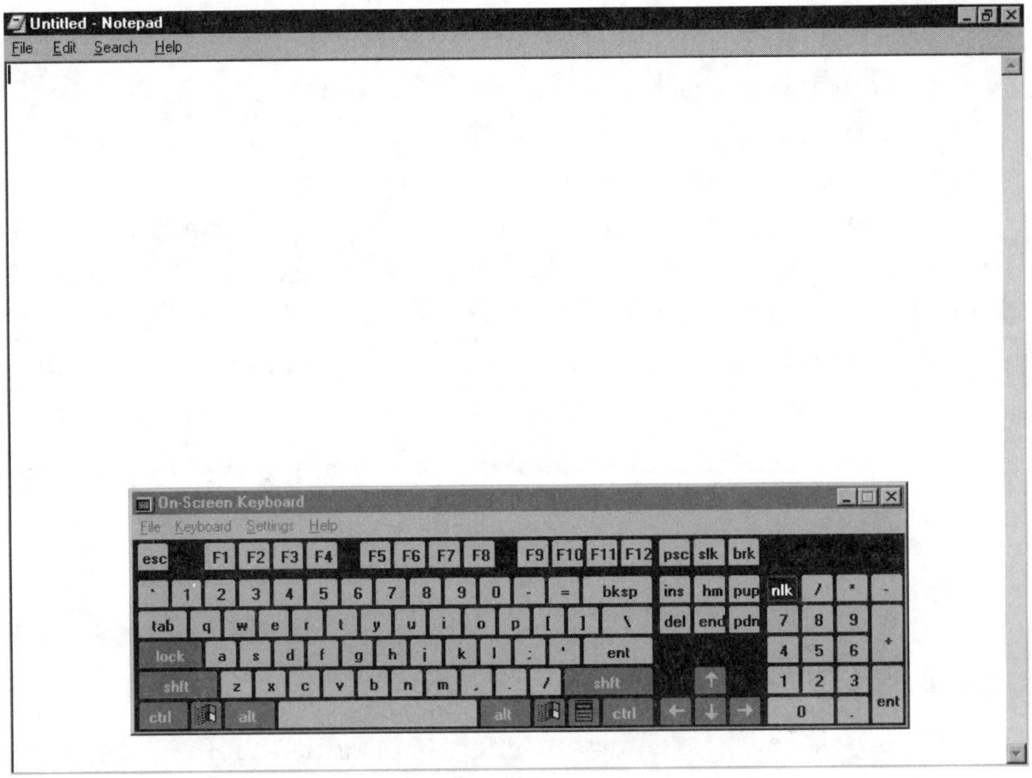

Figure 10-11 Click a key with the mouse to type on the screen.

3. Enter some text.

Click the keys with your mouse to enter text. You can alternate between "typing" and choosing menu commands. When you're finished, click Close to close both Notepad and the keyboard.

TIP *If you can't see a portion of the screen where you need to type, click the keyboard's title bar and drag the keyboard to a new location.*

Do You Need Special Eyeglasses for the Computer?

Since I periodically have this discussion with all my over-50 friends and some of those not even approaching 50, I thought I'd also have it with you. Wearing bifocals while working at the computer may be a pain in the neck—literally. Tilting your head to look through whichever portion of the lens is necessary places your neck and your shoulders in an awkward position and can produce considerable strain on the muscles involved. Over the years, I've found that at various times I've needed a special pair of computer glasses whose lenses were some midway point in strength between my distance lenses and my reading lenses. Some people solve this problem by just taking their glasses off, although this didn't work for me. I got a ferocious headache.

Now my eyes have progressed to the point that I can wear my single-vision reading glasses for viewing the computer screen. This makes at least one fewer pair of glasses to keep track of.

If you spend any amount of time at the computer, do yourself a favor and speak with your ophthalmologist about it. Computer eyestrain is not an uncommon problem these days, and your physician may be able to suggest options that neither you nor I have considered. One of my friends wears progressive lenses, which provide ranges for seeing at a distance, up close, and in the middle. She swears by them, but I could never get used to them. At any rate, your best bet is to seek some professional counsel, especially if you're having headaches, neck pains, or any difficulty focusing on the display. This is one of those challenges in life that can be resolved successfully.

Making the Keyboard Work More to Your Liking

You can use the Accessibility Wizard to modify the way the keyboard works, but you can also change some settings using the Keyboard applet in Control Panel. If you have more than a little difficulty typing at the keyboard, I suggest that you run the Accessibility Wizard and on the Set Wizard Options screen, select the I Have Difficulty Using The Keyboard Or Mouse check box. You can then modify how the keyboard works in some specific ways.

If you simply want to change the repeat delay, the repeat rate, or the cursor blink rate, use the Keyboard applet:

- The repeat delay is the amount of time that elapses before a character repeats when you hold down a key.
- The repeat rate is the speed at which a character repeats when you hold down a key.
- The cursor blink rate is, obviously, how fast or slow the cursor blinks on the screen.

To modify the keyboard, double-click the Keyboard icon in Control Panel to open the Keyboard Properties dialog box, as shown in Figure 10-12. Move the appropriate slider to change the rate.

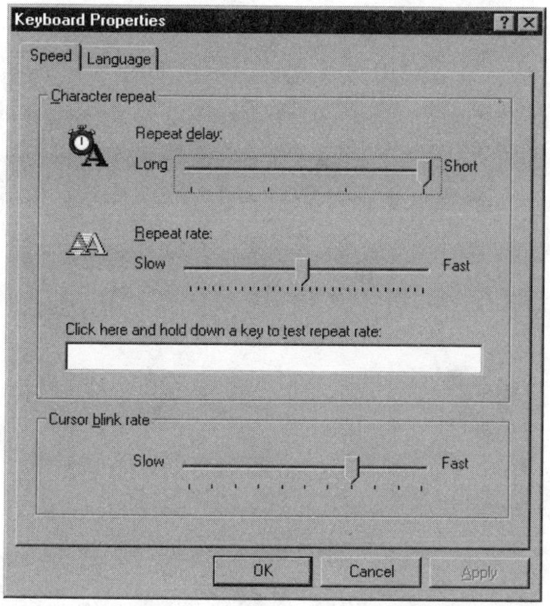

Figure 10-12 The Keyboard Properties dialog box.

By default, Windows installs the keyboard in English language mode. If you want to install and use the keyboard in a layout for other languages, you can use the options on the Language tab in the Keyboard Properties dialog box. For specific instructions, open Microsoft Help And Support (click the Start button and then click Help) and search on *language*.

Taking Charge of the Mouse

You can modify the way your mouse works using the options in the Accessibility Wizard, and you can also use the Mouse applet in Control Panel to modify the mouse. Why would you want to change the way the mouse works? Most notably, because the mouse is, by default, set up for a right-handed person. If you are left-handed, you'll probably want to change this setting as soon as possible after installing Windows or acquiring your computer. You can also adjust the double-click speed of the mouse, the size and shape of the mouse pointer, the speed at which the pointer moves, and other characteristics of the mouse.

You can make the changes in the Mouse Properties dialog box, which opens when you click the Mouse icon in Control Panel. Figure 10-13 shows the Mouse Properties dialog box open at the Buttons tab.

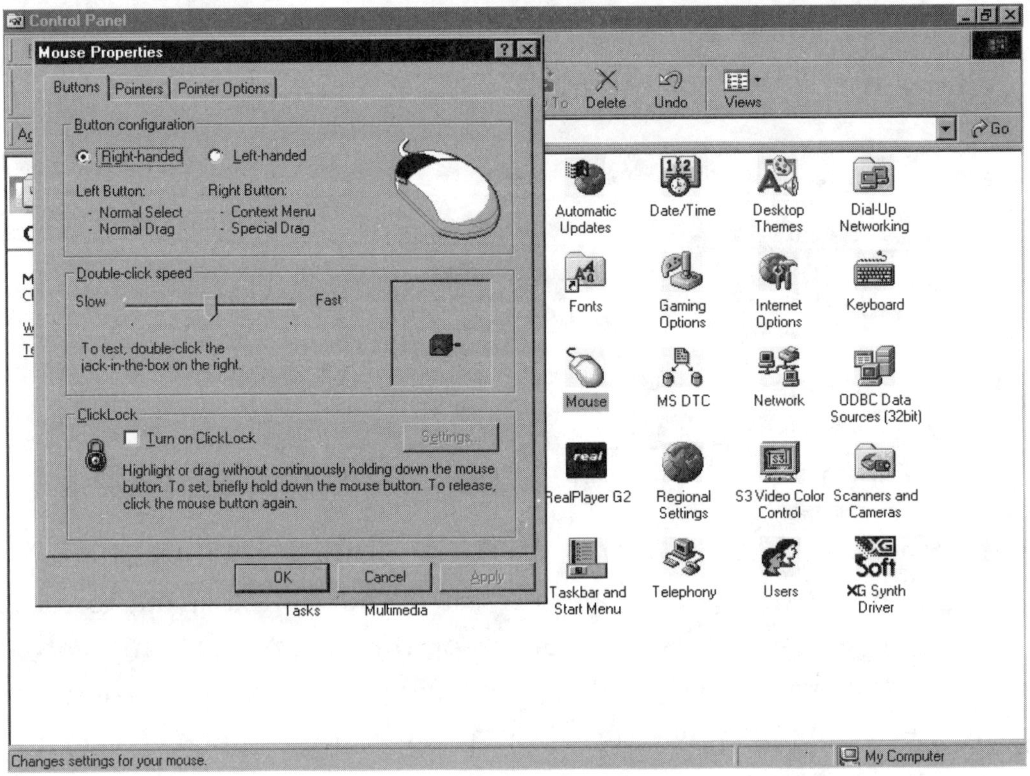

Figure 10-13 The Mouse Properties dialog box open at the Buttons tab.

To switch mouse buttons, simply click the Left-Handed option button. The mouse buttons then function exactly the opposite of the way I describe in this book. For example, to open a shortcut menu, you would click the left button. To open an item in a folder, you would double-click the right button.

If you want to increase or decrease the double-click speed, move the slider in the Double-Click Speed box. Click the little jack-in-the-box to check out the effect of your change. ClickLock is a feature that you can use to drag an item on the screen without continuously holding down the mouse button. If you want to use this feature, click the Turn

On ClickLock check box, and then click the Settings button to open the Settings For ClickLock dialog box, in which you can move the slider to set the amount of time you need to hold down a mouse button.

You can use the other tabs in the Mouse Properties dialog box to make the following modifications:

- Click the Pointers tab to change the size, color, or shape of the pointers that indicate what Windows is doing or what you can do in a certain situation.
- Click the Pointer Options tab to adjust the pointer speed and visibility options. In this tab you also tell Windows to move the pointer to the default button in a dialog box whenever you open a dialog box.

Customizing the Display

Since you can customize your screen display in many ways, I can't begin to describe all of them. I will, however, show you how to make the changes that you're most likely to use.

By default, the icons on your desktop are displayed against a teal background. As you saw earlier, you can display a Web page on your desktop if you are using the Active Desktop, but you have lots of other choices. Figure 10-14 shows a photograph of Yosemite National Park used as a desktop background; this photo is included with Windows.

Figure 10-14 Using a photograph as the desktop background.

Setting the Background

To set the background and to customize the Windows display in other ways, you use the Display Properties dialog box, as shown in Figure 10-15. You can open this dialog box in a couple of ways:

- Double-click the Display icon in Control Panel.
- Right-click an area not covered by an icon on the desktop, and choose Properties from the shortcut menu.

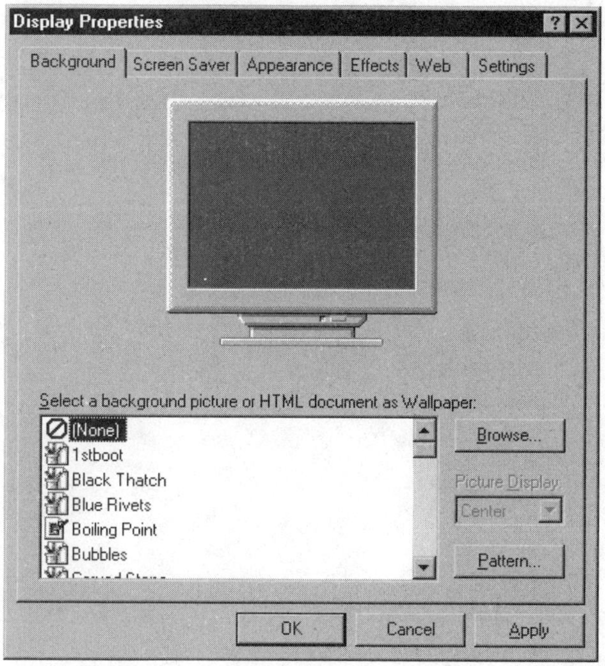

Figure 10-15 The Display Properties dialog box.

As background, you can use one of the files included with Windows, or you can use any picture that you have stored on your computer (a photo of your pet or your grandchildren, for example). To select a background from one of those supplied with Windows, click the Background tab in the Display Properties dialog box, select a background from the list, and then click OK. To select one of your files as the background, open the Display Properties dialog box, click the Background tab, and then follow these steps:

1. **Open the Browse dialog box, as shown in Figure 10-16.**

   Click the Browse button.

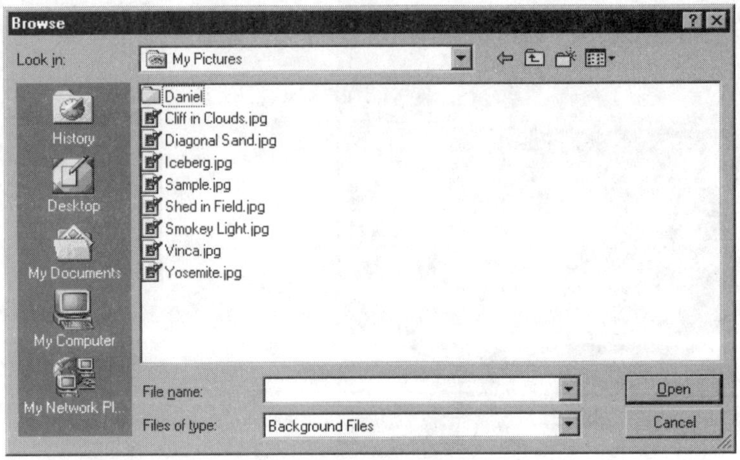

Figure 10-16 The Browse dialog box.

2. **Find the file you want to use.**

   Click the down arrow in the Look In box to locate the folder and the file, and then click Open.

3. **Position your picture.**

   Back in the Display Properties dialog box, click the Picture Display drop-down list, and then select how you want your picture positioned. You'll see a preview on the monitor in the top of the dialog box. When you like what you see on the preview, click OK. Figure 10-17 shows a photo I use as my background.

Figure 10-17 Using a photo as a desktop background.

Using a Screen Saver

A screen saver is an image that appears on your screen after the computer has been idle for a certain amount of time. As you learned in Chapter 1, the original purpose of a screen saver was to keep images from being burned into the screen if a program was allowed to continue running for a long period of time. Today, we no longer need to worry about this problem because technology has made it a nonissue, and screen savers are just for fun.

As with a background for your desktop, you can use any file on your computer as a screen saver, and there are some neat screen savers that you can download from the Internet. You can search on *screen savers* in Microsoft Internet Explorer to find sites.

To use one of the Windows screen savers, click the Screen Saver tab in the Display Properties dialog box, select something from the Screen Saver drop-down list, select a time to wait before the screen saver kicks in by selecting the number of minutes from the Wait spin box, and click OK.

If you have picture files saved on your computer, here's a really super way to use them as a screen saver:

1. **Move all the pictures you want to use into your My Pictures folder.**

   Open Windows Explorer, open your My Documents folder, and then move all the pictures you want to use into the My Pictures folder. (If you have any questions about how to do this, look back in Chapter 4.)

2. **Tell Windows to use the pictures in this folder.**

   In the Display Properties dialog box, click the Screen Saver tab, and in the Screen Saver drop-down list, select My Pictures Screen Saver. You'll see a preview in the little monitor in this dialog box.

3. **Tell Windows how to time and size the pictures.**

   Click the Settings button in the Screen Saver box to open the My Pictures Screen Saver Options dialog box, as shown in Figure 10-18. Use the sliders to specify how often pictures should change and the size of the pictures. If you want to use pictures in a different folder, click the Browse button to open the Browse dialog box and locate them. Use the options at the bottom of the My Pictures Screen Saver Options dialog box to tell Windows whether to stretch small pictures, show the filenames of pictures, use transition effects between pictures, and scroll through the pictures using the keyboard. When you're finished, click OK, and then click OK again in the Screen Saver tab of the Display Properties dialog box.

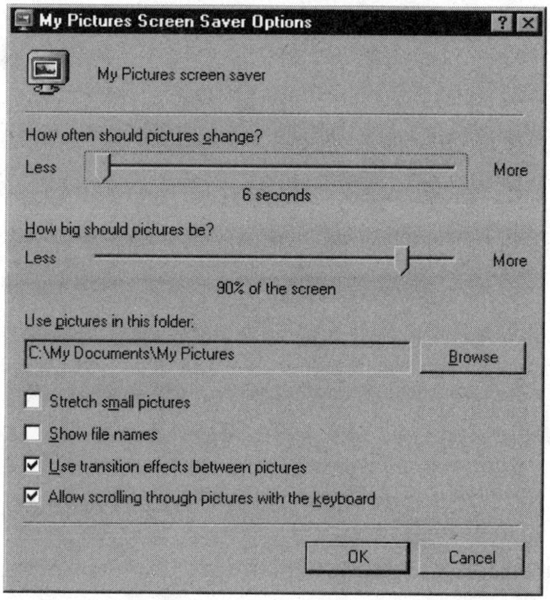

Figure 10-18 The My Pictures Screen Saver Options dialog box.

The Seven Most Important Things to Remember About Customizing Your Computer

1. You can use Control Panel to make most modifications to Windows.
2. If you customize Windows and you share a computer with someone, be sure to tell that person what you've done and how the system now works.
3. If the accessibility features supplied with Windows aren't sufficient to compensate for your particular disability, be sure to visit the Microsoft Accessibility site and check out the resources recommended there.
4. Check out the tabs in the Display Properties dialog box for more ways to customize your computer system than I've discussed in this chapter. If you need help with an option, click the Help button (the one with the question mark), and then click the option.

5. Using personal screen savers is a lot of fun. Set up a screen saver using photos that you've saved as files on your computer.
6. If you're left-handed, be sure to switch the mouse buttons when you install a new version of Windows.
7. To return to the default desktop background, open the Display Properties dialog box, click the Background tab, select None from the list, and click OK.

Summary

You don't have to live with Windows as it comes out of the box or as it was installed by the manufacturer of your computer. You can customize it so that it looks and acts as you prefer. In this chapter, we've looked at how to personalize settings using the applets in Control Panel, and we've taken a brief look at how to customize using the options in the Display Properties dialog box.

Chapter 11

GOT A PROBLEM?

Featuring:

- Getting Information About Your Computer
- Getting in Touch with Microsoft Product Support Services
- Using the Windows Troubleshooters
- Getting Online Help
- Troubleshooting Some Everyday Problems

What's the first thing you do when you run into a problem with your computer? Panic? Throw up your hands in despair? Curse your computer? Call a friend who you think might be more knowledgeable than you? The first three options are natural reactions but not helpful, except insofar as they release your frustration. The last option might or might not be helpful. Often those we think are more computer savvy are just more conversant with the technology and less inhibited in talking about it.

Unless your computer completely crashes, you can use Microsoft Windows itself and the Internet to get help and information that will solve your problems. As you'll see in this chapter, the solutions at your fingertips are numerous and really easy to come by. When you know how to find and use the help that Windows and the Internet provide, you may be the best-equipped person to solve your problem.

Getting Information About Your Computer

Regardless of how you go about troubleshooting a problem, your first step is to become armed with some information about your computer system. You need to know what version of Windows you are running, the type and speed of your computer's processor, the available space on your hard drive, and other similar facts. You can get this information in a couple of ways.

A quick way to find out how much space is being used on your hard drive and how much space is left is to open Windows Explorer (right-click the My Computer icon on the desktop, and choose Explore from the shortcut menu). In the Folders pane, select your hard drive. The pane on the right will display a pie chart that represents your hard drive and shows how much space is being used. Figure 11-1 shows the pie chart representing my drive C.

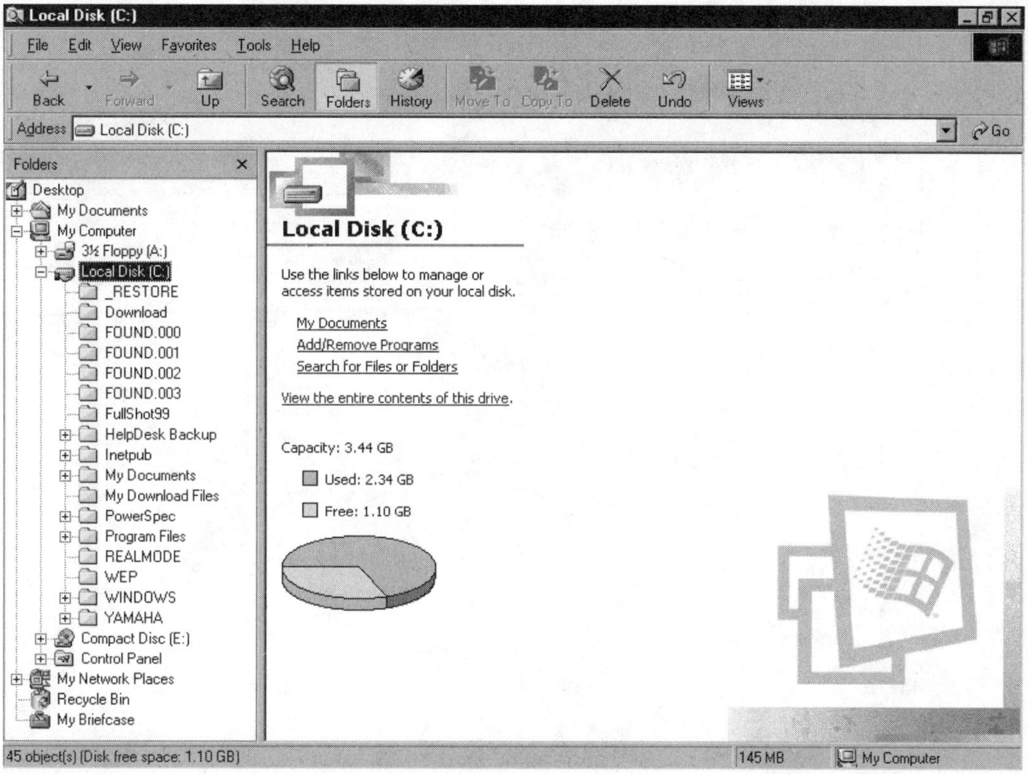

Figure 11-1 Finding out how space is being used on your hard drive.

You can get even more information about your system from the System Information tool. Click the Start button, click Programs, click Accessories, click Systems Tools, and then click System Information to display the screen shown in Figure 11-2. Using this screen, you can get details about every component in your system, including hardware, software, drivers, printers, and so on. Simply click the plus sign next to an item in the System Summary list, and then select a component to display details in the pane on the right. Whenever you go online or access other kinds of technical support, you'll want to have all the information about your system at hand.

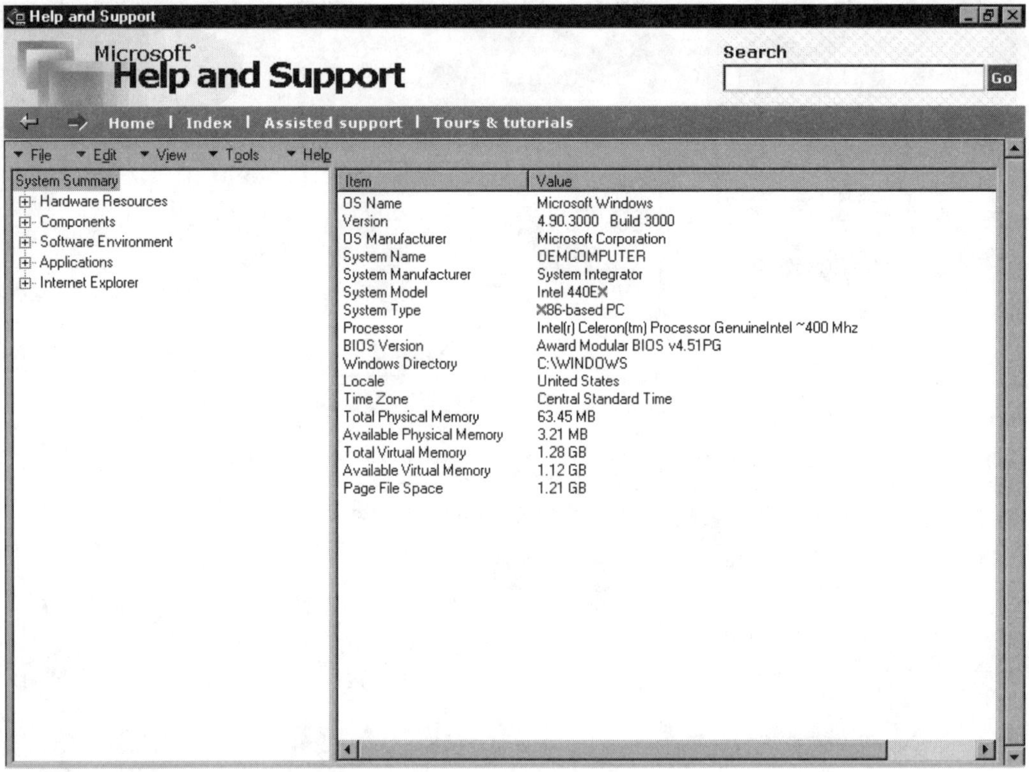

Figure 11-2 Getting information about your computer system.

Getting in Touch with Microsoft Product Support Services

Although I don't suggest that this be your first step when attempting to solve a computer problem, you can get in touch with Microsoft Product Support Services. If you acquired Windows and/or your computer as a stand alone retail product, you may be eligible for two no-charge personal support assists via the Web or the telephone. Before you use either, you need to be at your computer and have the following information readily available:

- The version of Windows you are using.
- The type of hardware you are using.

- The exact wording of any informational or error message that appeared on your screen.
- A description of what happened and what you were doing when the problem occurred.
- A description of how you tried to solve the problem.

You may also need your 20-digit PID (product identification) number, which you'll find on the General tab of the System Properties dialog box in the Registered To section. (Double-click the System icon in Control Panel.) Figure 11-3 shows the PID number for my system, which follows my name.

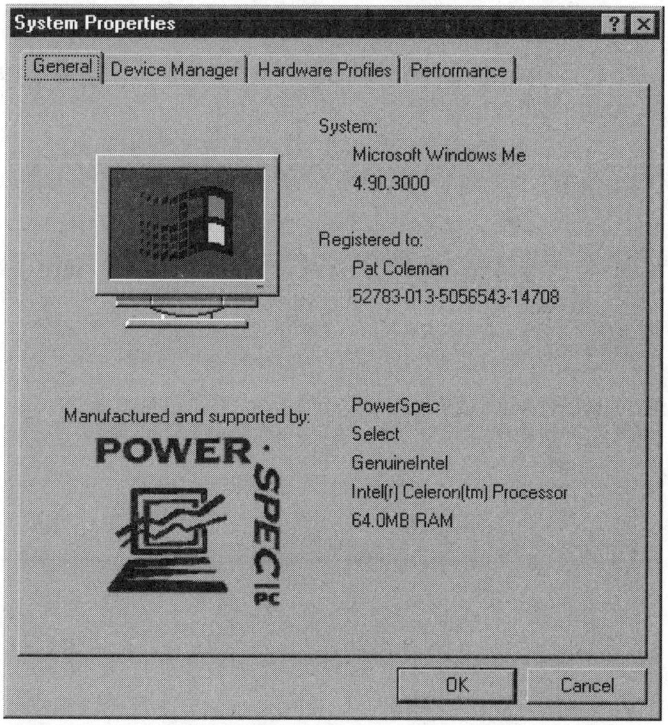

Figure 11-3 Finding your PID number.

To submit your question using the Web, go to *http://www.microsoft.com/support*. You will be notified when your solution is available. To call Product Support Services, dial 425-635-3311. This is not a toll-free number, and Product Support Services is located in Redmond, WA. Your call will be answered Monday through Friday between the hours of 5:00 AM and 9:00 PM (Pacific time) and on Saturday between the hours of 9:00 AM and 3:00 PM (Pacific time), excluding holidays.

Using the Windows Troubleshooters

If you've ever tried to call technical support at any computer company or any other customer service department at any company, you know that you could spend a great deal of time on hold listening to elevator music. A better first step when you run into a problem is the Windows troubleshooters. A troubleshooter is a type of wizard that guides you step-by-step through some questions and answers that attempt to isolate exactly what's going on and that tells you what to do to solve the problem.

To access the Windows troubleshooters, you use the Windows Microsoft Help And Support center (click the Start button, and then click Help). At the opening screen, click the Troubleshooting link in the What Would You Like Help With? list. You'll see the screen shown in Figure 11-4. The individual troubleshooters are nested in the categories listed under Troubleshooting.

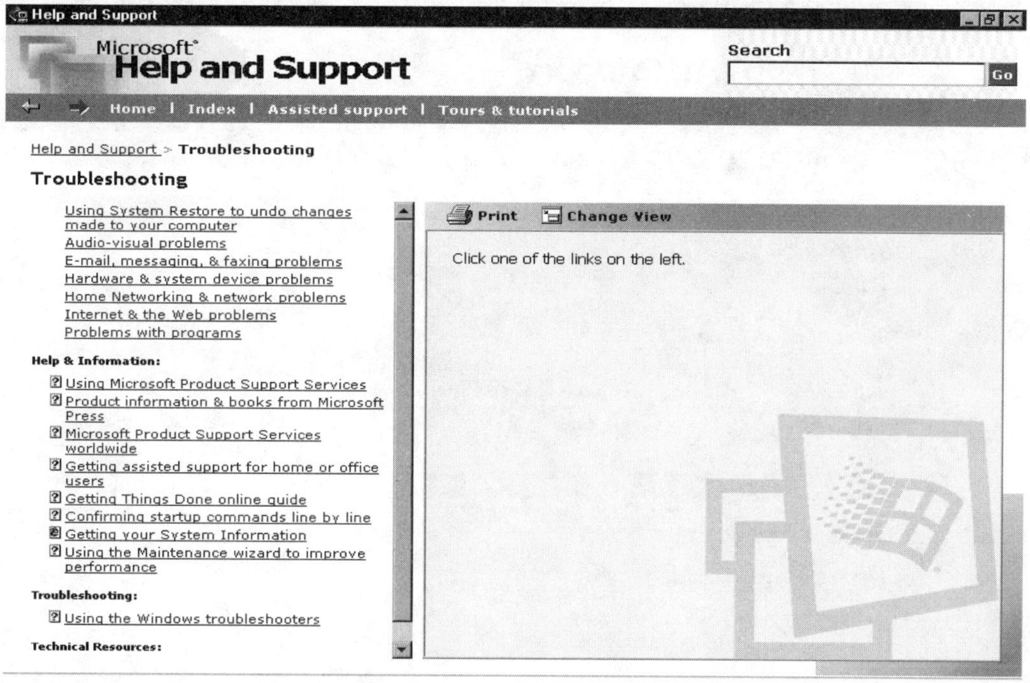

Figure 11-4 Accessing the Windows troubleshooters.

To see how a troubleshooter works, let's assume you're having a problem with your Internet connection. In the Troubleshooting list, click the Internet & The Web Problems link, and then in the next screen click the Internet Connection (ISPs) Troubleshooter link in the Troubleshooting list. Figure 11-5 shows how the troubleshooter starts to identify the problem by asking questions. Select the option that applies to your situation, click Next, and then continue to follow the onscreen instructions to help the troubleshooter sort out the difficulty.

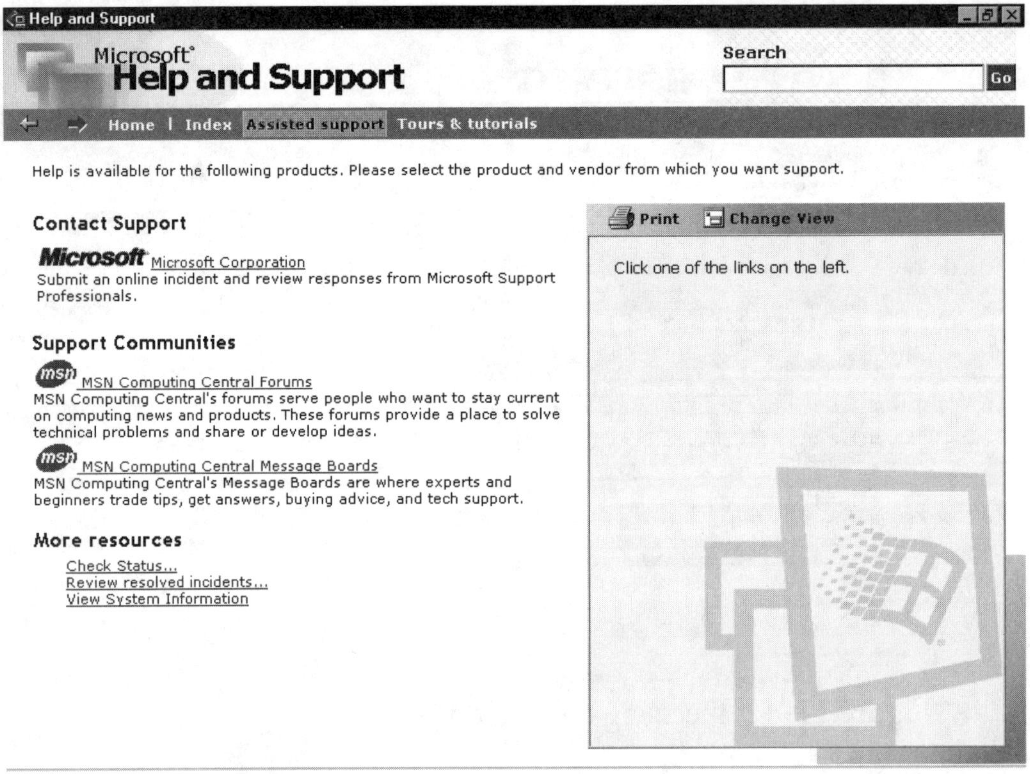

Figure 11-5 Using a Windows troubleshooter.

TIP *Sometimes you can access a troubleshooter from within a Windows program or tool. As you may recall from Chapter 5, you can access the Printing troubleshooter if your test page doesn't print correctly after you install a printer.*

Getting Online Help

If you have a computer problem but you can still get on the Internet, you have access to a ton of help resources. And you have several ways to get to those resources: from throughout Windows and Windows applications as well as through Microsoft Help And Support.

Let's start by looking at the Web resources you can access through the Help And Support screen. Open Help And Support (click the

Start button, and then click Help), and then click the Assisted Support tab near the top of the screen. You'll see the links shown in Figure 11-6.

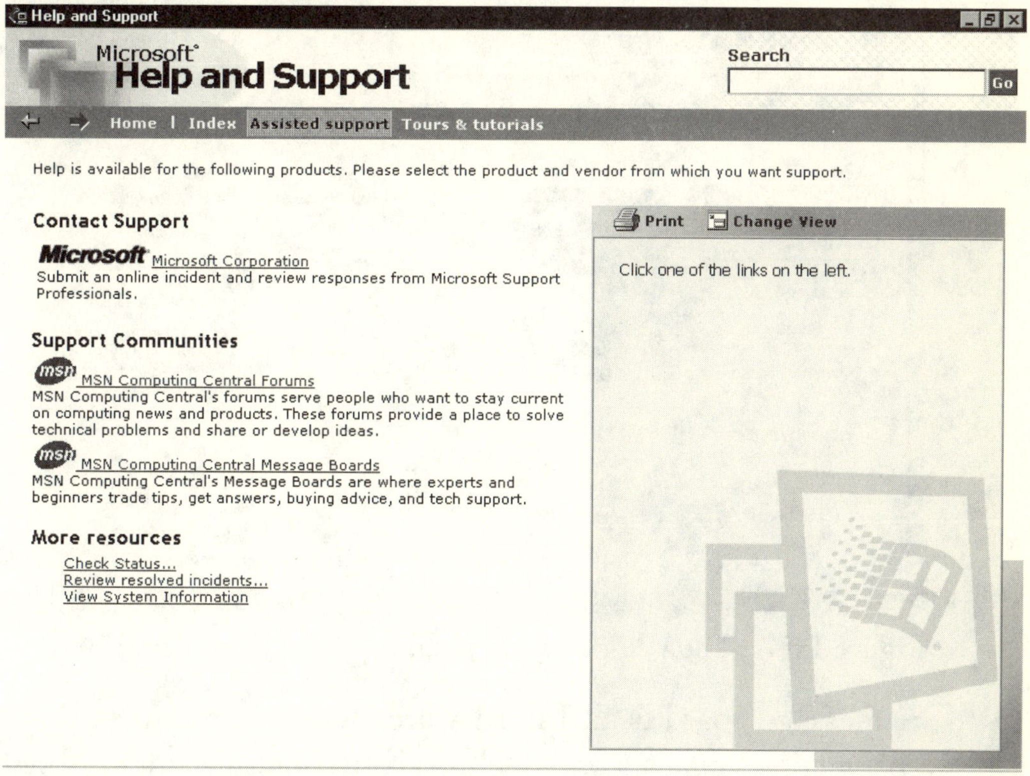

Figure 11-6 Accessing assisted support.

If you click the Microsoft Corporation link, you will be taken to the site for assisted Web support that I mentioned earlier in this chapter. Follow the onscreen instructions to sign in, get a password, and submit your question.

Clicking the MSN Computing Central Forums link opens a pane on the right that lists forums by topic. A forum is simply a site that provides information about a product. Figure 11-7 shows the forum for Windows Me, which is the version of Windows I'm using in this book. To open this page, click the Operating Systems Forum link in the list of forums, and then in the next page that opens, click the Windows Me link. To access support options, click the Support link at the top of this page.

Figure 11-7 The Windows Me forum.

A message board is an Internet area where computer users can exchange tips, get answers to technical questions, get advice about which products to buy, and get technical support. To go to a Windows message board, click the MSN Computing Central Message Boards link in the main Help And Support screen, and then in the list that is displayed on the right, click the Operating Systems Message Boards link. On the following page, click the link that represents your version of Windows. Figure 11-8 shows the page I opened for Windows Me. Click a link to read any posted message. To post a message to a message board, click the Post Message button. You'll need to register with the site by clicking the Sign Me Up! link. After you register, follow the instructions at the site to post a message.

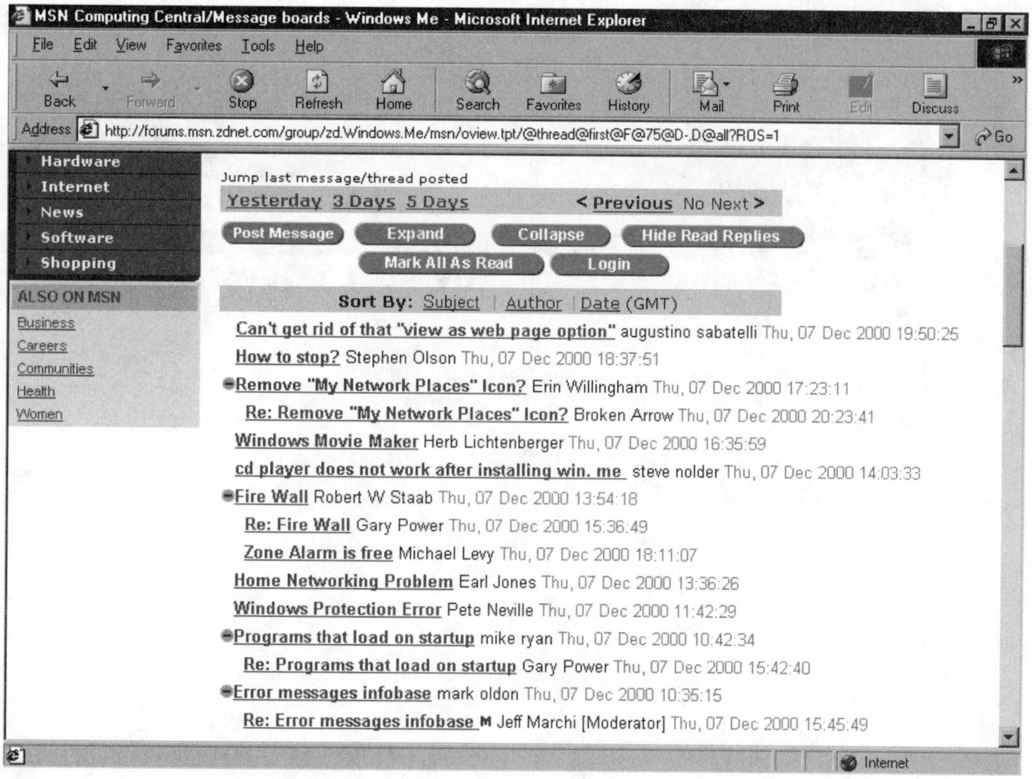

Figure 11-8 The Windows Me message board.

TIP *You can also open the system information screen by clicking the View System Information link on the Assisted Support page in Help And Support.*

You can also access excellent online troubleshooting help from within a Windows application. For example, in Outlook Express, click the Help menu, click Microsoft On The Web, and then click Frequently Asked Questions. You'll see the screen shown in Figure 11-9, which asks and answers questions specific to Outlook Express. Click a question to display the answer.

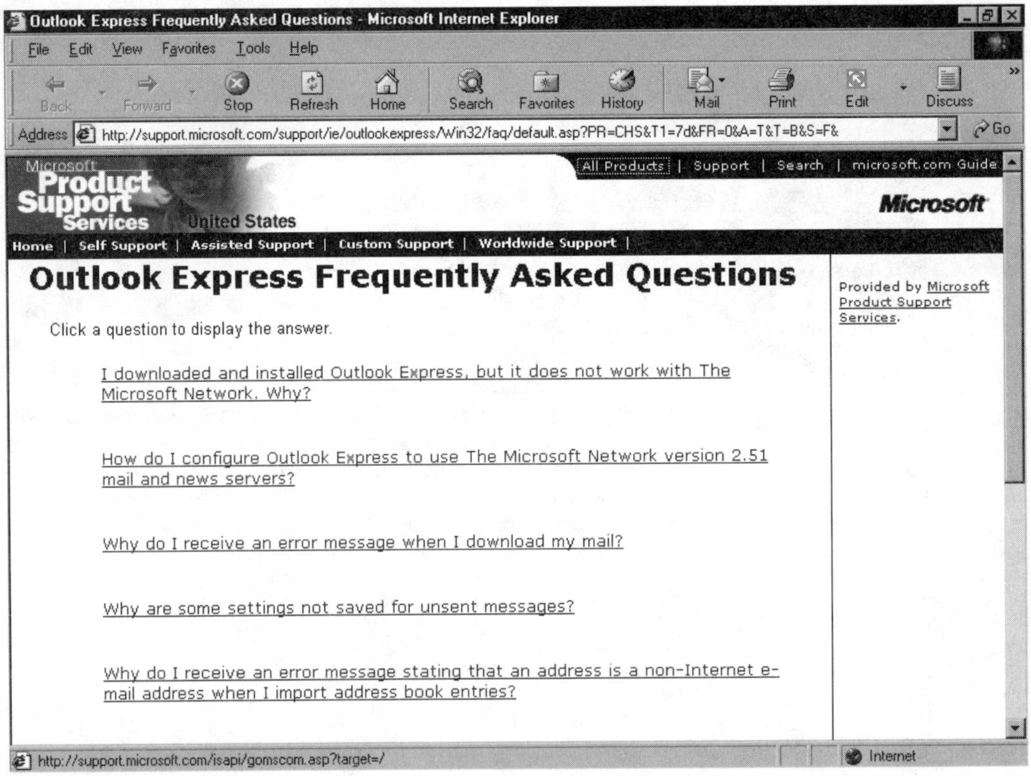

Figure 11-9 Frequently asked questions about Outlook Express.

Troubleshooting Some Everyday Problems

Some problems are more like annoyances than huge difficulties, but if you don't know what to do about them, you'll feel stuck. Here are some Windows annoyances that I seem to face more often than I'd like and some suggestions as to what to do about them.

An Application Stops Responding

No matter which key you press or what you click, nothing happens. Press Ctrl+Alt+Delete, and in the Close Program dialog box, select the program that seems to have died, and click the End Task button. You may lose unsaved information in the program, and you'll have to restart it to continue working with it.

Windows Stops Responding

Again, no matter which key you press or what you click, nothing happens. Press Ctrl+Alt+Delete to restart Windows.

Your Display Is Frozen and Pressing Ctrl+Alt+Delete Doesn't Restart Windows

Turn off your computer (press the On/Off button on the system unit), count to five, and then turn the computer back on. When you restart the system, Windows will probably run ScanDisk, which I described in Chapter 10.

Your Computer Just Keeps Beeping and Beeping

Is a book, your glasses case, or some other item resting on the keyboard? Continuous beeping indicates that the computer is getting too much keyboard input. If something is resting on the keyboard, remove it. If nothing was resting on the keyboard, the key may be stuck because it's dirty. Pull the key up, and take your keyboard to a computer shop for repair, although it's usually cheaper to buy a new keyboard. (I know. Our generation is not crazy about items that have to be thrown away rather than fixed.)

The Dog Chewed Through the Cord That Attaches Your Mouse to the System Unit

This happened to my system once, and I just reattached the little wires inside the cord and wrapped the cord with duct tape. The mouse has been working fine ever since, and that was three years ago. Mice aren't expensive though, so buying a new one is also an option.

In a Folder or on the Desktop, the Icons Are All Messed Up

Right-click an area outside the icons, choose Arrange Icons from the shortcut menu, and then click By Name in the submenu.

You See the Message "Nonsystem Disk or Disk Error" When You Start Your Computer

You have a disk in the floppy drive. Every time Windows starts, it looks first in the floppy drive for a disk that contains system files. If it doesn't find it, Windows next looks to the hard drive. If it finds a disk in the floppy drive that doesn't have system files on it, you'll see this message. Pop the floppy disk out, and press any key to continue booting your computer.

The Seven Most Important Things to Remember When Troubleshooting Your Computer

1. Don't panic.
2. In all likelihood, you didn't cause the problem, so don't beat yourself up.
3. If you have a serious problem and lose—I mean really, really lose—an important file, take time to grieve and be royally frustrated, but don't despair. This happened to me recently, and a friend gave me some very good advice: The document may not be on your computer, but it's still in your head. You can reconstruct it, and it won't take you nearly as long as writing it in the first place. He was right. I slept on it, and the next morning I was able to calmly and rationally retype the document, although, I hope that doesn't happen again soon.
4. Don't call Microsoft Product Support Services the minute something goes wrong. Try to solve the problem using the other resources I've described in this chapter.
5. If you have a problem but can still connect to the Internet, try to find a solution online.

6. Sometimes computer components wear out and break down. Be sure that you always back up any information you don't want to lose.
7. Get the name of a reputable computer repair service in your area so that if your hard drive crashes or some other piece wears out or needs repair, you can quickly get in touch with them. I even found a little company that will "make house calls," and knowing this gives me peace of mind when I'm working on a deadline, which is usually the case. Besides that, I can't lift my system unit.

Summary

Troubleshooting is a skill you will inevitably need to learn as you work with your computer. Never, ever think that you are the only person in the world to face any particular difficulty; we've all been there. What I hope is that you'll actually use the information in this chapter when you face a situation that needs troubleshooting. When you resolve a problem successfully all by yourself, you'll become a much more confident computer user.

Chapter 12

USING THE APPLICATIONS THAT COME WITH WINDOWS

Featuring:

- Creating an Address Book
- Using Calculator
- Using the Windows Word Processors
- Drawing with Paint
- Using the Imaging Program

In Chapter 1, I discussed some popular applications for doing things such as tracing your family tree, managing your finances, organizing your kitchen, and so on. I pointed out that these applications are not part of Windows but run on the Windows operating system.

A few basic applications, though, are included with Windows and are part of the operating system. These applications are called *accessories,* and you find them on the Accessories menu. In this chapter, I'm not going to discuss all of these applications, only those that I think you might have occasion to use. In the next chapter, I'll discuss some entertainment accessories.

Creating an Address Book

The accessory I use the most is Address Book because I store e-mail addresses in my Address Book. I mentioned in Chapter 8 that instead of typing an e-mail address in the To line in the New Message window, you can select it from your Address Book. Doing so is much faster and, of course, more accurate.

You can open Address Book from the Accessories menu or from within Outlook Express:

- From the desktop, click the Start button, click Programs, click Accessories, and then click Address Book.
- From within Outlook Express, click Addresses.

Figure 12-1 shows an empty Address Book, ready for contact information to be entered.

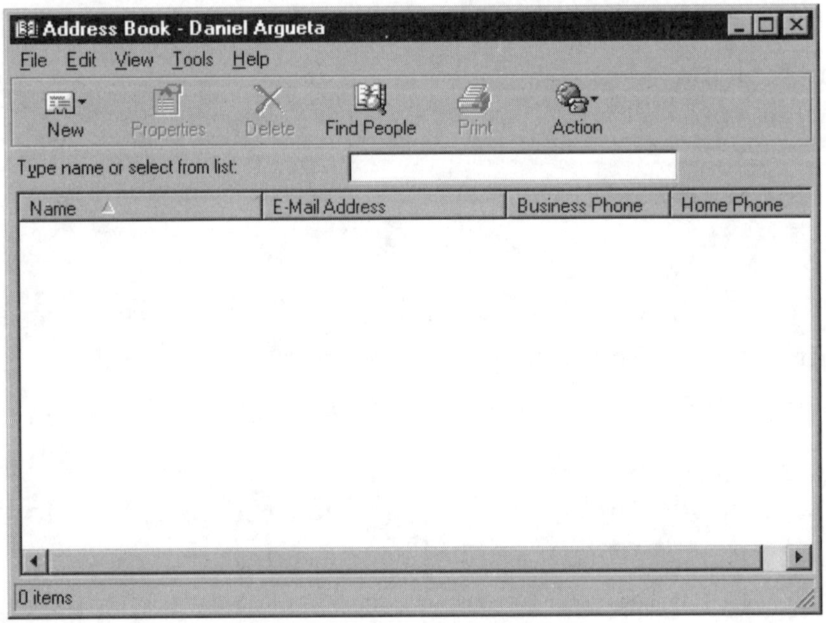

Figure 12-1 An empty Address Book.

Adding Contact Information for an Individual

The easiest way to get e-mail addresses into your Address Book is to reply to someone else's message. You do need to verify that you've set this up in the Options dialog box in Outlook Express. Click the Tools menu, and then click Options to open the Options dialog box. Click the Send tab, and be sure that the Automatically Put People I Reply To In My Address Book check box is selected.

You can use Address Book, to keep track of much more than e-mail addresses, including the following kinds of contact information:

- Full names, street addresses, phone numbers, fax numbers, home page URLs
- Business-related data such as job title, department, company, phone numbers, fax numbers, and pager numbers
- Personal information such as the names of spouse and children and birthday and anniversary dates
- Comments about a contact
- Conferencing and digital ID information

To add these types of information, you use the tabs on the Properties dialog box in Address Book. Follow these steps to add a new contact to your Address Book:

1. **Open the Properties dialog box, as shown in Figure 12-2.**

   In Address Book, click the New button on the toolbar, and then click New Contact.

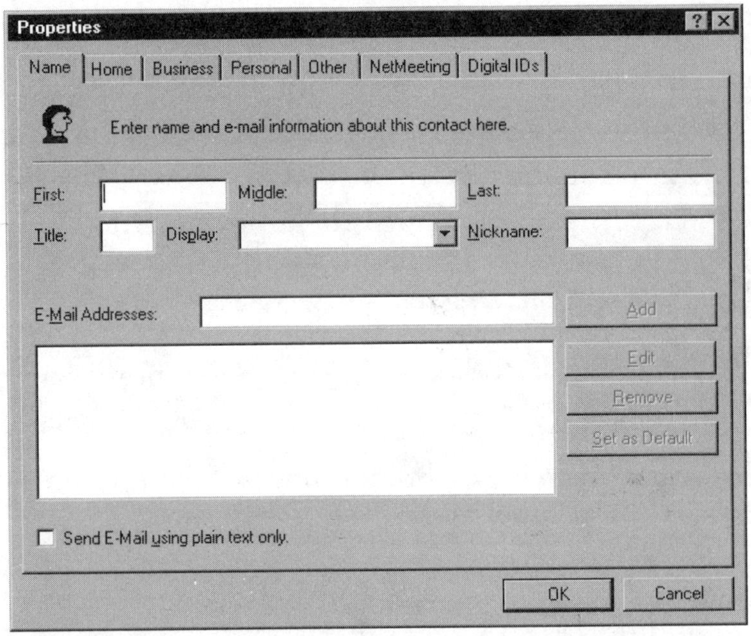

Figure 12-2 The Properties dialog box in Address Book.

2. **Add information about this person.**

   Click the Name, Home, Business, Personal, Other, NetMeeting, and Digital IDs tabs to add as much or as little information as you want. In a tab, press the Tab key to move from one field to the next.

3. **Close the Properties dialog box.**

   When you've finished adding all the information you want about this person, click the Close button. You'll see your new contact listed in the Address Book window.

To send e-mail to a person in your Address Book, in Outlook Express click the To button in the New Message window to open the Select Recipients dialog box, click the person's name in the list, click the To button, and then click OK.

Adding Group Contact Information

If you regularly send e-mail to a group of people, such as a club or an organization or family members, you don't have to select each address individually. You can set up a group in Address Book, and then simply send mail to the group. Figure 12-3 shows an e-mail message I sent to members of my book club. As you can see, rather than entering each person's name in the To line, I've set up a group and named it Book Club, and now I can just select Book Club from my Address Book and send the message to all our members.

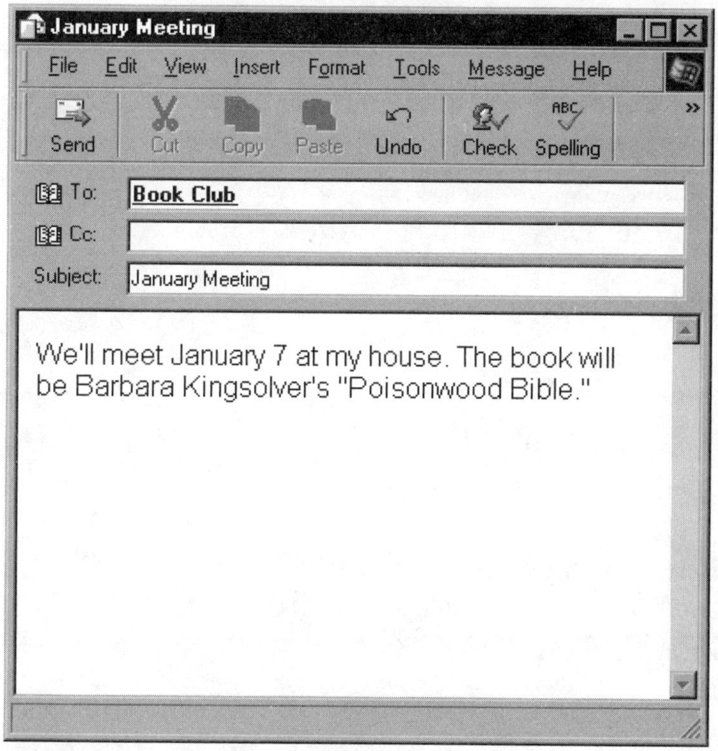

Figure 12-3 Sending mail to a group.

To set up a group, follow these steps:

1. **In Address Book, open the Properties dialog box for a group, as shown in Figure 12-4.**

   Click the New button, and then click New Group.

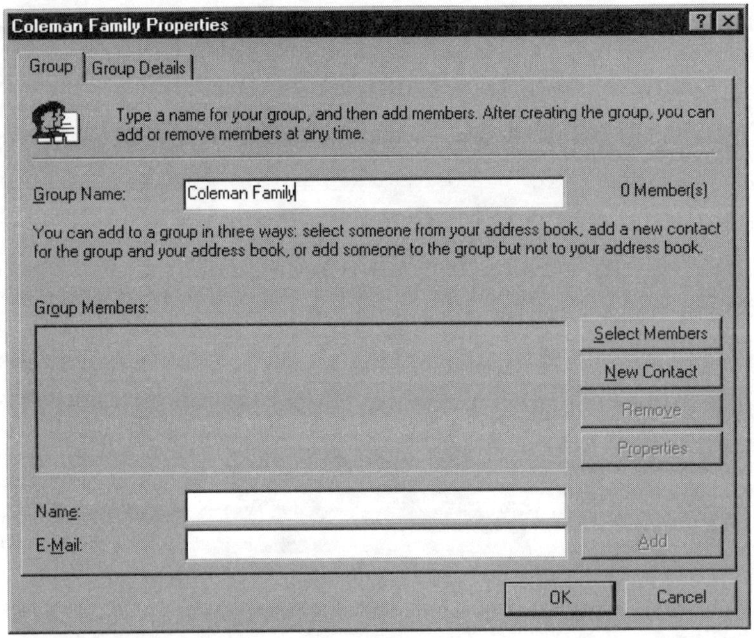

Figure 12-4 Setting up a new group in Address Book.

2. **Name the group.**

   In the Group Name box, type a name for your group.

3. **Add members to your group.**

   You can add members in the following ways:

   - Click the Select Members button to open the Select Group Members dialog box, select a name from the list, click the Select button, and then click OK.
   - Click the New Contact button to open the Properties dialog box for a new contact, enter contact information, and click OK to add a member to the group and to your Address Book.
   - In the Name and E-Mail boxes at the bottom of the dialog box, enter information to add someone to the group but not to your Address Book.

When you're finished creating your group, click OK. Now the group name will appear in boldface in the main Address Book window.

Finding Contact Information About People

A directory service on the Internet is really a giant electronic phone book that you can use to locate e-mail addresses as well as physical addresses and phone numbers. In Address Book, you can search several directory services. To do so, you use the Find People dialog box, which is shown in Figure 12-5. To open the Find People dialog box, click the Find People button on the toolbar.

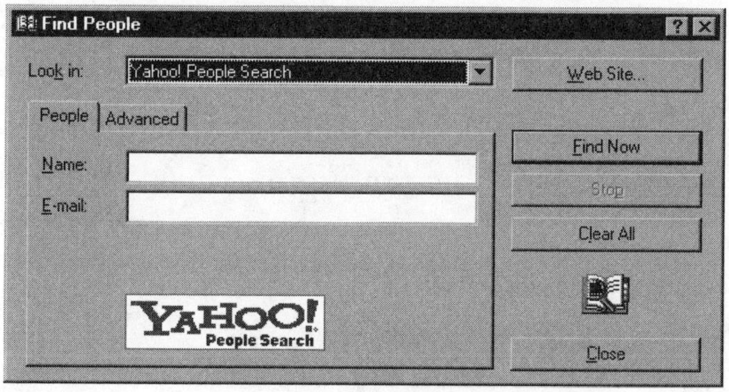

Figure 12-5 The Find People dialog box.

To locate contact information about someone, open the Find People dialog box, and then follow these steps:

1. **Select a directory service.**

   In the Look In drop-down list, select a service. It doesn't matter which one you select; if the first one doesn't turn up results, select another and try it.

2. **Enter some information about the person you're looking for.**

   In the Name or E-Mail box, fill in the information you know, and then click Find Now. If you get too many results, add more information; if you get too few, try searching only on the last name.

Printing Your Address Book

If you will be away from your computer and you keep all your contact information in Address Book, you can print it out and take it with you. You can print in three formats:

- Memo prints all the information you have stored.
- Business Card prints the information you'd typically find on a business card.
- Phone List prints only your contacts' names and telephone numbers.

To print in one of the formats, click the Print button on the toolbar to open the Print dialog box, as shown in Figure 12-6. Select whether you want to print a selection or all of your contacts, select a print style, specify the number of copies, and click OK.

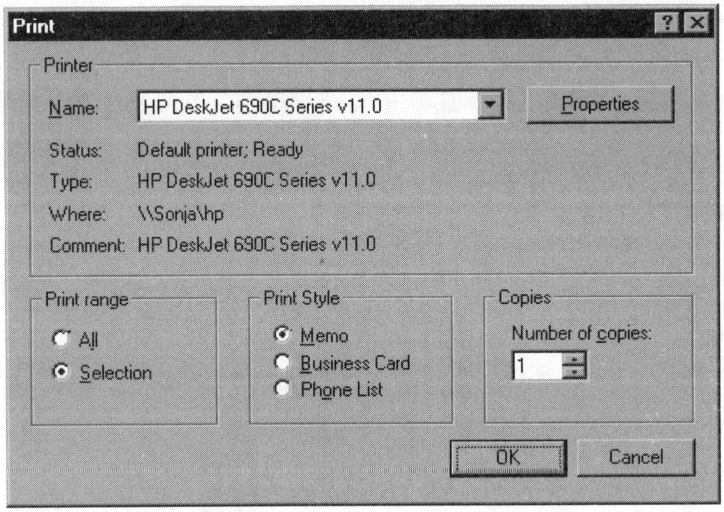

Figure 12-6 Printing your Address Book.

Creating and Printing a Map

This feature is another reason that Address Book is my most-used accessory. If you live in a large city or metropolitan area, it's become typical to include a map with an invitation to a party or some other gathering. But if a map is not included, you can easily create one using Address Book. You can print the map or print driving instructions to take along.

To create and print a map for a location that's not listed in your Address Book, follow these steps:

1. **Open the Properties dialog box.**

   Click the New button on the toolbar, and then click New Contact.

2. **Enter the address.**

   Click the Home tab or the Business tab, and enter the address information in the appropriate boxes.

3. **Create a map.**

   Click the View Map button. You'll see a map of the location in Microsoft Internet Explorer, as shown in Figure 12-7. (You may be required to provide some additional information before the map can display.) To get driving instructions, scroll down and click the Get Driving Instructions To This Location link.

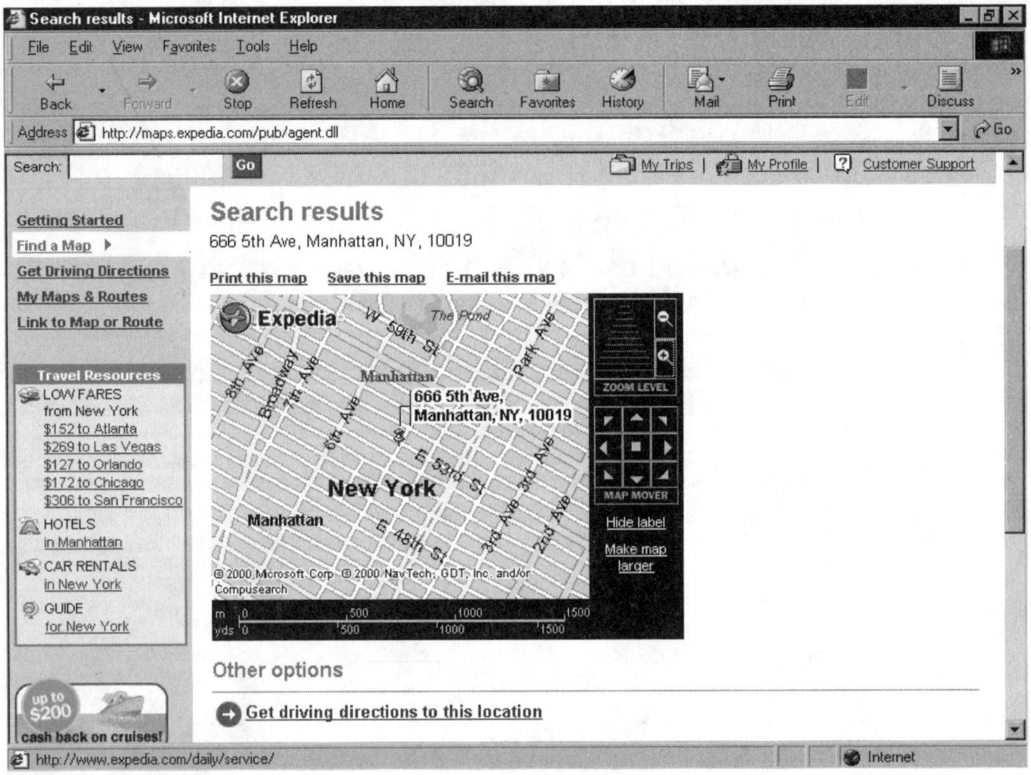

Figure 12-7 A map created using Address Book.

You can print this map, save it, or e-mail it to someone just as you would any other Web page.

NOTE *To create a map for a location that's already in your Address Book, simply select the address and click the View Map button.*

Using Calculator

The Windows Calculator accessory is simply an onscreen version of the handheld variety, and it works in much the same way. You can use it to perform standard operations or statistical operations. When you get a result, you can copy and paste it into other applications. (Click the Edit menu, and then click Copy.)

To open Calculator, click the Start button, click Programs, click Accessories, and then click Calculator. You can work with Calculator in two views: Standard and Scientific. In Figure 12-8, the Calculator on the left is in Standard view, and the Calculator on the right is in Scientific view. To change from one view to the other, click the View menu. When you close Calculator and then reopen it, it opens in whichever view was last displayed.

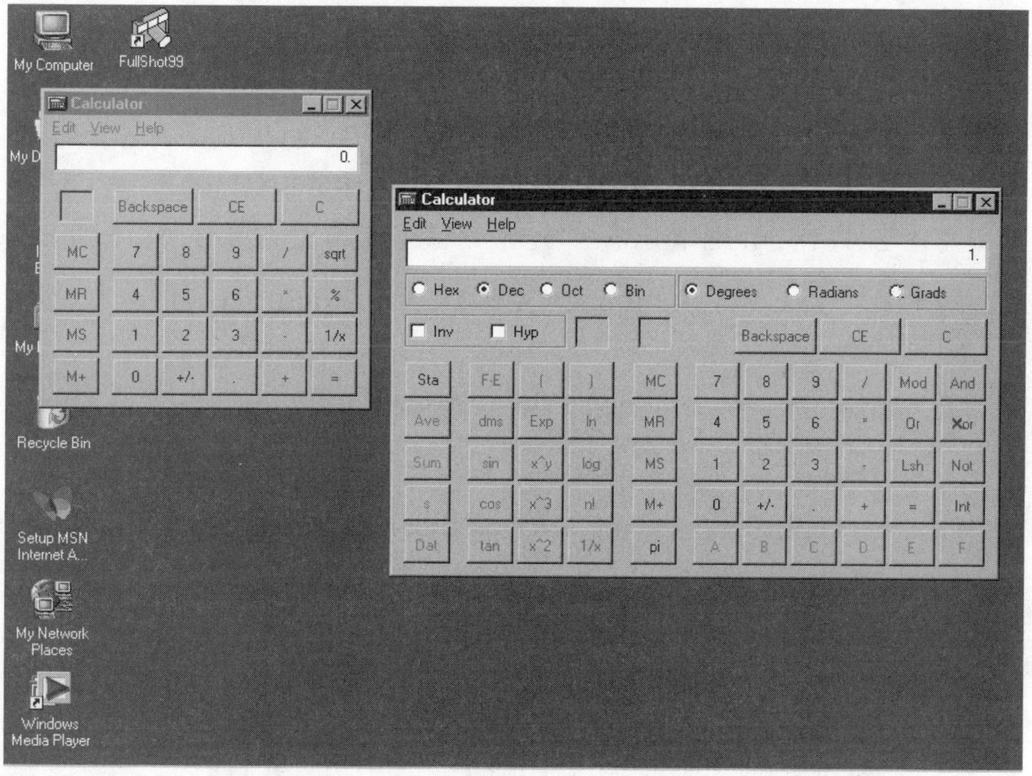

Figure 12-8 The Standard Calculator (on the left) and the Scientific Calculator (on the right).

When you open Calculator, the numbers on the numeric keypad become active. In other words, the effect is the same as if you pressed the Num Lock key. You can press the keys on the keypad to enter calculations, or you can click the numbers on Calculator with the mouse. In either case, you perform operations on the Windows Calculator just as you would on a handheld calculator.

In both Standard and Scientific view, Calculator has the following keys in addition to the number keys:

- * represents the multiplication sign and / represents the division sign.
- **Backspace** deletes a single digit.
- **CE** deletes the last entry. You can also press the Delete key to erase the last entry.
- **C** removes a calculation altogether. You can also press the Esc key to do this.
- **MC** clears a number from Calculator's memory.
- **MR** recalls a number from Calculator's memory.
- **MS** stores a number in Calculator's memory and removes whatever was already in memory.
- **M+** adds a number to the number in Calculator's memory.

In Standard view, Calculator also has the following keys:

- **sqrt** calculates the square root of a number. For example, if you enter 36 and then click sqrt, the result is 6.
- **%** lets you add, subtract, divide, and multiply a number by a percentage. For example, if you enter the number 10, click the plus sign (+), enter the number 50 followed by the percent sign (%), and then click equals (=), the result is 15.
- **1/x** is the Inverse key. You use it to divide 1 by a value.

For information about how to perform scientific and statistical calculations, click Calculator's Help menu to open Calculator Help, click the Performing Calculations link, and select either the Perform A Statistical Calculation topic or the Perform A Scientific Calculation topic.

Using the Windows Word Processors

Windows includes two word-processing applications: Notepad and WordPad. Notepad is a simple text editor, and WordPad is a simple word processor. Which you use depends on what you're doing, but most of the time these applications do not have the features that you'll want when you produce lengthy, complicated documents. In this section, I'll briefly describe both and show you the basics of how to use each.

Using Notepad

You may recall that when you view the source of a Web page in Internet Explorer, the HTML opens in Notepad. Notepad is a good application if you want to handcode HTML rather than using an application such as Microsoft FrontPage. The reason for this is that Notepad provides no special formatting, and HTML pages must be plain text (not boldface, italics, or other effects).

Consequently, if you ever use Notepad, it will only be to create a simple note or memo or the like. To be honest, about the only time I use Notepad is to open a Web page and look at the source. To open Notepad, click the Start button, click Programs, click Accessories, and then click Notepad. If you click the menus, you'll see that this application provides only basic functionality, such as the ability to save and print a simple document and to search for something within an open document. In addition, often when you install a new application on your computer, it will include a ReadMe file that contains late-breaking information about the product. A ReadMe file typically opens in Notepad. Figure 12-9 shows one of the ReadMe files that comes with Windows Me open in Notepad.

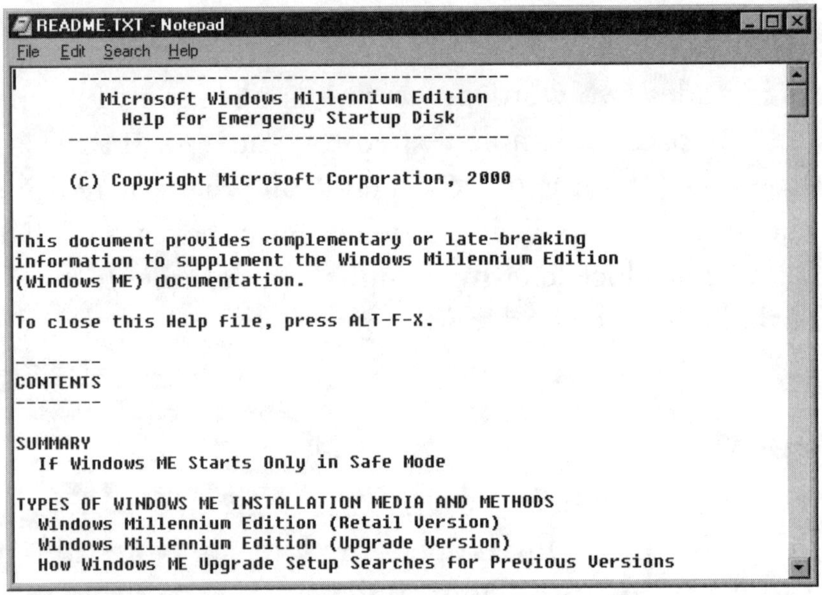

Figure 12-9 A ReadMe file open in Notepad.

Using WordPad

WordPad, unlike Notepad, is a real word processor, though not nearly as powerful or as full-featured as Microsoft Word or Corel Word Perfect or several others. If you have one of these sophisticated word processors installed on your system, the WordPad window, which is shown in Figure 12-10, will look familiar.

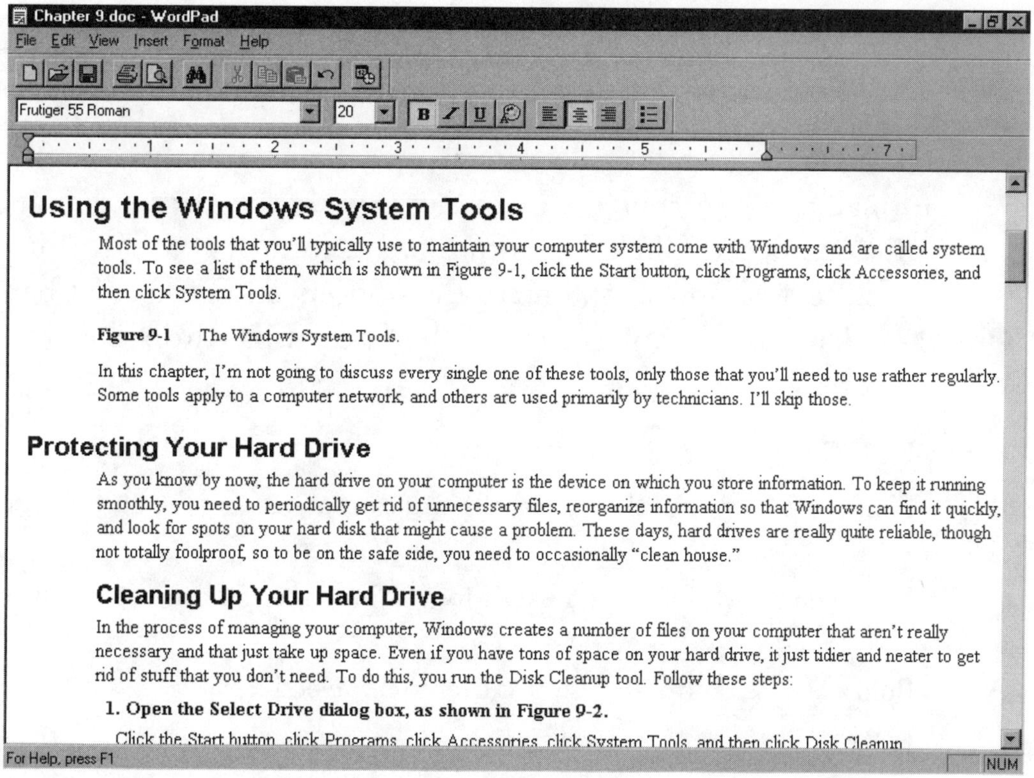

Figure 12-10 A chapter file from this book open in WordPad.

At the top of the WordPad window is the menu bar, and beneath that is the toolbar. Following are the Format bar and the ruler. If you don't see all these bars and the ruler in your screen, click the View menu, and then click to display the other elements. To display a ScreenTip that describes a button on any toolbar, point to the button.

The options on the menus are similar to those you find in most Windows applications. You use the buttons on the Format bar to add special effects to text. You can format as you go along, or you can enter all of the text of your document and then go back and format. To format as you go along, select an option on the Format bar and then enter your text. Click the option again to turn it off. To format selected text, simply click one of the options on the Format bar. Table 12-1 lists and describes each of the Format bar drop-down lists and buttons.

BUTTON	WHAT IT DOES
Font	Displays a list of fonts you can use for the current text selection.
Font Size	Displays a list of font point sizes you can use for the current text selection.
Bold	**Boldfaces** the current text selection.
Italic	*Italicizes* the current text selection.
Underline	Underlines the current text selection.
Color	Displays a list of colors you can use to color the current text selection.
Align Left	Aligns the current text selection with the left margin.
Center	Centers the current text selection horizontally.
Align Right	Aligns the current text selection with the right margin.
Bullets	Turns the selected paragraphs into a list of bulleted items.

Table 12-1 Options on the WordPad Format bar.

To create a simple document in WordPad, follow these steps:

1. **Open the New dialog box, as shown in Figure 12-11.**

   Click the File menu, and then click New.

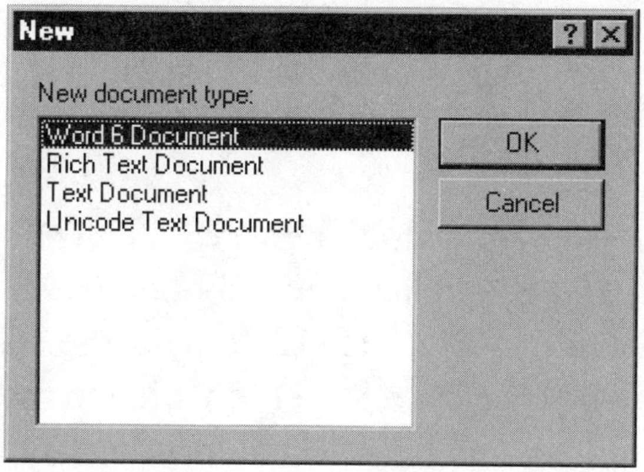

Figure 12-11 The New dialog box.

2. **Select a document type.**

   From the New Document Type list, select a document type. Most of the time you'll probably want to choose Word 6 Document, but for your information, here's an explanation of each of these types:

   - Word 6 Document: You can open and save the document in any version of Microsoft Word starting with version 6 and continuing to the latest version.
   - Rich Text Document: You can include character formatting and open the document in any of several word-processing programs.
   - Text Document: Your document will contain no text formatting.
   - Unicode Text Document: You can include characters from any of the world's writing systems, including Greek, Chinese, Cyrillic, and so on.

   Click OK after you select a document type.

3. **Create your document.**

   At the insertion point, start typing your document. To start a new paragraph, press the Enter key.

NOTE *WordPad doesn't include a spelling checker, so read over your document before you print it or otherwise distribute it.*

4. **Save your document.**

   When you've finished typing your document, you'll want to save it. Click the File menu, and then click Save to open the Save As dialog box, which is shown in Figure 12-12. This is the standard Windows Save As dialog box. Select a folder in which to save your document, give the document a name, select a document type, and then click the Save button. (If you have any questions about how to use this dialog box, look back in Chapter 4.)

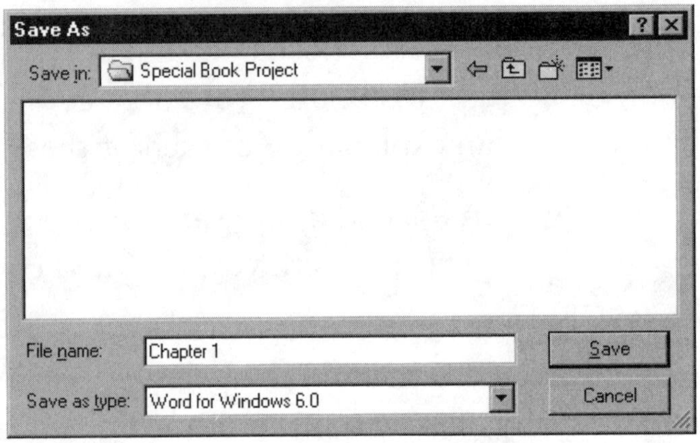

Figure 12-12 The Save As dialog box.

Drawing with Paint

Paint is a program that you can use to create and edit graphic images—simple diagrams, logos, scanned photographs, even complex artistic creations. To open Paint, click the Start button, click Programs, click Accessories, and then click Paint. Paint opens with a blank area in which you can draw, open an image from your scanner or digital camera, and so on, as shown in Figure 12-13.

Figure 12-13 The Paint program.

To draw in Paint, you use the items in the toolbox, which is to the left of the drawing area. Point to a tool to display a ScreenTip that describes what it is. To use a tool, select it, and then use it to draw in the drawing area. At the bottom left of the screen is the color box. You use the first part of the color box to set the background and foreground colors. To create a drawing, select a drawing tool; select a line width, a brush shape, or rectangle type. Then select a background color and a foreground color, and start drawing.

Using Paint takes some practice to become familiar with the tools and the way they work. For more information, click the Help menu, and then click Help Topics.

Using the Imaging Program

When you double-click an image file in Windows Explorer, it opens in Image Preview, which is part of the Imaging program. Imaging is similar to Paint in that you can use it to view and manipulate digital images, but Imaging provides many more tools and many more options. For example, you can annotate images; change their size, color, and resolution; and send images as e-mail attachments. Imaging even has a toolbar you can use with a scanner.

To open Imaging, click the Start button, click Programs, click Accessories, and then click Imaging. Figure 12-14 shows the Imaging window in which a scanned image is displayed. At the top of this window is the menu bar, and beneath that is the Standard toolbar. On the next row at the left is the Scanning toolbar, which is grayed out if you do not have a scanner attached to your computer, and at the right is the Imaging toolbar. In the lower left of the window is the Annotation toolbar.

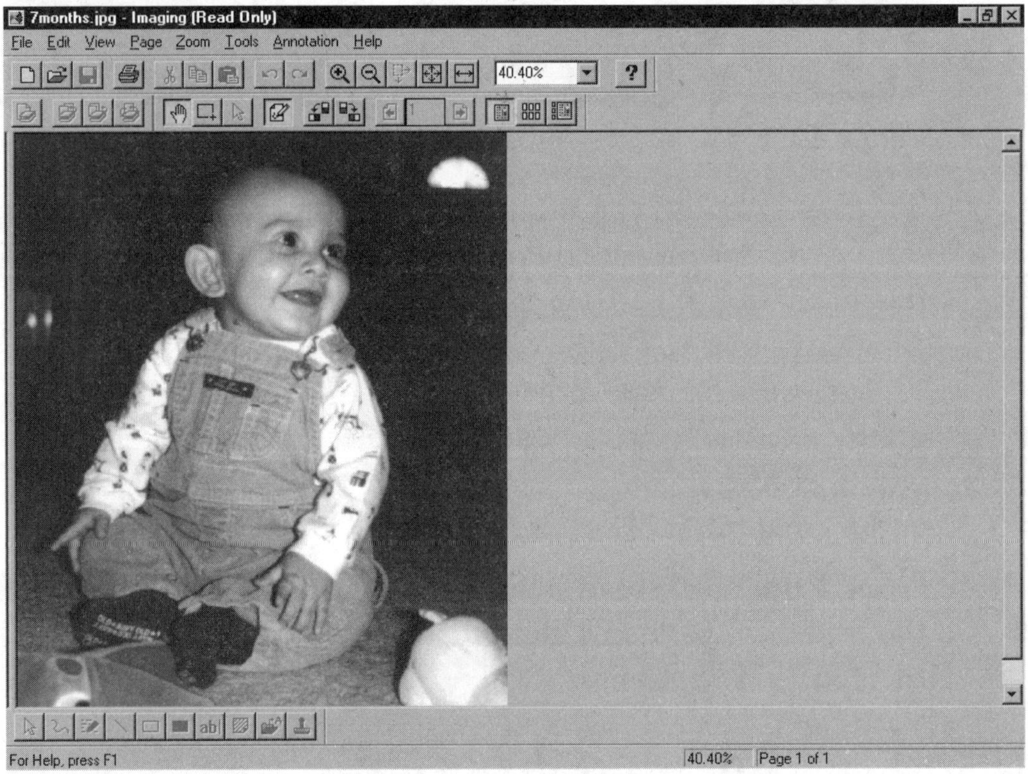

Figure 12-14 The Imaging window.

In this section, I simply want to introduce you to the Imaging program and show you how to use it to open and view images. For details, click the Help menu, and then click Imaging Help.

To open an image that is stored on your computer, click the File menu, click Open to display the Open dialog box, select the image, and click Open. The Open dialog box is a standard Windows dialog box that you have used many times already in this book. To change the size of the image display, click the Zoom menu. You can specify a certain percentage, you can zoom in and out, and so on.

The Seven Most Important Things to Remember About the Windows Applications

1. Entering contact information in Address Book lets you more easily and more accurately enter e-mail addresses in Outlook Express.
2. Print a map to almost any location using the View Map feature in Address Book.
3. Sometimes it's handier to access the Windows Calculator onscreen than it is to locate a calculator on your physical desktop.
4. When you view the source of a Web page in Internet Explorer, the HTML opens in Notepad.
5. Notepad is a simple word processor that you will probably use very seldom, but if you don't have a full-fledged word-processing program installed on your computer, you can use WordPad to create formatted documents. Read them carefully, however, because WordPad doesn't include a spelling checker.
6. The Paint program is a bit tricky to use, but if you want to experiment with computer graphics, using Paint is a good way to start.
7. If you have a digital camera or a scanner, explore the options in Imaging for viewing and manipulating your digital photos.

Summary

Several applications are included with Windows, and this chapter has briefly looked at those I think you might most often use. I encourage you to take advantage especially of Address Book for storing contact information. You can then automatically collect e-mail addresses of those who send you messages, which is a handy, neater alternative to sticky notes or a paper-and-pen address book.

Chapter 13

HAVING FUN

Featuring:

- Playing the Windows Games
- Playing Multimedia
- Customizing the Windows Sounds

More and more, Microsoft Windows and your computer are becoming an entertainment unit. If you are a computer games aficionado, this chapter is not for you. I'm not going to talk about force-feedback joysticks, 3-D flight simulators, online role-playing games, or how you can upgrade a standard computer to dream system configuration for zipping through the digital world.

This chapter concerns the games and entertainment features that come with the Windows operating system. If you have Windows Me, the latest version of Windows for home use and the version I use in this book, you may be pleased to find that there are some new games and access to multiplayer games on the Internet.

In the first part of this chapter, I'll talk about the games that come with Windows, and then I'll discuss how you can use Windows to play multimedia. Multimedia is a catchall term that describes a device that can produce more than one kind of output. For example, your TV is a multimedia device because it can produce video and sound. Your computer, though, is even more multimedia capable; it can produce advanced levels of animation, video, sound, and graphics while at the same time letting you interact as you view a presentation.

Playing the Windows Games

Windows Me includes two kinds of games: those you can play on your computer by yourself and those you can play with others when you are connected to the Internet. If you have an earlier version of Windows, you'll find the games on the Accessories menu that we looked at in the previous chapter. If you have Windows Me, click the Start button, click Programs, and then click Games to open the Games menu.

Playing Alone

Windows may include the following games that you can play by yourself or against the computer:

- Classic Hearts
- Classic Solitaire
- FreeCell
- Minesweeper
- Pinball
- Spider Solitaire

To start any game, simply select it from the Games menu. For the rules and instructions on how to play any game, click the Help menu, and then click Help Topics.

Classic Hearts

When you play Classic Hearts, you play against the computer. Click Classic Hearts to start Hearts, click the Games menu, and then click New Game to deal the cards. You'll see something similar to Figure 13-1.

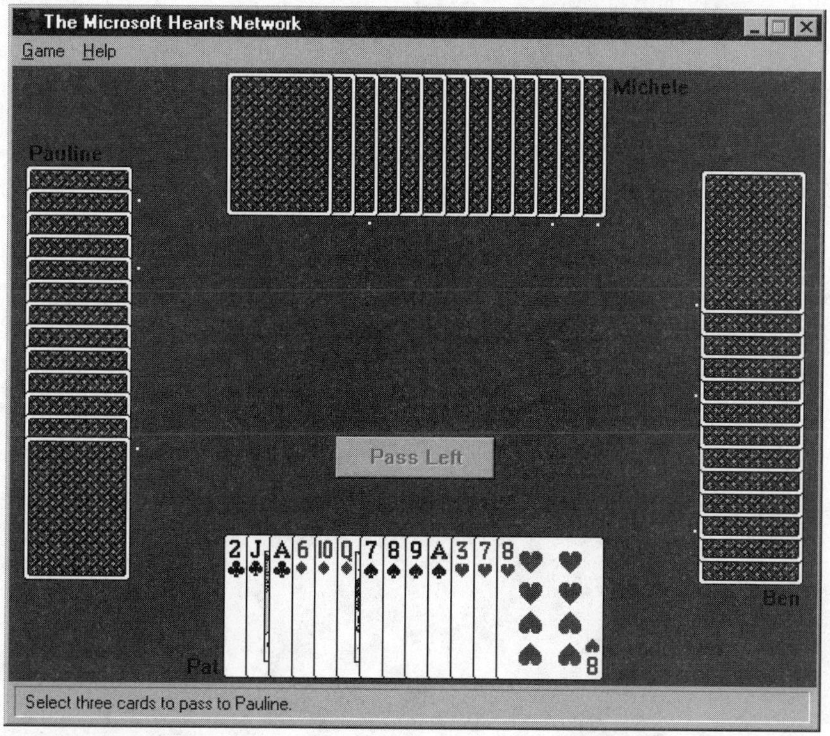

Figure 13-1 Playing a game of Hearts against the computer.

The object of Hearts is to collect as few tricks as possible that contain hearts and thereby have the lowest score at the end of the game. At the end of a hand, you get 1 point for each heart in your pile of tricks and 13 points if you get saddled with the queen of spades. The game continues until one player gets 100 points. If you win all the hearts and the queen of spades (called Shooting the Moon), you get no points, and each of the other players gets 26 points.

Each player first passes three cards to the player on the left, except for the fourth hand when no cards are passed. The player with the two of clubs leads it first. Each player in turn must play a card, following suit if possible. In any case, you cannot play a heart or the queen of spades on the first trick. The person who plays the highest card of the suit that was led takes the trick and then leads another card. You cannot lead a heart until a heart has been played on a previous trick. Play continues until all 13 tricks have been taken.

To change the speed of the animation or to rename the players, click the Games menu and then click Options to open the Hearts Options dialog box.

Classic Solitaire

When you open Solitaire, the first hand is dealt for you, as you can see in Figure 13-2. To deal a new game after you complete one, click the Games menu and then click Deal.

Figure 13-2 A hand of Solitaire, ready to be played.

To play Solitaire, first move any aces that are face up to the spaces at the upper right of the screen and then turn over the cards that were underneath the aces. (To display a face-down card, simply click it.)

Next, check to see whether you can make any plays on the piles. You must play black cards (spades and clubs) on red cards (hearts and diamonds) and red cards on black cards in descending order. You can move one pile in its entirety to another pile if its bottom card can be played on the other pile's card. To move a pile, click it and then drag it.

When you have made all available plays on the piles, click the deck to turn over the first three cards; only the top card is displayed. If you can play it on a pile, do so; if not, click the deck again. Continue clicking the deck and making plays. Whenever you free an ace, move it to the space at the top and then, as you uncover the appropriate cards, build on the aces in sequence from ace through king.

When you click completely through the deck, click the deck space to start over. You win when all the piles are empty and each of the four aces is built up completely. When you win, Windows rewards you with a little graphical surprise. If you run through all the cards in the deck without being able to play any of them, the game is over and you lose.

TIP *To minimize a game at any time, press the Esc key.*

FreeCell

Unlike Solitaire, it is believed (though not proven) that it is possible to win every game of FreeCell. Like Solitaire, in FreeCell you lay out a tableau of cards, then attempt to arrange them in their respective suits. The object of FreeCell is to move all the cards to the home cells, stacked by suits in order from ace through king.

To play FreeCell, open the game, click the Games menu, and then click New Game to deal a hand, as shown in Figure 13-3. The four free cells are in the upper left, and the four home cells are in the upper right. Before you make a move, locate the aces and the lower cards, especially twos and threes. If you are lucky enough to have some aces at the bottom of columns, click them first and then click a home cell to move them to it.

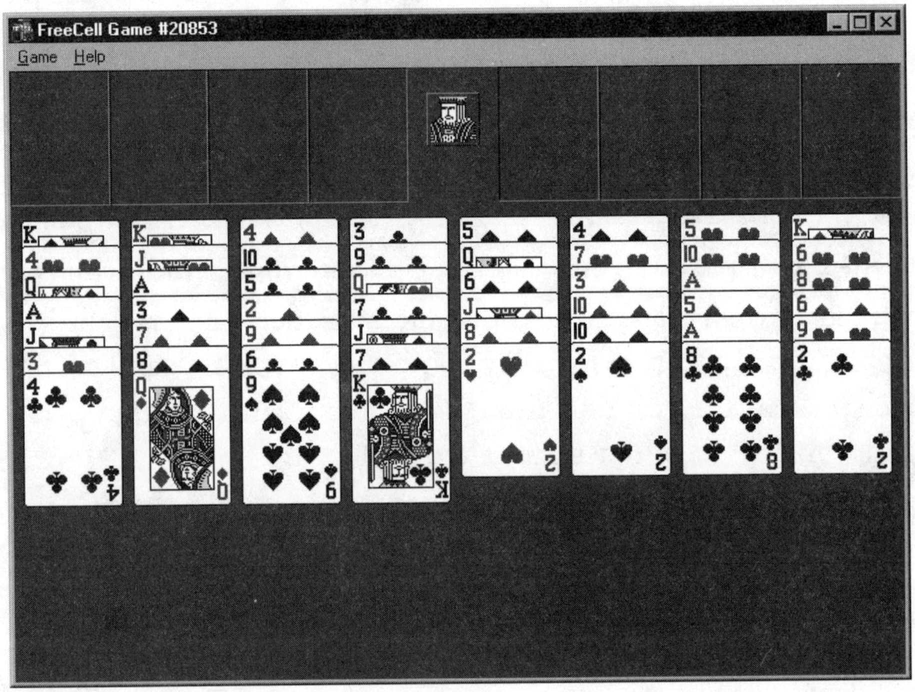

Figure 13-3 A hand of FreeCell.

Here are your basic moves in FreeCell:

- You can move the bottom card of a column to a free cell or to a home cell.
- You can move the bottom card of a column to another column if it follows in sequence. That is, you can place a red jack on a black queen, a black four on a red five, and so on.
- You can move a sequence of cards from one column to another if the other column has enough free space. To do so, click the top card of the sequence, and then click the bottom of the column where you want to move it. (You'll see a warning message if there is not enough free space.)

- You can move a card from a free cell to a home cell or to the bottom of a column if it follows in sequence.
- You can move any card to an empty column.

Minesweeper

Unlike the games we've looked at so far, Minesweeper is not based on a card game you might have played in pre-computer days. Minesweeper is strictly a computer game, and it has to do with deduction and logic. The object of Minesweeper, which is shown in Figure 13-4, is to uncover all the squares in a minefield that don't contain mines and to mark the squares that do contain mines as quickly as possible. (I prefer not to think about any real-world analogy to this game.)

Figure 13-4 A game of Minesweeper.

To begin, click any square to uncover it. There are two possibilities:

- The square could be blank, indicating that no mines are in the surrounding squares.
- The square could contain a number, indicating how many mines are in the surrounding squares.

When you click the second square, however, there is a third possibility: the square could contain a mine, in which case all mines are displayed and you lose the game.

The Mine Counter, which is to the left of the smiley face, displays the number of unmarked mines in the field. The Timer, which is to the right of the smiley face, shows the time elapsed since you uncovered the first square. If you think a square contains a mine, right-click it to mark it. If you just aren't sure about a square, right-click it twice to put a question mark in it. If you later want to uncover the square, click it again.

Pinball

Pinball is the electronic equivalent of the arcade machine. Unlike the other Windows games we've looked at so far, Pinball is played with the keyboard. The object is to launch the ball and earn lots of points by hitting bumpers, targets, and flags. To start a game, press F2, and then hold down the spacebar and release it to launch the first ball. The longer you hold down the spacebar, the more powerful your shot. Figure 13-5 shows a game of Pinball in progress.

Figure 13-5 A game of Pinball in progress.

You use the following keyboard controls to manipulate the pinball:

- Press the Z key to move the left flipper.
- Press the forward slash (/) to move the right flipper.
- Press the X key to nudge the table to the right.
- Press the period (.) to nudge the table to the left.
- Press the up arrow to nudge the table up.

TIP *If you have any problems figuring out how to play this game, check with a 12-year-old.*

Spider Solitaire

When you first open Spider Solitaire, you'll see a Difficulty dialog box, as shown in Figure 13-6. Select Easy, Medium, or Difficult, and then click OK to deal a hand, as shown in Figure 13-7.

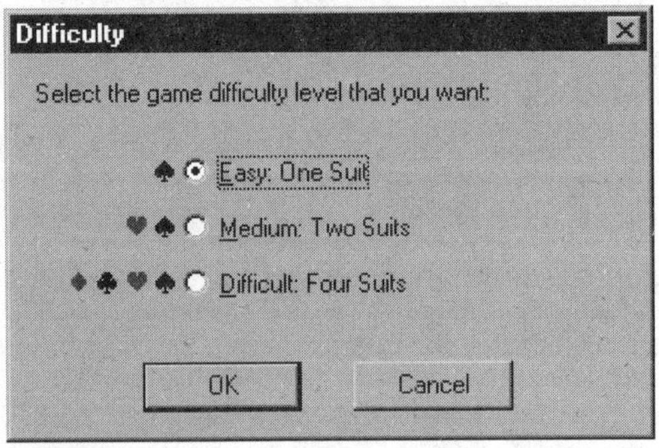

Figure 13-6 Select a game difficulty.

Figure 13-7 A hand of Spider Solitaire.

The object of this game is to remove all the cards from stacks at the top of the window in the fewest possible moves by lining up a suit of cards in order from king to ace. When you line up a complete suit, those cards are removed. To find out how Spider Solitaire is scored and to get tips for how to play the game, click the Help menu and then click Contents.

Playing Games with Others on the Internet

When you play the Internet games that come with Windows, you are connected to a games server called Zone.com. You can go to this site (*http://www.zone.com*) to download and play many other games, including Bridge and Chess.

In this section, I won't get into the details of how to play all the Windows Internet games, but I will look at one of them to give you an idea of what's involved when you play on the Internet. Let's take a look at how to play Internet Spades.

When you start any of the Windows Internet games, you'll see a screen that explains how Zone.com works. If you don't want to be bothered with this screen in the future, click the Show This Every Time check box to clear it. Click the Play button to start a game.

If the game server can't find actual people to play a game, you can play against the computer. Figure 13-8 shows a hand of Spades ready to be played. As you can see, you can choose to look at your cards before you bid or you can bid without seeing your cards for extra points.

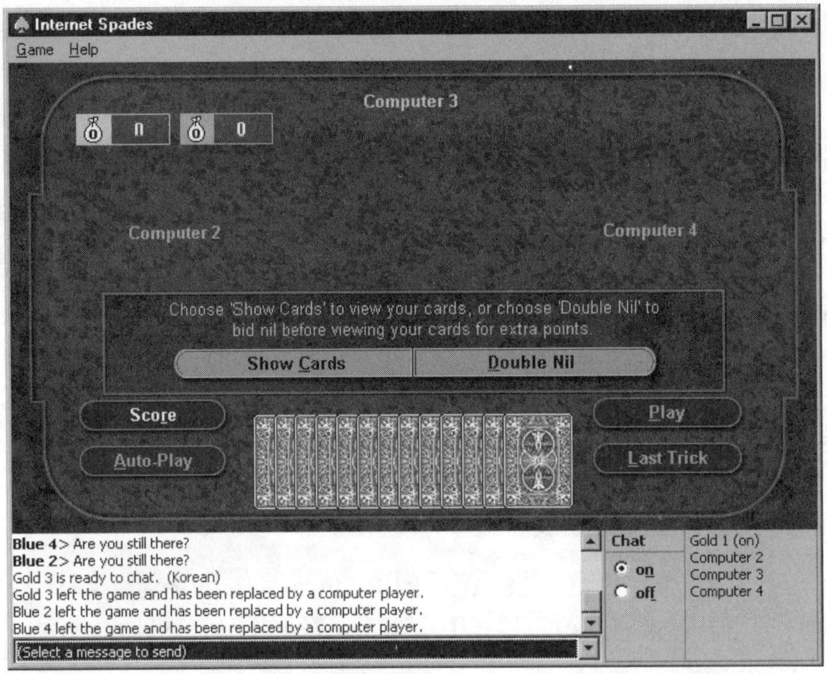

Figure 13-8 Starting a hand of Internet Spades.

Spades is a partnership game, and the object is to reach a contract between you and your partner that lets you correctly predict how many tricks you will take. To bid, you select a number in the chart that is displayed on the screen. To play a card, click it and then click the Play button. The card will be moved to the center of the play area, and the person who wins the trick will collect the cards.

If you want, you can chat with the other players by typing a message in the lower part of the screen. Remember, this is the Internet, and you may be chatting with people from all over the world who speak various languages.

TIP *For information about how to play any of the Internet games, click the Help menu and then click Help Topics for that game. You might also want to consult a good games book, such as* According to Hoyle: Official Rules of More Than 200 Popular Games of Skill and Chance with Expert Advice on Winning Play, *edited by Richard L. Frey and published by Fawcett Books.*

Playing Multimedia

If you are using Windows Me, the Windows Media Player is the tool you use to do any of the following:

- Listen to radio stations from all over the world.
- Play and copy your audio CDs.
- Find movies that are available on the Internet.

To open the Windows Media Player, click the Start button, click Programs, click Accessories, click Entertainment, and then click Windows Media Player. You'll see something similar to the screen in Figure 13-9 if you are connected to the Internet.

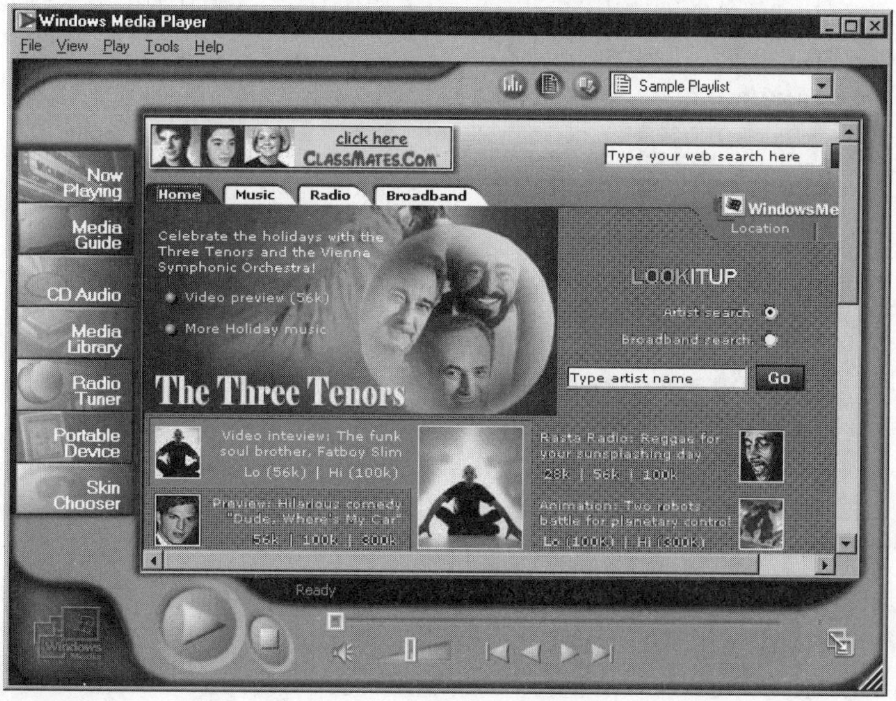

Figure 13-9 The Windows Media Player.

Is Your Computer Multimedia Ready?

Most computers that you buy these days include sound cards, speakers, various kinds of CD-ROM drives and/or a DVD-ROM drive, lots of memory, big hard disks, modems, and network cards that let you connect at high speeds. If you plan to get heavily involved in multimedia, you'll want the best and the most of these features that you can afford.

Even listening to a radio station over your computer at a fast modem speed is not satisfying, and trying to access Internet video is hardly worth the effort. In this section, I'm going to show you how to use the various multimedia features of the Windows Media Player, but if your computer is not outfitted with the necessary hardware and if you don't have some other devices, you won't be able to take advantage of these features.

If you want to upgrade your computer or buy a computer that will allow you quality access to multimedia, check out the Buyer's Guide at ZDNet.com. Go to *http://www.zdnet.com*, and click the Buying Guides link. You can then specify what you want to do with your computer, and the Buyer's Guide will give you a feature list and a range of prices for the system that will meet your needs.

Listening to the Radio

To find and tune in a radio station, click the Radio Tuner button on the left side of the screen. You'll see the screen shown in Figure 13-10, from which you can select a preset station to listen to or specify various criteria and search for a station.

Figure 13-10 Selecting a radio station.

To search for a radio station, you use the Station Finder. In the first drop-down list, select a format, band, language, location, and so on, and in the next drop-down list, further specify what you want to search for. For example, if you choose Format in the first list, you can then select from a variety of formats in the second list—Adult Contemporary, Big Band, Classical, and so on. The Windows Media Player then displays a list of stations. Double-click a station to connect to and listen to it.

You can create a playlist that contains links to the radio stations you most often like to listen to. You add a station to your playlist while you're listening to it. Click the File menu, click Add To Library, and then click Add Currently Playing Track to add the station to your All Audio playlist. To later select a station from the playlist, click the Media Library button in the main Windows Media Player window, click All Audio in the list on the left, and then click the link to the station in the list on the right.

Playing and Copying Your Audio CDs

I mentioned way back in Chapter 1 that you can play audio CDs on your computer. Simply pop a CD into your CD-ROM drive, and it will start to play automatically. In the Windows Media Player, click the Now Playing button on the left side of the screen to display a visualization of the sound (splashes of color and geometric shapes that change with the beat). Figure 13-11 shows the visualization on my screen while I was playing the Schubert "Trout" Piano Quintet. (I don't think the Water ambience had anything to do with the "trout" symbolism because I got the same graphic when I played "Eine Kleine Nachtmusik.")

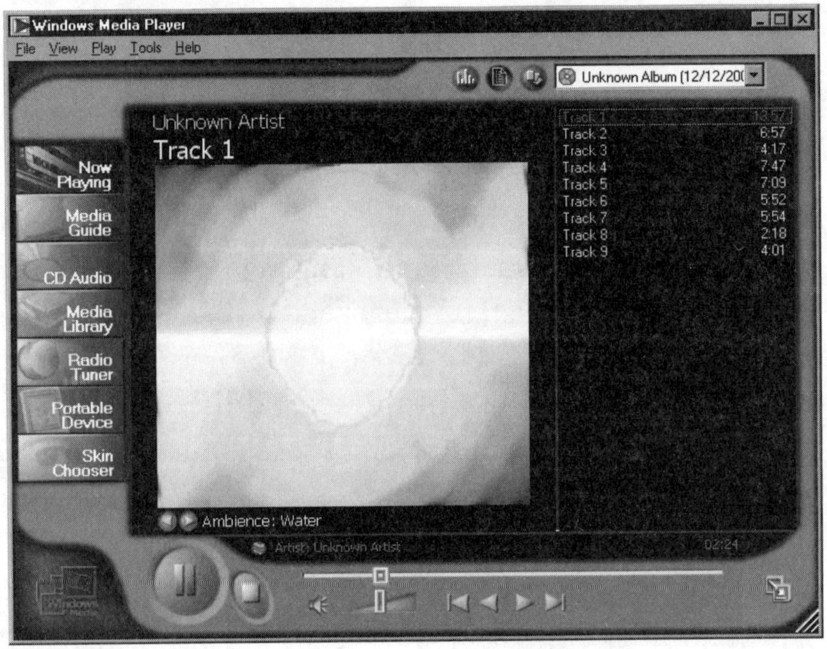

Figure 13-11 A visualization of a playing CD.

To stop, start, pause, and otherwise control the playing of a CD, use the controls across the bottom of the Windows Media Player window. Simply point to a control to display a ScreenTip that tells you what the control does.

You can also use the Windows Media Player to copy tracks from an audio CD to your hard drive. Why would you want to do this? Well, perhaps you're really fond of only two or three of the tracks from one CD, and then you like one track from another CD, and so on. You can copy individual tracks to your hard drive and then play them without switching out the CD in the CD-ROM drive.

When you copy a CD track, you'll want to be sure that you have sufficient space on your hard drive. Such files are not small, but they don't take a long time to copy. And the quality when you play a track from you hard drive is surprisingly good. My ear picks up almost no distortion.

Copying a CD track is a simple task. With the CD in its drive, click the CD Audio button. You'll see a list of the tracks, as shown in Figure 13-12. Clear the check marks from any track that you don't want to copy, and then click the Copy Music button. In most cases, you can copy a track while you listen to it. The Copy Status column will indicate the percentage of the track that has been copied.

Figure 13-12 Copying a CD track.

To listen to a track that you have copied to your hard drive, click the Media Library button, select the track, and then click the Play button at the bottom of the screen.

NOTE *In some cases, the Windows Media Player will recognize the album title and place information about it in the list.*

Finding Movies on the Internet

In the Windows Media Player, click the Media Guide button to open a guide with links to the latest movies, music, and video on the Internet. You'll see something similar to Figure 13-13. To view a trailer for an upcoming movie, click the Coming Attractions link and then click the link to a trailer. You can click any link to open and play the resource in the Windows Media Player. Again, the quality of your viewing and listening experience will depend on the speed of your Internet connection and the hardware setup of your computer.

Figure 13-13 A guide to movies and other media on the Internet.

Customizing the Windows Sounds

When Windows is installed on your computer, certain sounds are associated with certain events, such as exiting Windows, receiving e-mail, starting Windows, and so on. You can keep these sounds, you can silence your computer or select to play only sounds associated with particular events, or you can associate other sounds with these events. To customize the Windows sounds, you use the Sounds And Multimedia applet in Control Panel. Follow these steps:

1. **Open Control Panel.**

   Click the Start button, click Settings, and then click Control Panel.

2. **Open the Sounds And Multimedia Properties dialog box, as shown in Figure 13-14.**

   Click the Sounds And Multimedia icon in Control Panel.

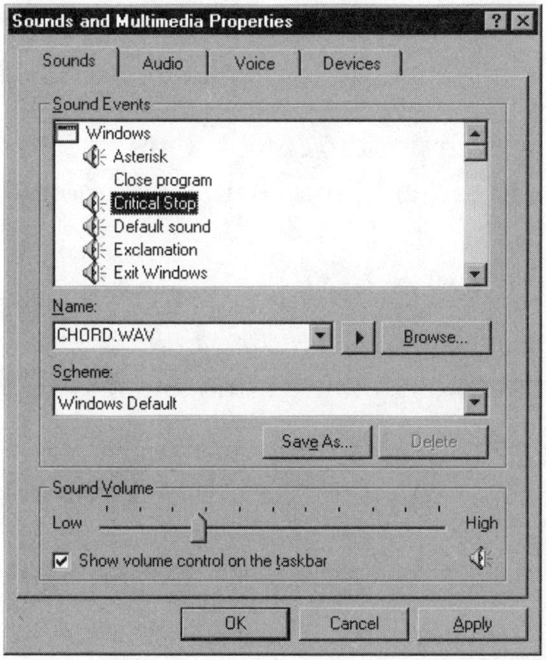

Figure 13-14 The Sounds And Multimedia Properties dialog box.

3. **Tell Windows which sounds you want to hear.**

   If you want to silence the sounds that Windows makes, click the Sounds tab (if necessary), click the Scheme drop-down list, and select No Sounds. To then associate sounds with only certain events, click the event in the Sound Events list, and then select a sound from the Name drop-down list. Click the right-arrow button next to the Name list to preview the sound. To change the volume, move the Sound Volume slider bar in the lower part of the dialog box. Click OK when you've made your selections.

The Seven Most Important Things to Remember About Games and Multimedia

1. FreeCell can be a very addictive game.
2. To minimize a game at any time, press the Esc key.
3. If you're a bridge player and sometimes can't scrape together a foursome, try playing bridge on the Internet. Depending on your level of expertise, you may even want to enter a tournament. The Zone.com site I mentioned earlier in this chapter is a good place to find a bridge game.
4. If you like to play casino games, such as Video Poker, Blackjack, or the slot machines, go to *http://www.gambling.com*. You can download the software for an online casino and play for fun or for real money.
5. If you find that you want to do a lot with multimedia, take that into consideration when you upgrade your computer or buy a new one. The same is true if members of your household or family play a lot of the popular games that you can purchase at a computer store or download from the Internet.

6. If you want to play audio CDs and your computer is in the bedroom or any other place where you might be disturbing people, consider buying a pair of earphones. They are inexpensive and plug into the speaker connection on the back of the system unit of your computer.
7. For links to all sorts of game-related sites, go to *http://dir.yahoo.com/Recreation/Games.*

Summary

According to some of my senior friends, the main reason for having a computer is to play games. And they, of course, don't get any arguments about that from their children and grandchildren. Some people are satisfied to play endless games of Solitaire, and others are always ready to investigate something new. Playing games on the Internet presents all sorts of possibilities for honing your skills and meeting new people who share your interests. In this chapter, I also introduced you to some of the multimedia features in Windows. If experimenting with multimedia is more your game, be sure to explore the Windows Media Player in depth.

Chapter 14

SETTING UP A HOME NETWORK

Featuring:

- Do You Need a Home Network?
- A Really Easy Solution
- Setting Up a Network with Windows Me

When you network your home computers, you connect them so that they can share files, a printer, and an Internet connection. In the recent past, setting up a home network could take the skills of an electrician and a computer programmer. Today, it can be as easy as plugging a computer into a power source and a telephone wall jack.

Creating home networks is becoming easier and cheaper by the month. The immediate benefits are significant if you have more than one computer in your household, but the benefits for the future are even greater. When we are able to network computers with household systems and appliances—and some experts predict that this may be possible within the next five years—an air-conditioning system that refuses to cool can call the repair person to request service.

In this chapter, I'm going to tell you about a couple of ways you can network your computers. However, the technology is improving so rapidly that by the time you read this, even these methods may be superceded. First, though, let's take a look at the reasons you might want to set up a home network.

Do You Need a Home Network?

In the year 2000, more than 21 million homes in the United Sates had more than one computer. If your home is among this number, you probably need to consider whether you should network your computers. The primary reason for networking is sharing resources. For example, in my home office, I have two computers, one printer, and one Internet connection. Because these computers are networked, I can open any file on either system on either computer, I can print from either computer, and I can access the Internet from either computer.

Mine is a simple network, and the computers are both in the same room. But it is also possible to network computers that are in various rooms throughout your house. If you have a computer upstairs in the bedroom, you can print on a printer that's physically connected to a computer in your downstairs office if the computers are networked. You can also play a game of Hearts or any other computer game on any computer in your home. In addition, multiple people can access the Internet simultaneously; one person can browse the Web, while another is sending and receiving e-mail, or both can browse the Web at the same time.

A Really Easy Solution

If you are running Microsoft Windows Me, it is now easier than ever to set up a home network, and in the next section I'll give you the steps. But even easier solutions are available.

AnyPoint Home Network is a hardware and software solution available from Intel. It costs about $100, and you'll need a kit for each computer on the network. AnyPoint comes in wireless and phone-line versions, it's easy to install, and it can access resources on other computers that are as much as 150 feet away, through walls and floors. AnyPoint works with DSL, cable modem, and an analog modem. You simply connect the AnyPoint device to the cable that's included in the kit, connect the cable to the computer's USB (universal serial bus) port, and run an install wizard that's on the CD in the kit. For more information, including system requirements, go to *http://www.intel.com/anypoint*.

NOTE *A USB port is a connection on the back of your computer's system unit to which you can attach one of 63 kinds of devices, such as printers, modems, and so on. Most computers have two such connections.*

Many other networking kits are available, and more are being developed all the time. For links to sites that contain the latest information, open Microsoft Internet Explorer and search on "networking kits."

Setting Up a Network with Windows Me

These days, setting up a home network is not expensive even if you go with a solution such as AnyPoint, but with a little more effort you may be able to do it for even less, especially if your computers are in the same room. In this section, I'm going to walk you through the steps for setting up a network of computers for a home office. One of the computers needs to be running Windows Me, but the other computers can be running Windows Me, Windows 98, or Windows 95.

The process I'll describe here is not as simple as connecting AnyPoint, but it isn't difficult, and, depending on how many computers you network, it shouldn't take you more than an afternoon. One of my friends describes the skill level needed to set up such a network as about the same as that for making a pot of coffee. I don't know about that comparison, but it's definitely easier than programming your VCR.

Determining What You Need

In this setup, you'll need three things in addition to the computers you want to network:

- A *network interface card* (NIC) for each computer in the network. The NIC is inserted in an empty slot on the motherboard in the system unit. (The *motherboard* is the main printed circuit board in a computer.) The slot can be of two types: Industry Standard Architecture (ISA) and Peripheral Component Interconnect (PCI). And you need a NIC of the same type as the slot. (Later in this section, I'll tell you how to find out which type you need.)
- A *hub*, which is the central device that connects all the computers on the network. The hub is a small metal box (mine is about 9 inches long and 5 inches wide) that has places to which you connect a cable that is connected to a computer on the other end. You need to buy a hub that has enough connections for the number of computers you want to connect.
- Some *cable* wiring. Cables are the physical connection between the computers on the network and the hub. How much cabling you need depends on the distance between your computers and the hub.

You can purchase this hardware separately or in a kit from a computer store or over the Internet. A kit that contains everything you need to connect two computers usually costs less than $100.

Most newer computers have PCI slots, and older computers have ISA slots. Here are some ways to find out the type of slot on the motherboard of your computer:

- Check the invoice that you received when you bought your computer. It will usually list the number and type of available slots.
- Look in the documentation that came with your computer.
- Go to the manufacturer's Web site and search for your computer model. Most manufacturers provide hardware specifications online, and these should list and describe the available slots on your computer.
- If all else fails, call the manufacturer of your computer. Be sure to have the model number handy.

Connecting the Computers

Once you have the necessary network hardware assembled, get yourself a small screwdriver and some good light to work by (you might also want a flashlight nearby), and you're ready to begin. Don't be timid. If you've ever put together a child's tricycle or a barbecue grill, you can certainly do this. Follow these steps:

1. **Open the case to the system unit of one of the computers.**

   First, turn off all computers, printers, and so on, and unplug them from the power supply. Turn the system unit so that you can easily get to it, and remove the screws from the case that covers the sides and top. (Put the screws where you can easily find them when you're finished.) Now slide the case off. If necessary, give it a tug. You won't hurt anything.

2. **Insert the NIC in the slot.**

   Locate the manufacturer's instructions that came with the NIC, and follow them to insert the NIC. Be sure that the card bracket is sitting snugly in the slot. Now, slide the case back on the system unit. You can replace the screws now or wait until you're sure that the card is working, which we'll do in step 4.

3. **Connect the cables.**

   Connect one end of the cable to the NIC (the prongs will protrude from the back of the system unit), and connect the other end of the cable to the hub, starting with the hub's first connection. Both ends of the cable are identical, so it doesn't make any difference which end you connect to the computer or the hub. Now, repeat steps 1, 2, and 3 for each computer that will be on the network.

4. **Power up the system.**

   Turn on the hub and all connected computers. You should see a light on the hub for each connected computer.

That's all there is to it. The first computer may take you awhile, but by the time you insert the last NIC, you'll realize how simple the process is and be doing it confidently and easily. You're now ready to tell Windows about the network you've just connected.

Telling Windows About Your Network

It's best to set up your Windows Me computer as the server on your network, so be sure that it is the computer on which the modem (or DSL or cable modem) is installed, and physically connect the printer to this computer. In the following steps, I'm going to set up a computer that has an analog modem rather than a high-speed connection and that is connected to other computers on the network via a hub, as shown in Figure 14-1. If you have a high-speed connection and your network is connected by phone lines or power lines rather than by cabling, open Microsoft Help And Support and search on "Home Networking" to find detailed instructions.

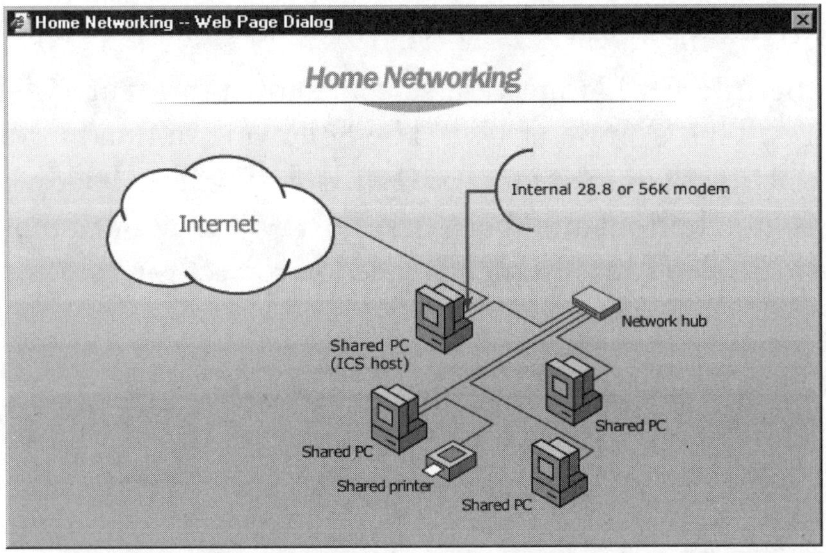

Figure 14-1 A typical home network.

To tell Windows about your network, you use the Home Networking Wizard. On your Windows Me computer, follow these steps:

1. **Start the Home Networking Wizard.**

   Click the Start button, click Programs, click Accessories, click Communications, and then click Home Networking Wizard. You'll see the screen shown in Figure 14-2. Click Next.

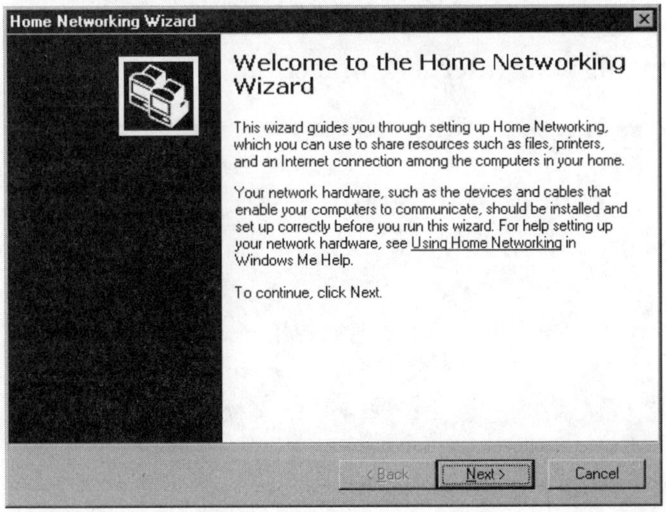

Figure 14-2 Starting the Home Networking Wizard.

2. **Tell Windows about your Internet connection.**

   On the Internet Connection screen, shown in Figure 14-3, click the Yes, This Computer Uses The Following option button, click the A Direct Connection To My ISP Using The Following Device option button, and then click Next. Windows will most likely have identified your Internet connection correctly in the drop-down list box.

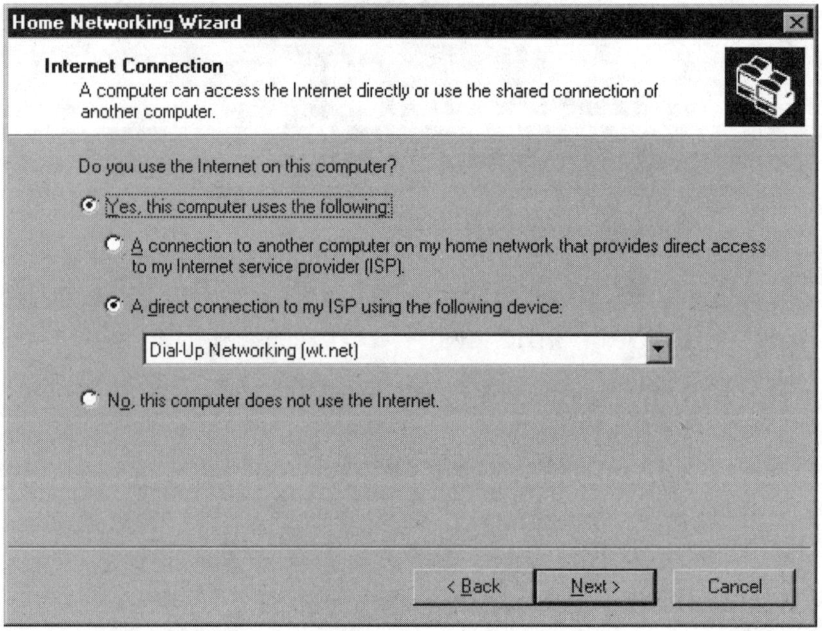

Figure 14-3 Identifying your Internet connection.

3. **Share your Internet connection.**

   In the Internet Connection Sharing screen, shown in Figure 14-4, click Yes, and then click Next.

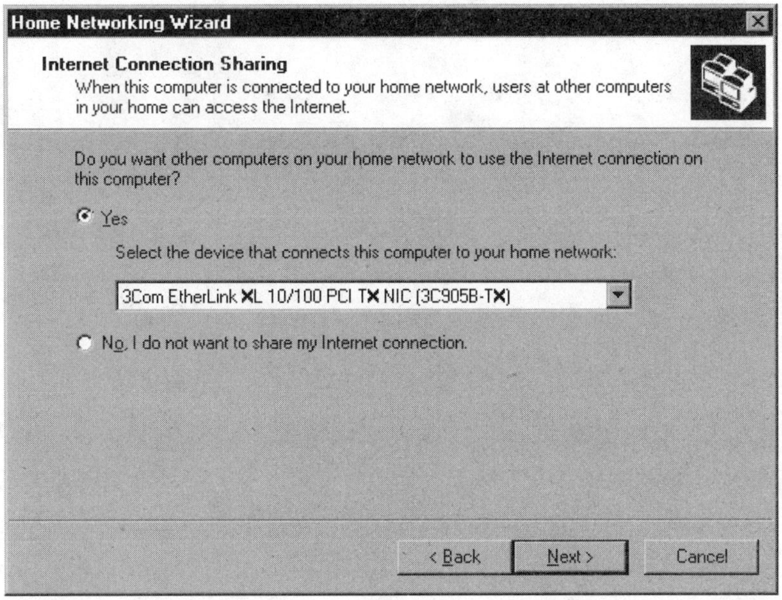

Figure 14-4 Sharing your Internet connection.

4. **Name the computer and your workgroup.**

   In the Computer And Workgroup Names screen, type a name for your computer in the Computer Name box. (Each computer on your network will need a unique name. Write this name down.) All the computers on your network belong to the same workgroup, and you can accept the default name of MSHOME or click the Use The Workgroup Name button and enter another name. (Write this name down.) After you do one or the other, click Next.

5. **Tell Windows whether you want to share your files and your printer.**

   In the Share Files And Printers screen, click the My Documents And All Folders In It check box. Click the Password button if you want other users on the network to type a password in order to open the files in your My Documents folder on this computer. If you don't want to password-protect your files, the wizard will warn you that you should, but you can continue without doing so. Click the check box for the printer you want to share, and then click Next.

6. **Create a Home Networking Setup disk.**

   If some computers on your network are not running Windows Me but are instead running Windows 95 or Windows 98, you'll need to create this disk so that you can run the Home Networking Wizard on those computers. Click the Yes, Create A Home Networking Setup Disk option button, and then click Next. Insert a disk in your floppy drive, and click Next to create the disk. When the disk is created, click Finish on the last screen of the wizard.

You'll now need to take your Home Networking Setup Disk to your non-Windows Me computers and run the Home Networking Wizard. Place the disk in the floppy drive, and then click the Start button and click Run to open the Run dialog box. In the Open box, type *a:\setup.exe,* and press the Enter key to start the wizard. As the wizard runs, do the following:

- On the Internet Connection screen, shown earlier in this chapter in Figure 14-3, click the Yes, The Computer Uses The Following option button, and then click the A Connection To Another Computer On My Home Network That Provides Direct Access To My Internet Service Provider (ISP) option button.
- On the Computer And Workgroup Names screen, be sure to give the computer a unique name and the same workgroup name you set up for the Windows Me computer.
- Specify whether to share the files in your My Documents folder, and if you are sharing the printer attached to the Windows Me computer, you'll see a Rendering Subsystem check box that is checked.

To share a file that is not in your My Documents folder, follow these steps:

1. **Open Windows Explorer.**

   Right-click My Computer, and choose Explore from the shortcut menu.

2. **Open the Properties dialog box for the file or folder.**

   Right-click the file name or folder name, and choose Sharing from the shortcut menu. Figure 14-5 shows the Properties dialog box for my My Download Files folder.

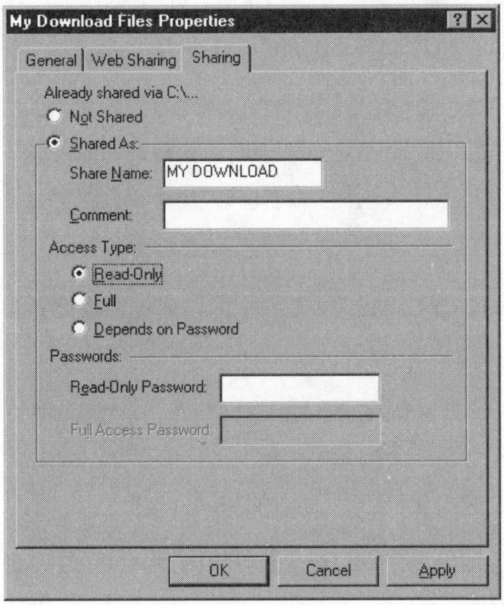

Figure 14-5 The Properties dialog box for a folder.

3. **Tell Windows how to share this resource.**

   On the Sharing tab, click the Shared As option button, and then enter a name for the file or folder or keep the name Windows suggests. You can also add a comment that describes this file or folder if you want to do so. In the Access Type section, specify whether a network user can open the file as read-only, have full access to the file, or open only with a password. With read-only access, a user can view the file but not make any changes to it. Enter a password if you want to password-protect the file. You will, of course, need to tell users the password if you want them to access the file. Click OK when you've finished describing how to share the file or folder.

The Seven Most Important Things to Remember About Networking Your Home Computers

1. If you find yourself schlepping a floppy disk from computer to computer in your house, consider setting up a network.
2. With some network kits, you need only one phone line and one Internet connection for all the computers on your network. You can even use the phone line for voice calls when someone else is browsing the Internet.
3. Setting up a network is not expensive these days, but as a rule of thumb, the more you pay, the less work is involved in setup.
4. You can use the Home Networking Wizard in Windows Me to quickly and easily set up a network of computers running Windows Me, Windows 98, and Windows 95.
5. Networking technology is developing at a rapid rate. If you're thinking about networking your home computers, periodically search the Internet for new products.
6. A great advantage of a network is that you can easily back up important files to another computer on the network.
7. If you have a high-speed connection, check with your ISP about how many users can share that connection and what is involved in doing so.

Summary

Setting up a home network of computers is becoming easier and cheaper every day. In this chapter, we've looked at two solutions: AnyPoint, and using Windows Me to set up a network that uses a hub and cabling. But many other options are available, including wireless and phone-line networks. The computers on a wireless network communicate over specially authorized radio frequencies. Phone-line networks use existing phone lines, but operate on a different frequency to avoid colliding with regular telephone calls. Check out these options when you are looking for a home network solution.

Appendix

INSTALLING AND UPGRADING WINDOWS

Featuring:

- Installing Windows Me on a Blank Hard Disk
- Upgrading to Windows Me

I mentioned in Chapter 2 that you don't need to upgrade every time a new version of Microsoft Windows is released, but that periodically you'll want to do so to take advantage of the features that deliver new technology or make existing technology easier to use. In this book, I've used the latest version of Windows for the home, Windows Me. If you have an earlier version of Windows and have been working along at your computer, you'll certainly have noticed features that aren't available on your system. A notable example is the Home Networking Wizard, which I discussed in Chapter 14.

In this appendix, I'll discuss how to install and upgrade to Windows Me. If you are upgrading to a different Windows operating system, follow the instructions in the booklet that came with the software for that version.

Installing Windows Me on a Blank Hard Disk

When you buy a new computer these days, an operating system is already installed, as well as some applications. About the only time you'll ever need to install Windows on a blank hard disk is when you add a new hard drive to your system. Even then you might want to do what I did: take your computer to a professional technician, who will install the hard drive and the operating system. Be sure that you also take along the setup CD-ROM.

If you decide to tackle this job yourself, you can use the detailed instructions that you'll find in the *Quick Start Guide* that's included in the Windows Me package.

Upgrading to Windows Me

When you upgrade to Windows Me, your previous operating system is replaced with Windows Me and your existing files and programs are retained. You can upgrade to Windows Me if you are currently running Windows 95, Windows 98, or Windows Second Edition. If you are currently running Windows 3.1, you will need to install Windows Me as if you were doing so on a blank hard disk. In the process, you must reformat your hard drive so all existing files and programs will be deleted. For instructions on how to install Windows Me on a computer that is currently running Windows 3.1, see the *Quick Start Guide* that's included in the Windows Me package.

Upgrading to Windows Me is really easy and should take you only about 30 minutes. To upgrade to Windows Me, your computer system must have the following:

- At least a Pentium, 150 megahertz processor.
- At least 32 megabytes of RAM.
- Enough free hard-disk space. A typical installation requires about 350 megabytes.

- At least a VGA (Video Graphics Adapter) monitor.
- A CD-ROM or DVD-ROM drive.
- A mouse or another compatible pointing device.

Almost any new computer you've bought within the last couple of years will meet these requirements. If you have any questions about these specifications, check the documentation that came with your computer.

Before you begin the upgrade, be sure that you have the following at hand:

- The Windows Me CD-ROM.
- A floppy disk. You'll need this to create a Windows Startup disk, which you can use to start Windows if you can't do so from your hard drive.
- The 25 letters and numbers of the product key. It's usually on a yellow label that's attached to the back of the CD-ROM case.

Now you need to take the follow preparatory steps:

1. **Run your antivirus program, if you have one.**
2. **Defragment your hard drive.**

   For information about how to do this, look back in Chapter 10.
3. **Back up all important data.**

   It is unlikely that you'll lose anything during the upgrade process (I never have), but you want to be on the safe side.
4. **Turn off any programs that run automatically.**
5. **Disconnect from the Internet.**

OK, you're ready to start. Follow these steps:

1. **Start your current version of Windows.**
2. **Insert the Windows Me CD-ROM in the CD drive.**
3. **When the Setup Wizard asks if you want to upgrade, click Yes.**

   Now just follow the instructions on the screen.

NOTE *During the upgrade, the Setup Wizard will automatically restart your computer several times. Don't be alarmed. This is part of the normal process.*

That's all there is to it. Upgrading requires almost no interaction on your part. When the upgrade is complete, you'll see the Enter Windows Password dialog box on your screen. You're now ready to start using Windows Me.

GLOSSARY

Accessibility Options

Features that can be used to customize Windows so that it is easier to use for people who have visual, mobility, hearing, cognitive, or language impairments.

Active desktop

A feature that, when enabled, makes your **desktop** look and work like a Web page.

Address Book

The Windows program you can use to store and access contact information.

applet

A small program in Windows. You use some applets to customize your installation of Windows.

application

A program that is designed for a specific task, for example, a word processor or a database.

attachment

A file that travels along with an e-mail message.

backup

An up-to-date copy of the files on your system.

boot

The process of starting or restarting a computer system.

byte

The basic unit of measurement in a computer. One byte stores one character.

cable modem

A high-speed connection that uses the wiring provided by your cable TV company.

Calculator

The Windows program that replicates onscreen the handheld variety.

cascade windows

To display windows like stacked sheets of paper.

CD-ROM drive

CD-ROM stands for Compact Disc–Read Only Memory. A CD-ROM disc is a storage medium that uses the same technology as music CDs.The advantage to a CD-ROM is that it can store huge amounts of information.

chat room

An area on a **Web site** where you can communicate with others in real time by typing on the **keyboard** or, if you have the necessary equipment, speaking into a microphone and listening through speakers or earphones.

check box

A little square box you can click to select or clear the option it identifies.

Control Panel

A folder of **applets** that you can use to modify the settings in Windows and the **devices** on your computer system.

CPU

An abbreviation for central processing unit. The CPU is the component that does the real work of computing; also referred to as the microprocessor, the processor, or the chip.

desktop

The screen you see after you **log on** to Windows.

device

Any hardware peripheral that can send and receive information, for example, a **printer,** a **modem,** and a **CD-ROM drive.**

dialog box

A little windowlike box that opens on the screen when Windows or a program needs more information from you.

digital camera

A camera that lets you take pictures without film and then display, edit, and print them from your computer.

digital video camera

A camera that lets you record moving images and display them on the computer in real time or create and save them as files to play back later.

directory

The term sometimes used to refer to a **folder;** this term was used in older versions of Windows.

Disk Cleanup

A system tool that you can use to identify and delete files that you no longer need.

Disk Defragmenter

A system tool that you can use to reconstitute the bits and pieces of files stored in various locations on your hard drive into contiguous units.

document

Anything you create on your computer and then save.

dots per inch

Abbreviated dpi. The measurement that indicates print quality. The higher the dpi, the better the quality of the printing and the slower the output.

drag-and-drop

Click an object with the **mouse,** hold down the mouse button, move the object to a new location, and then release the mouse button.

drop-down list

A list of items that is hidden until you click the drop-down arrow at the top of it.

DSL

An abbreviation for Digital Subscriber Line, a high-speed connection to the **Internet** that uses existing telephone lines but that transmits at higher frequencies than those used to transmit voice.

encryption

Encoding information so that unauthorized persons cannot access it.

external modem

A **modem** that resides on the outside of the **system unit.**

FAT

An abbreviation for File Allocation Table, the file system supported by DOS, Windows 3.*x*, and the first release of Windows 95.

FAT32

An abbreviation for File Allocation Table 32, the file system supported by Windows 95 release 2, and the following Windows 95 versions, Windows 98, and Windows Me.

favorite

A **Web site** whose **URL** you've placed in a list in **Internet Explorer** so that you can quickly and easily return to it. The **Netscape Navigator** equivalent is bookmark.

file system

The overall structure in an operating system that determines how files are named, stored, and organized.

firewall software

Special software that sits between your computer and the **Internet,** which prevents unauthorized access. Firewall software is important if you have a high-speed, always-on connection to the Internet.

floppy disk drive

A component of the **system unit** into which you insert a removable disk, called a floppy disk. The actual disk that's inside the plastic casing is very thin and floppy.

folder

The container for files on your system. In earlier versions of Windows and in some other operating systems, a folder is called a **directory.**

font

A particular typeface; a font is identified by type and size.

gigabyte

Abbreviated GB; stores approximately 1,000,000,000 characters.

hard drive

The disk drive inside the **system unit** that stores data on magnetically coated disks. The disk is sealed in the factory to prevent contamination.

hardware

All the physical electronic components of a computer system.

home page

The opening page of a **Web site.**

HTML

An abbreviation for HyperText Markup Language, the language used to create Web pages.

HTML tags

The basic building blocks used to create an **HTML** document.

HTTP

An abbreviation for Hypertext Transfer Protocol, the rules that specify how a **Web browser** and a Web **server** communicate.

hub

The central **device** that connects all the computers in a **network.**

icon

A little picture on the screen that represents a program, a **document,** or some other object in Windows.

identity

In **Outlook Express,** a type of mail user that you can set up if multiple people use your computer and, thus, Outlook Express.

Imaging

A program that's included with Windows. You can use it to view and manipulate digital images.

impact printer

A **printer** that makes an image on paper by hitting a print head or a key against a ribbon.

internal modem

A **modem** that resides on the inside of the **system unit.**

Internet

The world's largest computer network, connecting tens of millions of **users.**

Internet Explorer

The **Web browser** that's included with Windows.

Internet service provider

Abbreviated ISP. An organization that provides dedicated or dial-up access to the **Internet.**

intranet

A private corporate network that uses **Internet** technology.

ISDN

An abbreviation for Integrated Services Digital Network, a digital connection that is available through the telephone company that can be considerably faster than a **modem** connection.

joystick

The pointing device you need to play certain kinds of computer games.

keyboard

The computer component that looks like a typewriter.

keyword

A word or term that you enter in a field in a **search service.** Multiple keywords form a search string, a phrase that the search service compares with information it finds in its database.

kilobyte

Abbreviated KB; stores approximately 1,000 characters.

landscape orientation

A page that is printed horizontally.

link

Short for hyperlink. A word, a phrase, an image, or a symbol that forms a connection with a resource that can be located on your local computer, your local **network,** or the **Internet.**

local area network

Abbreviated LAN. A group of connected computers and other **devices,** such as a **printer,** that can share files, **applications,** and other resources.

local printer

A **printer** that is physically attached to your computer by a cable.

logging off

Signing off on a **network** or a computer.

logging on

Identifying yourself to a **network** or to a computer.

Magnifier

A **device** that displays a magnified portion of your screen in a separate window.

maximize

Display a window in the full size of the screen.

megabyte

Abbreviated MB; stores approximately 1,000,000 characters.

menu

A list of options from which you can choose.

menu bar

Contains words that are the title of a list of commands.

message rule

A filter that you can apply to block mail from certain senders and route mail to specific **folders.**

minimize

Reduce an open window to a button on the **taskbar.**

modem

A **device** that lets you transmit and receive information to and from other computers using a telephone line.

monitor

The part of your computer that looks like a TV.

mouse

The small hand control that has buttons you can click with your finger.

multimedia

A catchall term that describes a **device** that can produce more than one kind of output.

NetMeeting

A conferencing **application** included with Windows that you can use to finger chat over the **Internet,** audio conference, video conference, share applications, collaborate on **documents,** transfer files, and draw on the whiteboard.

Netscape Navigator

A **Web browser** that was first released by Netscape Communications Corp. in 1994.

network

A group of computers and peripherals devices (such as **printers, modems,** and so on) that are connected in some way so that their **users** can share files and other resources.

network printer

A **printer** that is attached to another computer on your **network.**

newsgroup

A collection of articles on specific topics that you can access from the news server of your **Internet service provider.**

NIC

An abbreviation for **network** interface card, an adapter that plugs into a slot on the motherboard of a computer and then is connected to the network **device,** such as a **hub.**

nonimpact printer

A **printer** that makes an image on paper by using copy machine technology, by spraying a fine jet of ink onto the paper, or by using heat to transfer an image onto specially treated paper.

Notepad

A simple text editor (word processor) that's included with Windows.

object

Any component of Windows.

offline file

A file that is stored on the **network** but that you make available to you while not connected to the network.

On-Screen Keyboard

A **keyboard** that displays on the screen and on which you can type by clicking keys with the **mouse.**

option button

A little round circle that is displayed next to an item; also called a radio button. Like the buttons on your car radio, option buttons are mutually exclusive. You can select only one at a time.

Outlook Express

The news and mail reader that's included with Windows.

pages per minute

Abbreviated ppm; the measurement used to indicate the speed of a **printer.**

Paint

A program that's included with Windows. You can use it to create and edit graphic images.

password

A combination of characters you enter during the process of **logging on.**

path

The exact route Windows must take when finding and opening a file.

peer-to-peer network

A **network** in which all computers are equals. Each computer has its own **hard drive** and can see and communicate with all the other computers on the network. In addition, each computer can share its resources.

personalized menu

A **menu** that displays only the commands you most often use. Personalized menus are a feature of Windows that you can enable or disable.

Plug and Play

A feature of Windows that automatically configures a new piece of hardware when you install it in your computer.

POP

An abbreviation for Post Office Protocol, which retrieves messages from an e-mail **server.**

port

The interface through which information passes between a computer and a **device,** such as a **printer** or a **modem.**

portrait orientation

A page that is printed vertically.

post

To send an e-mail message to a **newsgroup** or a mailing list.

print server

A **network printer.**

printer

A peripheral **device** attached to your computer that reproduces on paper the contents of anything you see on the screen.

properties

Characteristics of an **object** or a **device.**

protocol

A formal specification that defines the rules whereby data is transmitted and received.

Quick Launch toolbar

The left portion of the **taskbar** that contains **icons** for starting **Internet Explorer** and **Outlook Express,** and for minimizing all open Windows and displaying the **desktop.**

RAM

An abbreviation for random access memory. RAM is an area in your computer's memory where information is stored while you are working on it. In general, the more RAM you have, the faster your computer works.

Recycle Bin

The container that holds deleted items until they are permanently deleted from your system.

restore

Display a window on the **desktop** at about one-third of its maximized size.

right-clicking

The process of using the right **mouse** button rather than the left. You can right-click almost anywhere in Windows and produce something useful.

ScanDisk

A system tool that searches your hard disk for errors and repairs any damaged areas it finds.

scanner

A **device** that converts paper images to digital images and stores and displays them on your computer.

screen

The part of the computer monitor that looks like a TV screen; also called the display.

screen resolution

The number of pixels on the screen and the number of colors that can be displayed at the same time. Some typical resolutions are 640 by 480, 800 by 600, and 1024 by 768.

screen saver

A utility that displays a specified image on the screen after the computer has been idle for a certain amount of time. Originally, screen savers prevented images from being permanently etched on the monitor's screen. Today's monitors need no such protection.

search engine

A program that indexes resources on the **Internet** and puts that information into a searchable database. Search engines are also known as search tools.

search service

A program that can search a file, a database, or the **Internet** for keywords and retrieve resources in which those words are found.

Security zone

An **Internet Explorer** setting that specifies the types of Web sites that a **user** of your computer can access.

server

A **network** computer that provides services, such as printing, storage, and communications.

sharing

Making a resource available to others on the **network.**

shortcut

An **icon** on the **desktop** that represents an **application,** a file, a **document,** a **printer,** or any other **object** in Windows.

shortcut menu

A **menu** of related commands that appears when you **right-click** an **object;** also sometimes referred to as a context menu or a right-click menu.

signature

In **Outlook Express,** a text file that you can append to the close of your e-mail messages. A typical business signature contains your name, title, the name of your organization, perhaps its physical address, and your phone number.

slider

A control on a bar that you can move to select a setting from a range of settings.

SMTP

An abbreviation for Simple Mail Transfer Protocol, which sends messages to an e-mail **server.**

software

A collection of computer programs that tell the hardware what to do and how to do it.

start page

The **Web site** you see when you first open **Internet Explorer.** You can choose any site you want as your start page.

stationery

A preformatted background that you can use to compose messages in **Outlook Express** using **HTML.** You can also create your own stationery.

status area

The area at the far end of the **taskbar** that, by default, contains the Volume **icon** and the clock.

system unit

In a personal computer, the large heavy box into which all the separate components are connected. The system unit stands on the floor or slides into a cabinet.

tabs

The separate pages of a **dialog box.** A dialog box includes tabs when it contains more information than can be displayed in a single screen.

taskbar

The **toolbar** at the bottom of the **desktop** that contains **icons** you can use to quickly access programs.

terabyte

Abbreviated TB; stores approximately 1,000,000,000,000 characters.

text box

An area in a **dialog box** where you type text.

tile windows horizontally

To display windows horizontally so that all have equal amounts of space on the **desktop** and arrange them so that their edges don't overlap.

tile windows vertically

To display windows vertically so that all have equal amounts of space on the **desktop** and arrange them so that their edges don't overlap.

title bar

The bar at the top of a window that displays the name of the **document** and the name of the program running inside the window.

toolbar

Contains buttons that are graphic representations of **menu** items that you use frequently.

Troubleshooter

A tool included with Windows Help that you can use to solve problems with various **devices,** such as **printers, modems, network** adapters, and so on.

URL

An abbreviation for Uniform Resource Locator, an address for a resource on the **Internet.**

user

Any person that is allowed to access a computer or a **network.**

user account

Identifies a **user** on a **network** or on a computer by his or her user name and **password.**

virus

A malevolent program that can attach itself to your computer system without your knowledge or permission and wipe out your **hard drive.**

wallpaper

A graphical image that serves as a background on your **desktop.**

Web browser

A program that you can use to explore **Internet** resources.

Web site

A collection of Web pages that are connected by means of **links** (or hyperlinks).

WebTV

A small boxlike appliance that turns a television screen into a computer monitor.

Windows Explorer

The program that you use to see and manage the drives, **folders,** and files on your Windows computer.

wizard

A Windows component that steps you through a process, such as setting up a **network** connection, connecting to the **Internet,** and so on.

WordPad

A word processor that's included with Windows. Though far from a fully featured program, such as Microsoft Word or Corel WordPerfect, WordPad is sufficient for creating basic, formatted **documents.**

Index

B

C

D

E

F

G

H

I

J

K

L

M

N

O

W

X

Y

Z

The manuscript for this book was prepared and submitted to Redmond Technology Press in electronic form. Text files were prepared using Microsoft Word 2000. Pages were composed using PageMaker 6.5 for Windows, with text in Frutiger and Caslon. Composed files were delivered to the printer as electronic prepress files.

Project Editor

Paula Thurman

Technical Editor

Carolyn M. Connally

Layout

Minh-Tam S. Le

Indexer

Julie Kawabata